Abstracts of the
TESTAMENTARY PROCEEDINGS
of the
PREROGATIVE COURT OF MARYLAND

Volume XXV: 1746-1749

Liber: 32 (pp. 23-256)

by
V. L. Skinner, Jr.

CLEARFIELD

Printed for Clearfield Company by
Genealogical Publishing Company
Baltimore, Maryland
2010

ISBN 978-0-8063-5486-6

Made in the United States of America

INTRODUCTION

Purpose of the Prerogative Court.

The Prerogative Court was the central point for probate for Provincial Maryland. It was mirrored after the Prerogative Court of Canterbury. There was a judge as well as clerk(s) of the court. Initially, all probate was brought directly to the Prerogative Court, located in the Provincial Capital. As the Province became more populous, all documents were still to be filed with the Prerogative Court; however, administration of probate was delegated to the various county courts. Even so, there are documents only in the Prerogative Court and not in the appropriate county, and vice versa.

Documents filed in the Prerogative Court.

The following documents were filed in the Prerogative Court: administration bond, will, inventory, administration accounts, and final balances. The testamentary proceedings contain the administration bond and the docket for the court. If the administrator is lax in filing documents, then a summons is also recorded.

Equity Court

The Prerogative Court was also the court for equity cases—resolution of disputes over the settlement and distribution of an estate. The case was brought before the judge and could take several years to resolve. Often depositions were taken and recorded in the minutes.

Notes on the Abstraction.

1. The left hand column contains the liber/folio number. The folio numbers are presented just as they appear in the actual document, e.g., 32a, 78½.
2. The right hand column contains the abstraction text.
3. Various libers specify a particular session for the Prerogative Court, e.g., 1678; or, September Court 1742. This information is presented as "Court Session:" followed by the appropriate session. Should no session have been specified, then the phrase "no

date" is used.
4. An ellipsis (...) is used to indicate a continuation of the previous information, but no relevant genealogical information is present.
5. The following symbols are used in the abstraction:
   - ? - difficult to read.
   - # - pounds of tobacco.
   - ! - [sic].

Abbreviations.

The following abbreviations have been used throughout this abstraction:

AA - Anne Arundel Co.
ACC - Accomac Co.
BA - Baltimore Co.
CE - Cecil Co.
CH - Charles Co.
CR - Caroline Co.
CV - Calvert Co.
dbn - de bonis non
DE - Delaware
DO - Dorchester Co.
ENG - England
FR - Frederick Co.
g - gentleman
GB - Great Britain
HA - Harford Co.
IRE - Ireland
JP - justice of the peace
KE - Kent Co. MD
KEDE - Kent Co. DE
LaC - letters ad colligendum
LoA - letters of administration

LoD - list of debts
MA - Massachusetts
MD - Maryland
MO - Montgomery Co.
NE - New England or "non est"
NEI - "non est inventar"
NY - New York
NYC - New York City
p - planter
PA - Pennsylvania
PG - Prince George's Co.
PoA - power of attorney
QA - Queen Anne's Co.
SM - St. Mary's Co.
SMC - St. Mary's City
SO - Somerset Co.
TA - Talbot Co.
VA - Virginia
WA - Washington Co.
WO - Worcester Co.

This volume is a continuation of the series, covering 1746 to 1749. The Court is meeting every 2 months to review the docket, and to take appropriate actions. Except for spurious entries, the information is presented in chronological order, as recorded by the Register.

By 1739, all mainstream processing of probate records has been delegated to the Deputy Commissaries.

32:23 26 September. Mr. Nehemiah King (SO) to examine accounts of:
- Samuel Wilson acting executor of Margaret Lindow (SO).

Exhibited from TA:
- additional accounts of William Martin & his wife Ann executrix of Loftus Bowdle.

29 September. Mr. John Thompson (CE) to examine accounts of:
- Michael Tully & his wife Rachel administratrix of Robert Crocker (CE).

2 October. Exhibited from BA:
- accounts of Burridge Scott (AA) administrator of James Powell.

Exhibited from CE:
- additional accounts of Augustina Ward administratrix of John Ward.

13 October. Walter Hanson (g, CH) exhibited:
- will of Alexander Willson.
- inventory of Samuel Burgess.
- inventory of James Ross.
- additional inventory of Leonard Green.
- accounts of Matthew Clubb surviving executor of John Clubb.
- accounts of Margaret Jenkins administratrix of William Jenkins.
- additional accounts of Prudence Green executrix of Leonard Green.
- accounts of Thomas Coleman executor & James Greenfield Wood & his wife Martha executrix of Thomas Coleman.

Mr. Walter Hanson (CH) to examine accounts of:
- John Alexander & Gerrard Fowke administrators of Sarah Fowke (CH).
- Ignatius Gardner & James Middleton executors of Vincent Askin (CH).
- Henry Barnes, Jr. administrator of Thomas Barnes (CH).
- Andrew Chunn administrator dbn of Richard Chunn (CH).
- Robert Whythill & his wife Elisabeth

administratrix of John Theobalds (CH).
- Henry Barnes acting executor of Martha Barnes (CH).
- Frances Bryan administratrix of Daniel Bryan (CH).

32:24 **20 October.** Thomas Bullen (g, TA) exhibited:
- bond of Henry Sworden (DO) & Thomas Smith administrators of Henry Sworden. Sureties: William Webb Haddaway, Benjamin Cooper. Date: 11 October 1746.
- inventory of Barnaby Stapleford, Jr.
- inventory of James Berry.
- inventory of Daniel Macdaniel.
- accounts of Mary Ann Robotham administratrix of Ralph Robotham.
- accounts of Richard Dove & his wife Rachel administratrix of William Ardery.
- additional accounts of Elisabeth Stevens administratrix of John Stevens.

21 October. Mr. Gabriel Parker (CV) to examine accounts of:
- Betty Sedwick executrix of Benjamin Sedwick (CV).
- Sarah Scarff administratrix of Nicholas Scarff (CV).
- William Williams & John Howarton executors of Elisabeth Young (CV).
- Clarana Winall administratrix of William Winall (CV). Additional accounts.

28 October. Benton Harris (g, WO) exhibited:
- will of George Truitt, constituting Elisabeth Truitt executrix. Also, widow's election. Said Elisabeth was granted administration. Sureties: Abraham Outten, Daniel Wells. Date: 13 September 1746.
- will of Elisabeth Tingle, constituting Daniel Tingle executor. Said executor was granted administration. Sureties: Benjamin Davis, Hugh Tingle, Jr. Date: 19 July 1746.

- will of William Ennis, constituting Rebeckah Ennas & William Ennis executors. Said executors were granted administration. Sureties: Daniel Wells, Littleton Townsend. Date: 5 September 1746.
- will of John Langston.
- will of William Turvill, constituting Margery Turvill executrix. Said executrix was granted administration. Sureties: John Turvill, William Gault. Date: 13 October 1746.
- bond of Elisabeth Longo administratrix of James Longo. Sureties: James Macdanald, William Oshahanus, Peter Becketts. Date: 24 July 1746.
- inventory of Turvill Pointer.
- inventory of Selby Claywell.
- accounts of George Jarman administrator of Absolem Bessicks.

32:25   29 October. Mr. Benton Harris (WO) to examine accounts of:
- Bridgett Kennett executrix of Martin Kennett (WO).
- Joshua Morss & his wife Mary administratrix of John Burton (WO).
- Joseph Robinson administrator of John Robinson (WO).
- Lucretia Claywell & Peter Claywell executors of Peter Claywell (WO).
- William Lathinghouse & his wife Mary administratrix of William Smith (WO).
- David Smith one of sureties of Martha Harvey administratrix of John Harvey (WO).

1 November. Mr. Thomas White (BA) to examine accounts of:
- Richard Dallam administrator of Peter Farmer (BA).

3 November. William Tilghman (g, QA) exhibited:
- will of Worner Chance.
- inventory & LoD of Daniel McClean.
- inventory of Peter Countiss.
- additional inventory of John Jackerman.

- accounts of Abraham Williams & his wife Rebecca executrix of Peter Hand.
- accounts of Phineas Wilson & his wife Ann administratrix of John Jackerman.

Nehemiah King (g, SO) exhibited:
- will of John Tunstall.
- inventory & LoD of William Jones.
- inventory of Richard Wallace.
- accounts of Marcy Fountain administrator of William Copsey.
- accounts of Mary Fountain & Marcy Fountain executors of Nicholas Fountain.
- accounts of James Gunby surviving executor of John Gunby.
- accounts of Mary Goslee administratrix of James Goslee.
- accounts of John Caldwell & his wife Mary (alias Mary Vaughn) acting executrix of William Vaughn.
- accounts of Sarah Jones executrix of James Jones (Baron Creek).

Exhibited from AA:
- inventory of Dr. Samuel Chew.

5 November. Exhibited from BA:
- will of John Cockey.

32:26 7 November. William Tilghman (g, QA) exhibited:
- will of James Tounsend, constituting Jane Tounsend executrix. Said executrix was granted administration. Sureties: Thomas Soden, John Cahell. Date: 9 October 1746.
- will of Elisabeth Clouds.
- bond of William Burch & his wife Rachael administrators of Stephen Sweatnam. Sureties: Robert Reynolds, Reuben Taylor. Date: 6 October 1746.
- inventory of James Powell.
- additional inventory of James Hicks.
- inventory of Richard Mason.

Mr. William Tilghman (QA) to examine accounts of:

- James Daley executor of John Dailey (QA).
- Anne Hicks & Giles Hicks executors of John Hicks (QA).
- Matthew Weeks & Stephen Weeks executors of John Weeks (QA).
- Vincent Price administrator of Timothy Lane (QA).
- William Dulany executor of William Dulany (QA).
- Patrick Robertson & Alexander Robertson executors of Patrick Robertson (QA).
- Rebecca Costin administratrix of Henry Costin (QA).

10 November. Exhibited from PG:
- 2nd additional accounts of James Drane & his wife Elisabeth executrix of Samuel Pottinger.

William Rogers (g, AA) exhibited:
- will of Francis Peirpoint.
- bond of Patrick Creagh administrator of Joel Hutchisson. Sureties (Annapolis): Simon Duff, Thomas Smith. Date: 17 September 1746.
- bond of Philip Jones administrator of Richard Smith. Surety: Benjamin Wright. Date: 20 October 1746.
- bond of Sarah Trott executrix of Thomas Trott. Sureties: Lewis Levin, Lewis Jones. Date: 9 September 1746.
- inventory of Richard Tootell.
- inventory of Thomas Ruley.
- inventory of James Macklannen.
- inventory of Gassaway Watkins.

32:27

Court Session: 11 November 1746.

Docket:
- Sheriff (PG) to render attachment to Lingan Wilson (PG) administrator of Joseph Wilson (PG) to render inventory.
- Sheriff (PG) to summon James Wilson (brother) & Henry Wright Wilson (nephew) of Joseph Wilson (PG, dec'd) to show cause why they do not sign inventory as next of kin.
- Thomas Sligh & Henry Morgan sureties

on estate of Buckler Partridge (BA) vs. Jane Partridge administratrix of said dec'd. Sheriff (BA) to render attachment to defendant to render accounts.

- Thomas Clark on behalf of Margaret & Susannah Clark minors & orphans of Abraham Clark (CV, dec'd) vs. John Griffen administrator of said dec'd. Sheriff (CV) to summon defendant to show cause why he conceals certain chattel of dec'd.

32:28
- Henry Hooper, Jr. administrator of Rosannah Reed (DO) vs. Sarah Dodd (DO). Sheriff (DO) to render attachment to defendant to show cause why she conceals estate of dec'd.

- Raymond Stapleford, Charles Stapleford, & Thomas Stapleford executors of Elisabeth Taylor (DO) vs. Dorothy Gollothon (DO) & Dorothy Loockerman (DO). Sheriff (DO) to summon defendants to show cause why they conceal estate of dec'd.

- Sheriff (SO) to summon Thomas Morrison & his wife widow of Philip Ellis (DO) to take LoA on his estate.

- S.B. for Lawrence Macnemara & his wife Elisabeth (CH) vs. Edward Dorsey procurator for Mary Ann Atcherson executrix of John Atcherson. Libel.

32:29
- S.B. for Baptist Barber & his wife Elisabeth (SM) vs. William Cumming, Esq. procurator for Samuel & Richard Southern executors of John Johnson Southern. Libel.

- Executors of Richard Tootell creditors to estate of Nicholas Hammond (AA) vs. Mary Hammond (AA) administratrix of said dec'd. Sheriff (AA) to summon defendant to render accounts.

- E.D. for executors of Godfrey Milner (BA) vs. Stephen Bordley, Esq. procurator for Thomas White. Libel, answer.

Court Session: 1746

12 November. Exhibited from QA:
* bond of Elisabeth Wilson
  administratrix of Robert Wilson.
  Sureties: Samuel Blunt (p, KI), John
  Grainger (p, KI). Date: 12 November
  1746.

MM Beddenfield Hands (KE), Simon Wilmer
(KE), Joseph Nicholson (KE), & William
Dames (KE) to appraise estate of Richard
Lux (KE).

13 November. Exhibited from CH:
* accounts of Peter Wright & his wife
  Ann executrix of Rowland Evans.

32:30   14 November. Exhibited from CV:
* 2nd additional accounts of John
  Skinner (merchant) & his wife
  Eleanor executrix of Capt.
  Posthumus Thornton.
* affidavit of Mr. William Thornton
  (of full age, Annapolis, nephew of
  said Posthumus Thornton). Mentions:
  Isaac Milner, Mr. Charles Sewall.
  Date: 14 November 1746.

Thomas Bullen (g, TA) exhibited:
* will of Mary Sherwood.
* will of Francis Armstrong.
* additional inventory of Wollman
  Gibson.
* inventory of Nathaniel Santee.
* inventory of Richard Story.
* inventory of Isaac Edwards.
* inventory of John Davis.
* inventory of John Tibbels.
* inventory of Thomas Thompson.
* inventory of John Studham.
* additional accounts of William
  Trippe & his wife Elisabeth acting
  executrix of Wollman Gibson executor
  of Jacob Gibson administrator dbn of
  Sarah Wollman.
* additional accounts of Mary Davis &
  Perry Benson executors of John
  Davis.
* additional accounts of William
  Trippe & his wife Elisabeth acting
  executrix of Wollman Gibson.
* accounts of Robert Spencer & his
  wife Mary administratrix of Thomas

Page 7

Russell.
- accounts of Jeremiah Nicols administrator of Michael Fletcher.

32:31 14 November. Mr. Thomas Bullen (TA) to examine accounts of:
- Thomas Dudley administrator of John Batcheldor (TA).

Francis Day (AA) creditor on estate of Mary Covill (AA) vs. said estate. Caveat against passing accounts.

Joseph Baron son & representative of Sarah Baron legatee of Thomas Sockwell (TA) vs. Peter Corke (TA) who married Mary widow & executrix of said dec'd. Sheriff (TA) to summon defendant to show cause why he does not pay plaintiff.

15 November. Exhibited from TA:
- additional accounts of Cassandra White executrix of William White.

Exhibited from PG:
- inventory of Benjamin West.
- will of John Parr.

18 November. Thomas Bullen (g, TA) exhibited:
- will of Richard Eubanks, constituting Tamson Eubanks executrix. Also, widow's election. Said executrix was granted administration. Sureties: Richard Porter (g), Thomas Porter (g). Date: 13 November 1746.
- accounts of John Small & his wife Sarah executrix of Henry Oldfield.

Mr. Thomas Bullen (TA) to examine accounts of:
- Thomas Bozman administrator dbn of Jonathan Taylor (TA).

20 November. Exhibited from PG:
- bond of George Beckwith & Basil Beckwith administrators of Ann Miller. Sureties: John Clagett (p), Sabrit Clagett (p). Date: 20 November 1746. Also, renunciation of

32:32   John Miller (widower). Date: 5
November 1746. Witness: John Night.
Appraisers: Mr. Thomas Hodgkins,
John Boon.

21 November. Exhibited from PG:
* additional accounts of Mareen
Duvall, Jr. executor of John Soper.

22 November. Exhibited from QA:
* accounts of Thomas Cooper & his wife
Amelia administratrix of Robert
Walters.

Exhibited from AA:
* accounts of Edward & John Hall
executors of John Hall.

24 November. Thomas Aisquith (g, SM)
exhibited:
* will of Margaret Miles.
* will of Hugh Hopewell, constituting
Joseph Hopewell executor. Said
executor was granted administration.
Sureties: George Aisquith, John
Horn. Date: 3 October 1746.
* bond of Teakly Joy administratrix of
Enock Joy. Sureties: James
Thompson, Oswell Thompson. Date: 7
August 1746.
* bond of James Mills administrator of
Edward Austain. Sureties: Gilbert
Ireland, Thomas Alstone. Date: 2
September 1746.
* bond of Mary Railey administratrix
of John Railey. Sureties: John
Lucas, Lazarus Ross. Date: 2
September 1746.
* bond of John Hilton administrator of
Andrew Hilton. Sureties: Robert
Ludel, Burch Swann. Date: 6 August
1746.
* inventory & LoD of Luke Hopkins.
* inventory of Joseph Owens.
* inventory & LoD of Elener Astin.
32:33 * inventory of Clement Gardiner.
* inventory & LoD of Mary Jones.
* inventory & LoD of Margret Alvey.
* inventory of Enock Joy.
* accounts of Rachel Billingsly
administratrix of Bowles Billingsly.
* accounts of John Gibbins

administrator of Martha Gibbins.
- accounts of Mary Bean & John Bean executors of John Bean.
- accounts of Thomas Alstone & his wife executrix of Samuel Bagley.
- accounts of Jane Watts executrix of William Watts.
- accounts of James Dickson administrator of George Boyd.
- accounts of Alice Gibson executrix of John Gibson.
- accounts of William Doxkey & his wife Agnes executrix of John Pembrook.

Gabriel Parker (g, CV) exhibited:
- bond of James Russell administrator of Francis Drake. Sureties: John Wilkinson, George Maxwell. Date: 13 October 1746.
- bond of Thomas Ireland, Jr. administrator of Jesse Bourne. Sureties: Thomas Ireland, William Ireland. Date: 16 September 1746.
- bond of Elisabeth Talbott administratrix of Daniel Talbott. Sureties: Richard Talbott, Joseph Talbott. Date: 29 October 1746.
- inventory of John Brooke.
- accounts of Thomas Cullinbur administrator of Thomas Cullinbur.
- accounts of James Fraizer executor of Daniel Fraizer.
- additional accounts of Clarana Winall administratrix of William Winall.

Mr. William Tilghman (QA) to examine accounts of:
- Joseph Nennam & his wife Sarah administratrix of Hercules Cook (QA).

32:34   Mr. Thomas Aisquith (SM) to examine accounts of:
- Pricilla Burn administratrix of Michall Burn (SM).
- Mazatin Forgoe administrator of Alexander Forgoe (SM).
- Meveril Lock administrator of George Wallis (SM).
- Rachel Bussey (CV) executrix of

Hezekiah Bussey (SM).
- Peter Johnson executor of John
  Johnson (SM).
- John Maddox executor of Samuel
  Maddox (SM). Additional accounts.

26 November. Mr. Charles Hynson (KE)
to examine accounts of:
- Mary Riley & Nicholas Riley
  executors of Nicholas Riley (KE).
- Elisabeth Tharp acting executrix of
  John Tharp (KE).
- Armerall Webb administratrix of John
  Webb (KE).

29 November. Mr. Walter Hanson (CH) to
examine accounts of:
- Mary Hamersley administratrix of
  Francis Hamersley (CH).

26 November. Charles Hynson (g, KE)
exhibited:
- will of William Goodson.
- will of Johannah Greenwood.
- will of John James.
- will of John Tilden, constituting
  John Tilden executor. Said executor
  was granted administration.
  Sureties: William Rasin, Perrigrine
  Browne. Date: 14 October 1746.
- will of Martha James.
- will of Nathaniel McClannahan,
  constituting Mary McClannahan
  executrix. Said executrix was
  granted administration. Sureties:
  Hugh Wallace, Philip Brooks. Date:
  20 November 1746.
- bond of Thomas Lynch & his wife Anne
  administrators of Edward Carwarden.
  Sureties: Nicholas Lynch, Edmund
  Lynch. Date: 29 October 1746.
- bond of Samuel Wallace administrator
  of John Tennant. Sureties: John
  Wallace, Henry Bodien. Date: 18
  September 1746.
- bond of John March, Jonathan Turner,
  & James Greenwood administrators of
  James Greenwood. Sureties:
  Alexander Brisco, Francis Lamb.
  Date: 1 November 1746.

32:35
- additional inventory of John Tharp.
- inventory of William Brown.

Page 11

Court Session: 1746

- additional inventory & LoD of Nicholas Riley.
- additional inventory of Robert Due.
- additional inventory of William Crow.
- inventory of John Webb.
- inventory of Edward Worrell.
- accounts of William Taylor administrator of Francis Wetherell.
- accounts of Katherine Simpson administratrix of Thomas Simpson.
- additional accounts of Lambert Wilmer executor of Elisabeth Young.
- accounts of Elisabeth Miller administratrix of Nathaniel Miller.
- accounts of Elisabeth Hickman & Henry Truelock administrators of John Hickman.

29 November. Thomas White (g, BA)
exhibited:
- will of David Thomas. Also, bond of Elisabeth Thomas acting executrix. Sureties: Thomas Wheeler, Benjamin Wheeler. Date: 20 September 1746.
- will of John Cole.
- will of Martha Paca.
- bond of Patience Stinchcomb administratrix of Nathaniel Stinchcomb. Sureties: John Stinchcomb, Christopher Randall. Date: 14 September 1746.
- bond of James Rowles administrator of James Scarff. Sureties: John Sarjant, Peter Dowell. Date: 5 November 1746.
- bond of Thomas Sheredine administrator of John Frederick. Sureties: Parker Hall, John Hattan. Date: 18 October 1746.
- bond of Jacob Hanson executor of Sarah Taman. Sureties: Hudson Davidge, James Osborn. Date: 18 November 1746.
- inventory of Peter Farmer.
- accounts of Susanna Butler executrix of Henry Butler.
- accounts of Richard Dallam administrator of Peter Farmer.

32:36   1 December. Benton Harris (g, WO)
exhibited:

Page 12

- will of Hampton Hopkins, constituting Betty Hopkins executrix. Said executrix was granted administration. Sureties: John Scarbrough, Samuel Wise. Date: 28 October 1746.
- will of Matthew Rain.
- inventory of William Ennis.
- inventory of Levin Disharoon.
- accounts of Joseph Robison administrator of John Robison.
- accounts of Alexander Buncle administrator of James Ewart.

Mr. Benton Harris (WO) to examine accounts of:
- John Aydelet, Sr. administrator of William Salmon (WO).
- Mary Hudson administratrix of Richard Hudson, Jr. (WO).
- Warren Burross & his wife Pricilla administratrix of John Willeys (WO).
- Isaac Bell & John Rickords executors of Elisabeth Smith (WO). 2nd additional accounts.

2 December. Peter Dent (g, PG) exhibited:
- will of Anne Thomas, constituting William Tenaly executor. Said executor was granted administration. Sureties: John Lanham, Benjamin Norris. Date: 11 October 1746.
- will of Anne Weaver, constituting John Veach executor. Said executor was granted administration. Sureties: Charles Hays, Charles Bussey. Date: 27 August 1746.
- bond of Martha Page administratrix of Bingly Page. Sureties: William Sadd, Thomas Clayland. Date: 28 August 1746.
- accounts of Josiah Beall & Lucey Beall executors of Virlinda Beall executrix of John Beall.
- additional accounts of William Robinson & his wife Dianna administratrix of John Williams.
- accounts of Elisabeth Riggs executrix of James Riggs.

Court Session: 1746

Exhibited from BA:
- inventory & LoD of John Wright.

32:37   Exhibited from PG:
- accounts of Priscilla Wilson executrix of Thomas Wilson.

Gabriel Parker (g, CV) exhibited:
- accounts of Capel King administrator of Sarah Malden.
- additional inventory of Henry Austin. Also, additional accounts of Samuel Austin surviving executor.

3 December. Ennalls Hooper (g, DO) exhibited:
- will of John Quatermus, constituting Sarah Quatermus executrix. Said executrix was granted administration. Sureties: George Hutton, George Andrew. Date: 18 August 1746.
- will of William Robinson, constituting William & Andrew Robinson executors. Said executors were granted administration. Sureties: Hugh Cannon, Jacob Bramble. Date: 15 September 1746.
- will of Daniel Hubbert, constituting Mary Hubbert executrix. Said executrix was granted administration. Sureties: Arthur Whitely, Thomas Taylor. Date: 25 September 1746.
- will of Lewis Griffith, constituting Lewis Griffith executor. Said executor was granted administration. Sureties: Henry Leack, Thomas Wheatley. Date: 12 November 1746.
- bond of Ann Foxson administratrix of James Foxson. Sureties: Henry Leak, Arthur Whitely. Date: 12 November 1746.
- bond of Sarah Phillups administratrix of Thomas Phillups. Sureties: Benjamin Keen, Henry Keen. Date: 19 September 1746.
- bond of James Cullen administrator of William Cullen. Sureties: John Stewart, Jr., Thomas Manning. Date: 28 August 1746.
- inventory of David Rogers.

32:38
- inventory of Richard Nuttawell.
- inventory of George Williams.
- inventory of Adam Mears.
- inventory of William Spencer.
- inventory of Charles Wheeler.
- inventory & LoD of William Edmondson.
- inventory of Howes Goldsborough.
- inventory & LoD of Thomas Eccleston.
- inventory of John Hughs.
- inventory & LoD of Edward Tunis.
- inventory of Samuel Cornish.
- inventory of Henry Turner.
- inventory of John Quarturmus.
- inventory of John Turpin.
- accounts of Ailce Warren administratrix of John Warren.
- additional accounts of Rachael Jones administratrix of Walter Hunter.
- accounts of William Perray administrator of Adam Mears.
- accounts of William Twyford administrator of William Twyford.
- accounts of Hannah Reed administratrix of Ezekiel Reed.
- additional accounts of William Bartlett & his wife Margaret executrix of William Harper.
- accounts of John Pattison & Moses Lecompte & his wife Mary executors of St. Leger Pattison.
- accounts of John Brown & his wife Modlin administratrix of Thomas Windstandley.
- accounts of Elinor Phillips administratrix of Thomas Phillips.
- accounts of Martha Connerly executrix of Owen Connerly.
- accounts of Rebeccah Wall executrix of Charles Stapleford.
- accounts of Josias Moor administrator of John Jameson.
- accounts of Sarah Chillcutt executrix of George Chillcutt.
- additional accounts of Elisabeth Jones executrix of Leonard Jones.
- accounts of William Guy & his wife Sarah executors of John Creek.

32:39 Burridge Scott administrator of James Powell (BA) was granted continuance.

[Omitted from f. 17.]
- 13 September. Notice to Mr. John Lewis (PG). William Tenally was granted LoA on estate of Ann Thomas (PG).
- 20 September. William Tennally deposed.
- Hugh Daly (PG), of full age, deposed.

3 December. John Owings (BA) to appraise estate of William Mattingly (BA).

4 December. Mr. Peter Dent (PG) to examine accounts of:
- Jos. Ryan executor of John Orchard (PG).
- Peter Butler & his wife Elisabeth administratrix of William Beckwith (PG). Additional accounts.

32:40   8 December. Exhibited from AA:
- accounts of John Ballson administrator of Richard Randall.

9 December. Peter Dent (g, PG) exhibited:
- will of Jayne Mackbee, constituting Dr. James Doull executor. Said executor was granted administration. Sureties: Lewis Lee, James Eliott. Date: 27 November 1746.
- will of Henry Cramphin, constituting Mary Cramphin executrix. Said executrix was granted administration. Sureties: Edward Willett, William Willett. Date: 27 November 1746.
- bond of Thomas Waring administrator of Samuel Waring. Sureties: Osborn Sprigg, Thomas Hilleary. Date: 28 November 1746.
- bond of Thomas Hillery administrator of Eleanor Hillery. Sureties: Osborn Sprigg, Thomas Waring. Date: 28 November 1746.
- inventory of Anne Weaver.
- inventory & LoD of Robert Tyler.

10 December. William Tilghman (g, QA) exhibited:

- will of William Farrell, constituting Mary Farrell & John Farrell executors. Also, widow's election. Said executors were granted administration. Sureties: William Mason (QA), Edmond Farrell (TA). Date: 27 November 1746.
- bond of Benjamin Kirby & Nicholas Clouds executors of Elisabeth Clouds. Sureties: John Davis, William Baxter. Date: 4 December 1746.
- bond of Sarah Price administratrix of Andrew Price. Sureties: James Browne (g), Benjamin Kirby (g). Date: 4 December 1746.
- additional inventory of Henry Costin.
- inventory of James Maud.
- inventory of Charles Connor.
- inventory & LoD of Henry Price.
- inventory of Thomas Tully.
- inventory of John Bryant.
- accounts of Ann & Giles Hicks executors of James Hicks.
- accounts of Matthew Weeks & Stephen Weeks executors of John Weeks.

32:41

11 December. Mr. William Tilghman (QA) to examine accounts of:
- Bridget Primrose administratrix of William Primrose (blacksmith, QA).

20 December. Mr. Peter Dent (PG) to examine accounts of:
- Susanna Magruder executrix of Alexander Magruder (PG).

William Rogers (g, AA) exhibited:
- bond of Mary Elliott administratrix of Matthew Elliott. Sureties: Thomas Elliott (p), Joseph Bickerton (p), John Little (p). Date: 3 December 1746.
- bond of Philip Hammond administrator of Henry Slaughter. Surety: Thomas Williamson (g, Annapolis). Date: 1 December 1746. Also, renunciation of Mary Slawter (widow), recommending Philip Hammond. Date: 5 November 1746. Witness: John Hammond.

Court Session: 1746

- inventory of Thomas Trott.
- inventory of John Howard.

Gabriel Parker (g, CV) exhibited:
- bond of Benjamin Johns administrator of Richard Johns (Fuller). Sureties: Richard Johns, Richard Johns (of Angelica). Date: 9 December 1746.
- bond of Nathaniel Magruder administrator of Elisabeth Smith. Sureties: John Magruder, William Smith. Date: 8 December 1746.

Court Session: 13 January 1746

32:42 Docket:
- Sheriff (PG) to render attachment to Lingan Wilson (PG) administrator of Joseph Wilson (PG) to render inventory.
- Sheriff (PG) to summon James Wilson (brother) & Henry Wright Wilson (nephew) of Joseph Wilson (PG, dec'd) to show cause why they refuse to sign inventory as next of kin.
- Thomas Sligh & Henry Morgan sureties on estate of Buckler Partridge (BA) vs. Jane Partridge administratrix of said dec'd. Sheriff (BA) to summon defendant to render accounts.
- Thomas Clark on behalf of Margaret & Susanna Clark minors & orphans of Abraham Clark (CV, dec'd) vs. John Griffen (CV) administrator of said dec'd. Sheriff (CV) to summon defendant to show cause why he conceals certain chattel from inventory.

32:43
- Henry Hooper, Jr. administrator of Rosannah Reed (DO) vs. Sarah Dodd (DO). Sheriff (DO) to render attachment to defendant to show cause why she conceals estate of dec'd.
- Raymond Stapleford, Charles Stapleford, & Thomas Stapleford executors of Elisabeth Taylor vs. Dorothy Gollothon (DO) & Dorothy Loockerman (DO). Sheriff (DO) to render attachment to defendants to show cause why they conceal estate

Court Session: 13 January 1746

of dec'd.

- Sheriff (SO) to summon Thomas Morrison & his wife widow of Philip Ellis (DO) to take LoA on his estate.
- S.B. for Lawrence Macnemara & his wife Elisabeth (CH) vs. E.D. for Mary Ann Atcherson executrix of John Atcherson. Libel, answer. Sheriff (CH) to summon to testify for plaintiff: Benjamin Boswell, John Hamill, Robert Haislip, John Moore. Sheriff (PG) to summon to testify for plaintiff: Capt. John Stoddert.
- S.B. for Baptist Barber & his wife Elisabeth (SM) vs. W.C. for Samuel & Richard Southern executors of John Johnson Southern. Libel.

32:44
- Executors of Richard Tootell creditor to estate of Nicholas Hammond (AA) vs. Mary Hammond (AA) administratrix of said dec'd. William Thornton (sheriff, AA) to summon defendant to render accounts.
- E.D. for executors of Godfrey Milner (BA) vs. S.B. for Thomas White. Libel, answer, replication.
- Joseph Baron son & representative of Sarah Baron legatee of Thomas Sockwell (TA, dec'd) vs. Peter Corke (TA) who married Mary widow & executrix of said dec'd. Jacob Henderson (sheriff, TA) to summon defendant to show cause why he does not pay plaintiff his mother's legacy.

Court Session: 1746

32:45 24 January. Mr. Thomas White (BA) to examine accounts of:
- James Rigbie administrator of Samuel Cooper (BA), during minority of Lydia Cooper.

29 January. Walter Hanson (g, CH) exhibited:
- will of Mary Speake, constituting Marmaduke Semmes & Joseph Milburn Semmes executors. Said executors were granted administration. Sureties: James Semmes, Augustine

Court Session: 1746

Ward. Date: 24 November 1746.
- will of Samuel Turner, Sr.
- bond of James Russell administrator of Jonathan Davies, Jr. Sureties: Allen Davies (g), George Maxwell (g). Date: 13 November 1746.
- bond of Mary Willson executrix of Alexander Willson. Sureties: William Middleton, James Middleton. Date: 5 November 1746.
- accounts of Richard Nalley & his wife Elisabeth administratrix of Thomas Goley.
- accounts of Anne Scott administratrix of William Scott.
- additional accounts of Joseph Lancaster executor of Anne Howard.
- additional accounts of Walter Scott administrator of James Scott.
- accounts of Andrew Chunn administrator dbn of John Chunn.
- accounts of Alexander McLoud administrator of John Malony.
- accounts of James Middleton & Ignatius Gardner executors of Vincent Askin.

10 February. Peter Dent (g, PG) exhibited:
- bond of Andrew Gibbs administrator of William Mason. Sureties: James Adams, Thomas Monro. Date: 12 January 1746/7.
- inventory of James Cox.
- accounts of Mary & Zachariah Wade executors of Zachariah Wade.
- 2nd additional accounts of Alexander Norton & his wife Anne administratrix of Henry Jones.
- accounts of John Holly administrator of Humphry Deverson.
- additional accounts of Peter Butler & his wife Elisabeth administratrix of William Beckwith.

32:46   Exhibited:
- petition of Darby Lux attorney in fact for Jonathan Forward (merchant, London). Said Forward has a suit in Provincial Court against Rebecca Tilly executrix of Capt. John Prichard. Bond on said estate

assigned to petitioner.

11 February. Rachel Richardson
(spinster, AA) vs. Thomas Richardson
surviving executor of Richard Richardson
(AA). Sheriff (AA) to summon defendant
to render answer.

12 February. Mr. Charles Hynson (KE)
to examine accounts of:
* Isaac Crow administrator of William
  Crow (KE).
* Samuel Miller executor of Martha
  Miller (KE).
* Elisabeth Ringgold administratrix
  dbn of William Buckham (KE). 2nd
  additional accounts.

14 February. Exhibited from AA:
* will of Henry Wright.

32:47   Mr. Walter Hanson (CH) to examine
accounts of:
* Penelope Brown administratrix of
  John Brown (CH).
* Margret Chapman administratrix of
  John Chapman (CH).
* Mary Neale executrix of Benjamin
  Neale (CH).
* Elisabeth McHone administratrix of
  Robert McHone (CH).
* Anne Smoot & Thomas Smoot executors
  of Barton Smoot (CH).
* Sarah Hawkins administratrix of
  Thomas Hawkins (CH). Additional
  accounts.

16 February. William Tilghman (g, QA)
exhibited:
* will of John Wheatley. Also, bond
  of William Wheatley acting executor.
  Sureties: William Griffin (p), John
  Roe (p). Date: 22 January 1746.
  Also, renunciation of Daniel
  Wheatley executor of John Wheatley,
  Jr. Date: 21 January 1746.
  Witness: William Griffin. Also,
  renunciation of John Wheatley.
  Date: 22 January 1746. Witness:
  Richard Tilghman Earle.
* will of Robert Norrest Wright,
  constituting Nathan Wright executor.

Said executor was granted administration. Sureties: Thomas Harris, William Clayton. Date: 8 January 1746.
- will of Thomas Persons.
- bond of Mary Trickey administratrix of Thomas Trickey. Sureties: David Herrington, Thomas Bostock. Date: 12 February 1746.
- bond of Patrick Money & his wife Ann administratrix of William Nevil. Sureties: Francis Rochester, Jr., John Fouracres. Date: 12 February 1746.

32:48
- inventory of William Saunders.
- accounts of William Roberts administrator of Edward Jones.
- accounts of Rebecca Costin administratrix of Henry Costin.
- accounts of William Dulany executor of William Dulany.

Patrick Grey (BA) vs. Patrick Doran (AA) administrator of John Handling (AA). Sheriff (AA) to summon defendant to render inventory.

18 February. Thomas Bullen (g, TA) exhibited:
- will of Patrick Spence.
- will of Robert Goldsborough.
- will of Thomas Clark, constituting Sarah Clark executrix. Also, widow's election. Said executrix was granted administration. Sureties: Edward Neall, Francis Neall, George Prouse. Date: 4 February 1746.
- bond of William Standley administrator of John Standley. Sureties: Samuel Abbott, Erassmus Hollerin. Date: 15 December 1746.
- bond of Robert Morris (factor) administrator of Henry Colson. Sureties: Risdon Bozman, Richard Porter. Date: 26 January 1746.
- inventory & LoD of George Robins.
- inventory of Thomas Spry.
- inventory of Thomas Greenhough.
- inventory of Thomas Alexander.
- inventory of James Robson.
- accounts of Evan Jones & his wife

Susannah administratrix of William Clark.

Mr. Thomas Bullen (TA) to examine accounts of:
- Thomas Dudly administrator of John Batchelder (TA).
- Elisabeth Storey administratrix of Richard Storey (TA).
- William Alexander administrator of Thomas Alexander (TA), during minority of John Alexander.
- Rosannah Barwick executrix of William Barwick (TA).
- Eve Macdaniel administratrix of Daniel Macdaniel (TA).
- Christopher Spry executor of Thomas Spry (TA).
- Thomas Bozman administrator dbn of Jonathan Taylor (TA).

32:49 Capt. Anthony Bacon petitioned to pass accounts on estate of Mr. Anthony Richardson. The widow desires to be present. Mentions: Mr. Philip Walker married said widow.

19 February. Mr. William Tilghman (QA) to examine accounts of:
- Nicholas Glen (TA) & his wife Mary administratrix of Robert Jones (QA).

20 February. John Thompson (g, CE) exhibited:
- will of Abraham Wattson. Also, renunciation of executors. Also, bond of Elisabeth Wattson administratrix. Sureties: William Wattson, Henry Jackson. Date: 9 September 1746.
- will of William Becke. Also, bond of Nicholas Hyland administrator. Sureties: John Kankey, John Hyland. Date: 22 November 1746.
- bond of Ann Freeman administratrix of William Freeman. Sureties: Hugh Terry, Benjamin Terry. Date: 27 November 1746.
- bond of Terresa Allman & Dr. Hugh Mathews administrators of Joseph Allman. Sureties: Edward Rumsey, Walter Deven. Date: 21 January

1746.
- bond of Margaret Reynolds administratrix of Hugh Raney. Sureties: Richard Reynolds, Jacob Harper. Date: 6 February 1746.
- bond of William Robinson administrator of Patrick Macgren. Sureties: William Mackewn, John Armstrong. Date: 7 December 1746.
- bond of Margaret Silcock & John Cooper administrators of Gabriel Silcock. Sureties: Nicholas Dorrell, David Ricketts. Date: 12 January 1746.
- bond of Mary Jones administratrix of Peter Jones. Sureties: Thomas Davis, Robert Mercer. Date: 24 November 1746.

32:50
- bond of William Baily administrator of William Baily. Sureties: Thomas Taylor, Thomas Elliot. Date: 12 January 1746.
- bond of Margaret Reynolds administratrix of John Reynolds. Sureties: Jacob Harper, Richard Reynolds. Date: 6 February 1746.
- inventory of Abram Allman.
- inventory of John Sluyter.
- inventory of James Wright.
- inventory of William Freeman.
- additional accounts of John Harper administrator dbn of Robert Withers.
- accounts of Margaret Allman executrix of Abraham Allman.
- accounts of John & Thomas Rickets executors of Samuel Jones.
- accounts of Joseph Thomas & John Rickets executors of Roger Mirick.

Mr. John Thompson (CE) to examine accounts of:
- George Rock & his wife Mary administratrix of Robert Story (CE).
- John Cockson & James Ogleby executors of John Ogleby (CE).
- Ann Freeman administratrix of William Freeman (CE).

25 February. Walter Hanson (g, CH) exhibited:
- bond of William Sympson administrator of James Sayers.

Sureties: John Wathen (p), Thomas Sympson, Jr. (p). Date: 4 February 1746.

- bond of Mary Fewell administratrix of John Fewell. Sureties: William Sesson, Hugh Perrie. Date: 18 February 1746.
- bond of Mary Walker administratrix of Edward Walker. Sureties: John Blackwood, Benjamin Thompson. Date: 18 February 1746.
- bond of Jemima Sias administratrix of Robert Sias. Sureties: David Southerland, Jr., Rhodam Trussitt. Date: 18 February 1746.
- bond of Timothy McCan administrator of John Weathers. Sureties: James Muncaster, Bartholomew Hatton. Date: 18 February 1746.
- inventory of John Waters.
- inventory of Alexander Willson.
- accounts of Andrew Chunn administrator dbn of Richard Chunn.
- additional accounts of Frances Bryan administratrix of Daniel Bryan.
- accounts of Henry Barnes acting executor of Matthew Barnes.
- accounts of Henry Barnes administrator of Thomas Barnes.
- accounts of Mary Hamersley administratrix of Francis Hamersley.

32:51 Mr. Walter Hanson (CH) to examine accounts of:
- Jane Brent executrix of William Brent (CH).
- John Alexander & Gerrard Fowke administrators of Sarah Fowke (CH).
- Anne McDaniel executrix of Daniel McDaniel (CH).
- Mary Goodrick, Edward Goodrick, & Francis Goodrick executors of Francis Goodrick (CH).
- James Muncaster executor of Richard King (CH).
- Mary Chapman executrix of Richard Chapman (CH).

Lawrence Macnemara & his wife Elisabeth vs. Mary Ann Atcherson executrix of John Atcherson. Sheriff (PG) to summon Benjamin Bazel (PG) to testify for plaintiffs.

Exhibited from TA:
* Thomas Bullen (TA) deposed that he gave Philip Walker & his wife Elisabeth notice to appear before the Commissary General. Date: 23 February 1746. Signed: Thomas Bozman.

28 February. Exhibited from TA:
* 2nd additional inventory of Anthony Richardson. Also, additional accounts of Capt. Anthony Bacon executor.

Mr. John Thompson (CE) to examine accounts of:
* Margaret Reynolds administratrix of Thomas Reynolds (CE).
* John Baldwin & his wife Mary administratrix of Dominick Carroll (CE). Additional accounts.

Mr. Thomas White (BA) to examine accounts of:
* John Bailey administrator of Mary Smith (Spesutia, BA).

Mr. Gabriel Parker (CV) to examine accounts of:
* John Wood administrator of William Wood (CV).

32:52   5 March. Mary Parr & Anthony Parr executors of John Parr (PG) vs. Benjamin Clarey (PG) one of witnesses to will of said dec'd. Sheriff (PG) to summon defendant to prove said will.

Mary Parr & Anthony Parr executors of John Parr (PG) vs. John Hobbs (AA) one of witnesses to will of said dec'd. Sheriff (AA) to summon defendant to prove said will.

9 March. Thomas Aisquith (g, SM) exhibited:
* will of John Abell, constituting Frances Abell executrix. Said executrix was granted administration. Sureties: Samuel

Court Session: 1746

Abell (son of John), Francis
Hutchins. Date: 8 November 1746.

- will of Richard Deaver, constituting
Assilla Deavour executrix. Also,
widow's election. Said executrix
was granted administration.
Sureties: Hugh Hopewell, Jr., John
Woodward. Date: 17 November 1746.
- will of Matthew Harbert,
constituting Grace Harbert
executrix. Said executrix was
granted administration. Sureties:
Francis Harbert, Bennet Fenwick.
Date: 20 January 1746.
- will of John Heard, constituting
James Heard executor. Said executor
was granted administration.
Sureties: Matthew Heard, Peter Peek.
Date: 20 January 1746.
- bond of Charles Joy administrator of
Ann Joy. Sureties: Richard Finwick,
Thomas Spaulding (son of Peter).
Date: 27 November 1746.
- bond of Roger Tole administrator of
John Tole. Sureties: William
Harrison, Darby Morris. Date: 2
December 1746.
- inventory of John Railey.
- accounts of Rachal Green executrix
of John Green.
- accounts of Athanasius Notingham
executor of Stephen Notingham.
- accounts of Peter Mugg & his wife
Ann administratrix of Matthew
Vowles.
- accounts of Jane West administratrix
of William West.
- accounts of Kenelm Boult, Edward
Hilliard Hebb, & Ann Boult executors
of Thomas Boult.

10 March. Exhibited from QA:
- accounts of William Stavely & his
wife Mary executrix of Jacob
Winchester.

32:53   William Rogers (g, AA) exhibited:
- will of Mordecai Hammond.
- inventory of George Vennam.
- inventory of Matthew Elliott.

Page 27

Court Session: 10 March 1746

Docket:
- Sheriff (PG) to summon Lingan Wilson (PG) administrator of Joseph Wilson (PG) to render inventory.
- Sheriff (PG) to summon James Wilson (brother) & Henry Wright Wilson (nephew) of Joseph Wilson (PG, dec'd) to show cause why they do not sign inventory as next of kin.
- Thomas Sligh & Henry Morgan sureties on estate of Buckler Partridge (BA) vs. Jane Partridge administratrix of said dec'd. Sheriff (BA) to render attachment to defendant to render accounts.
- Thomas Clark on behalf of Margaret & Susanna Clark minors & orphans of Abraham Clark (CV, dec'd) vs. John Griffen (CV) administrator of said dec'd. Sheriff (CV) to summon defendant to show cause why certain chattel is not included in inventory.
- Henry Hooper, Jr. administrator of Rosannah Reed (DO) vs. Sarah Dodd (DO). Sheriff (DO) to render attachment to defendant to show cause why she conceals estate of dec'd.
- Raymond Stapleford, Charles Stapleford, & Thomas Stapleford executors of Elisabeth Taylor (DO) vs. Dorothy Gollothon (DO) & Dorothy Loockerman (DO). Sheriff (DO) to render attachment to defendants to show cause why they conceal estate of dec'd.
- Sheriff (SO) to summon Thomas Morisson & his wife widow of Philip Ellis (DO) to take LoA.
- Stephen Bordley & William Cumming procurators for Lawrence Macnemara & his wife Elisabeth (CH) vs. Edward Dorsey procurator for Mary Ann Atcherson executrix of John Atcherson.
  Text of libel. Plaintiff is late Elisabeth Macfall widow of James Macfall & daughter of John Atcherson (PG, dec'd). Said John married Margaret Steuart by whom he had Elisabeth (plaintiff) & then said

32:54

Page 28

John married Mary. Said Mary Ann
lives in CH; plaintiff is the only
child.

32:55 ...

32:56 Mentions: John Hamill (CH),
32:57 Samuel Hanson (sheriff, CH), Col.
Robert Hanson, Dr. Gustavus Brown.
Text of answer.

32:58 Mentions: William Downs (person of
no worth), John Dunn (person of no
worth), William Warder (person of no
worth), Daniel Williams.

32:59 Said Mary Ann calls said Elisabeth a
bastard & not the same person as
Elisabeth McFall mentioned in will
of said dec'd.

32:60 William Mauduit Sheriff (CH) to
summon to testify for plaintiff:
Benjamin Boswell (CH), John Hamill
(CH), Robert Haislip (CH), John
Moore (CH). William Mauduit
(sheriff, PG) to summon to testify
for plaintiff: Capt. John Stoddert
(PG), Benjamin Bazel (PG). Said
Stoddert is cited as N.E.
— Robert Haislip deposed.
Ruling: plaintiff. Mentions: Negro
Jemmy (man).

32:61 • S.B. for Baptist Barber & his wife
Elisabeth (SM) vs. William Cumming,
Esq. procurator for Samuel & Richard
Southren executors of John Johnson
Southren. Libel.

• Executors of Richard Tootell
creditors to estate of Nicholas
Hammond (AA) vs. Mary Hammond (AA)
administratrix of said Hammond.
Sheriff (AA) to render attachment to
defendant to render accounts. To be
left off.

• E.D. for executors of Godfrey Milner
(BA) vs. S.B. for Thomas White.
Libel, answer, replication.

• Joseph Baron (son of Sarah Baron
legatee of Thomas Sockwell (TA,
dec'd)) vs. Peter Clarke (TA) who
married Mary widow & executrix of
said Sockwell. Sheriff (TA) to
summon defendant to show cause why
he does not pay plaintiff legacy due
his mother.

• Patrick Grey (BA) vs. Patrick Doran

Court Session: 10 March 1746

       (AA) administrator of John Handling
(AA). William Thornton (sheriff,
AA) to summon defendant to render
inventory. Inventory exhibited.
- Mary Parr & Arthur Parr executors of
John Parr (PG) vs. Benjamin Clary
(PG) one of witnesses to said will.
Sheriff (PG) to summon defendant to
prove said will.

32:62 • Mary Parr & Arthur Parr executors of
John Parr (PG) vs. John Hobbs (AA)
one of witnesses to said will.
William Thornton (sheriff, AA) to
summon defendant to prove said will.
N.E.
- E.D. for Rachel Richardson (AA) vs.
Stephen Bordley procurator for
Thomas Richardson surviving executor
of Richard Richardson. Libel.
William Thornton (sheriff, AA) to
summon defendant to render answer.

Court Session: 1746

10 March. Exhibited from SM:
- LoD on estate of John Johnson
Sothoron.

11 March. Exhibited from AA:
- additional inventory of Loyd Harris.

12 March. Capt. John West who married
one of residuary legatees of Samuel
Maccubbin, Jr. (BA) vs. Joseph Lane
(AA) executor of said dec'd. William
Thornton (sheriff, AA) to summon
defendant to render full accounts.

32:63 14 March. Benton Harris (g, WO)
exhibited:
- bond of John Campbell administrator
of William Simpson. Sureties:
Thomas Powell, Sr., Thomas Powell,
Jr. Date: 5 December 1746. Also,
renunciation of Mary Allen (sister),
recommending John Campbell. Date:
19 November 1746. Witness: Mary
Campbel.
- bond of Sarah Johnson administratrix
of Leonard Johnson. Sureties: John
Atkinson, Peter Claywell. Date: 26
December 1746.

- inventory of James Longoe.
- inventory of Hutten Hill.
- inventory of Leah Parker.
- inventory of Hugh Bratten.
- inventory of Leonard Johnson.
- inventory of David Murray.
- inventory of William Simpson.
- accounts of John Jarman administrator of Martha Walton.
- accounts of John Aydelot, Sr. administrator of William Salmon.
- accounts of William Lathinghouse & his wife Mary administratrix of William Smith.
- renunciation of Robert Watson, Sr. on estate of his son John Watson. Date: 19 January 1743/4.
- renunciation of Alice Robinson widow of Joseph Robinson. Date: 3 April 1745.
- renunciation of Robert Gill on estate of Christopher Topham, recommending William Burton. Date: 2 February 1743/4.
- renunciation of John Jarman on estate of his father. Date: 12 July 1744.

32:64
- renunciation of Frances Burton widow of William Burton, recommending her 2 sons John & Joshua Burton. Date: 30 March 1745.
- renunciation of Sarah Schoolfield, recommending her son Joseph Schoolfield. Date: 14 October 1745. Witnesses: John Ake, Benjamin Scholfield.

10 March. Exhibited from AA:
- bond of Lewis Stinchcombe executor of Henry Wright. Sureties: William Lewis, Phillip Pettibone. Date: 17 February 1746.

14 March. Charles Hynson (g, KE) exhibited:
- nuncupative will of Jonathan Evans.
- will of William Crow.
- will of Jacob Glenn. Also, widow's election.
- will of James Gray, constituting Elisabeth Gray executrix. Said executrix was granted

administration. Sureties: Dr. Lewis Williams, William Millit. Date: 7 February 1746.

- will of Patrick Handraty. Also, bond of Neil McClean & Patrick Keran administrators. Sureties: Mathew Dreadman (p), John Wibb (g). Date: 17 February 1746. Also, renunciation of Ann Handraty (widow), recommending Neil McClean & Patrick Keran (one special creditor, other best friend). Date: 16 February 1746/7. Witnesses: Robert Dallas, Mathew Deadman.

32:65
- bond of James Claypoole administrator of John James. Sureties: Joseph Garnet (saddler), Phillip Davis. Date: 19 January 1746.
- bond of John McKey administrator of Crispin Buttler. Sureties: John Holeadger, Thomas Rickford. Date: 12 December 1746.
- ' bond of Sarah Blakiston administratrix of Ebenezar Blakiston. Sureties: William Wilmer, Henry Hurt. Date: 19 January 1746.
- inventory & LoD of John Hamilton.
- inventory of John Tennant.
- inventory of Edward Carwarden.
- inventory of John Tilden.
- inventory of William Rice.
- inventory & LoD of Nathaniel McClannahan.
- accounts of Mary Riley & Nicholas Riley executors of Nicholas Riley.
- accounts of Isaac & Jacob Caulk executors of Mary Pearce.
- accounts of Elisabeth Tharp acting executrix of John Tharp.
- accounts of Elen Farguson executrix of Robert Dew.
- accounts of Armerell Webb administratrix of John Webb.

Exhibited from AA:
- additional accounts of Dr. Charles Carroll executor of Margaret Macnemara.

Court Session: 1746

Exhibited from SM:
- additional accounts of Samuel Sothoron & Richard Sothoron executors of John Johnson Sothoron.

Exhibited from BA:
- bond of William Cockey & Joshua Owings executors of John Cockey. Sureties: Thomas Cockey (p), Elisabeth Cockey (widow). Date: 5 November 1746.

Exhibited from PG:
- inventory of Jane Mockbee. Also, accounts of James Doull administrator.

16 March. Nehemiah King (g, SO) exhibited:
- will of Charles Revell, constituting Randall Revell & William Revell executors. Said executors were granted administration. Sureties: David Wilson, Samuel Wilson. Date: 6 December 1746.

32:66
- will of George Baley.
- bond of John Elsey executor of William Caldwell. Sureties: David Wilson, Capell King. Date: 30 October 1740.
- inventory of William Miles.
- inventory of John Blewer.
- accounts of Samuel Wilson acting executor of Margrett Lindow.
- accounts of Robert King administrator of William Collins.

Mr. Nehemiah King (SO) to examine accounts of:
- Purnell Newbold administrator of Thomas Newbold (SO).
- Samuel Collins surviving executor of Richard Chambers (SO). Additional accounts.

Mr. Benton Harris (WO) to examine accounts of:
- Joshua Morss & his wife Mary administrators of John Burton (WO).

17 March. Exhibited from BA:
- will of James Presbury.

- will of William Fell, constituting Sarah Fell & Joseph Taylor executors. Said executors were granted administration. Sureties: Thomas Bond, Jr., John Bond. Date: 13 February 1746.
- will of Thomas Rutter.
- will of Thomas Brerewood, constituting William Dallam executor. Said executor was granted administration. Sureties: Richard Dallam, Richard Ruff. Date: 6 February 1746.
- will of Edward Day, constituting John Day executor. Said executor was granted administration. Sureties: Parker Hall, William Young. Date: 13 February 1746.
- will of Isaac Butterworth, constituting Jane Butterworth executrix. Said executrix was granted administration. Sureties: Ignatius Wheeler, Leonard Wheeler. Date: 13 February 1746.
- will of Roland Vine, constituting Sarah Vine executrix. Said executrix was granted administration. Sureties: John Chocke, William Amos. Date: 27 February 1746.
- will of Dugal Macquain.
- bond of William Dallam administrator of John Ward. Surety: Talbot Risteau. Date: 20 February 1746.

32:67
- bond of Avarilla Perrigoe administratrix of Edward Perrigoe. Sureties: Samuel Bowen, Peter Dowell. Date: 14 January 1746.
- bond of Samuel Bowen administrator of Martha Bowen. Sureties: Jonas Bowen, Peter Dowell. Date: 14 January 1746.
- bond of John Combest administrator of George Henry March. Surety: Jacob Combest. Date: 20 December 1746.
- bond of Frances Coleman administratrix of Nicholas Coleman. Sureties: Thomas Franklin, John Long. Date: 6 March 1746.
- inventory & LoD of Nathaniel Stinchcomb.

- inventory & LoD of William Smith.

Exhibited from CV:
- LoD on estate of Richard Lane.

23 March. Gabriel Parker (g, CV) exhibited:
- will of William Dawkins, Jr., constituting Dorcus Dawkins executrix. Said executrix was granted administration. Sureties: John Brome, James Mackall. Date: 10 March 1746.
- bond of Mary Card administratrix of Abraham Card. Sureties: William Williams, William Wilmott. Date: 19 March 1746.
- bond of Jonathan Hollyday administrator dbn of Catharine Hollyday. Sureties: Thomas Morgan, James Dobson. Date: 11 February 1746.
- bond of Young Parran administrator of Moses Parran. Surety: Alexander Parran. Date: 13 February 1746.
- inventory of Daniel Talbott.
- inventory of Thomas Cranford.
- inventory of Elisabeth Smith.
- inventory of Francis Drake.
- accounts of Elisabeth & John Fryer executors of Richard Fryer.
- accounts of William Williams & John Howerton executors of Elisabeth Young.
- accounts of Nathaniel Magruder administrator of Elisabeth Smith.

24 March. Mr. William Tilghman (QA) to examine accounts of:
- Benjamin Hines administrator of Jacob Deford (QA).
- Sarah Hays administratrix of John Hays, Jr. (QA).

32:68   17 March. Henrica Beatty (PG) widow of John Beatty (PG) was granted LoA on his estate. Appraisers: Stephen Julian, James Reed. Mr. Thomas Beatty to administer oath.

26 March. Mr. Charles Hynson (KE) to examine additional accounts of:

- Rev. James Sterling & his wife Rebecca administratrix of Rev. Arthur Holt (KE).

2 April. Exhibited from PG:

- 2nd additional accounts of Andrew Scott & his wife Mary executrix of John Abington.

3 April. Mr. Thomas Aisquith (SM) to examine accounts of:

- Mary Phippard executrix of William Phippard (SM).
- Thomas Simpson & his wife Mary executrix of John Fanning (SM).
- Joseph Pile surviving executor of Henry Wharton (SM).
- William Yates executor of William Bradburne (SM).
- Mary Sledmore administratrix of John Sledmore (SM).
- Margaret Graves administratrix of John Graves (SM).

4 April. Capt. John West who married one of residuary legatees of Samuel Maccubbin (BA) vs. Joseph Lane (AA) executor of said dec'd. William Thornton (sheriff, AA) to render attachment to defendant to render full accounts. On 18 June, 3rd additional accounts exhibited.

7 April. Peter Dent (g, PG) exhibited:

- will of Joseph Williams, constituting Catherine Williams executrix. Said executrix was granted administration. Sureties: Thomas Holly (p), Thomas Athy (p). Date: 16 February 1746.
- inventory of Anne Miller.
- inventory of Anne Thomas.

32:69 9 April. Mr. Ennalls Hooper (DO) to examine accounts of:

- William Smith administrator of John Hodson Secundus (DO).
- Ramond Stapleford, Charles Stapleford, & Thomas Stapleford executors of Elisabeth Taylor (DO).

- Anne Hill administratrix of Daniel Hill (DO).
- George Slacum & his wife Frances executrix of Lewis Griffith (DO).
- Samuel Stanford executor of William Stanford (DO).
- Anne Tregoe & William Tregoe administrators of William Tregoe (DO).
- Phillis Clarkson executrix of Robert Clarkson (DO).
- Thomas Hutchings & his wife Hannah executrix of Ephraim Trotter (DO).
- James Langril executor of Sarah Langril (DO).
- Margaret Arnett & Andrew Arnett administrators of William Arnett (DO).
- James Peterkin executor of Mary Peterkin (DO).
- Mary Smith administratrix of Henry Smith (DO).
- Thomas Wheeler executor of Charles Wheeler (DO).
- John Pollard, Jr. administrator of George Williams (DO).
- Elisabeth Turner administratrix of Henry Turner (DO).
- James Cullen administrator of William Cullen (DO).
- Joanna Alcock administratrix of Burtonwood Alcock (DO).
- Mary Whiteacre administratrix of Joseph Whiteacre (DO).
- Elisabeth Edmondson & William Edmondson executors of William Edmondson (DO).
- Josias Moore administrator of John Jamison (DO). Additional accounts.
- Richard Perry administrator of Hugh Perry (DO). Additional accounts.
- Anne Coburn administratrix of Stephen Coburn (DO). Additional accounts.
- Edward Trippe & his wife Anne administratrix of John Trippe (DO). Additional accounts.
- William Bartlett & his wife Margaret executrix of William Harper (DO). 2nd additional accounts.
- John Pattison executor & Moses Lecompt & his wife Mary executrix of

St. Leger Pattison (DO). 2nd
additional accounts.
- William Phillips administrator of
Catherine Phillips (DO).

10 April. Benton Harris (g, WO)
exhibited:
- will of Robert Watson, constituting
Charles Watson executor. Said
executor was granted administration.
Sureties: William Nelson, Charles
Davis. Date: 3 April 1747.
- bond of George Parker executor of
Tabitha Parker. Sureties: Joseph
Davis, Samuel Parker. Date: 6 March
1746.
- bond of Areada Rain executrix of
Mathew Rain. Sureties: George
Johnson, Samuel Parker. Date: 4
March 1746.
- inventory of Tabitha Massey.
- accounts of Mary Hudson
administratrix of Richard Hudson.
- accounts of Lucretia & Peter
Claywell executors of Peter
Claywell, Sr.
- accounts of Bridgett Kennett
executrix of Martin Kennett.

32:70   10 April. Mr. Benton Harris (WO) to
examine accounts of:
- William Toadvine administrator of
John Blewett (WO).
- John Teague administrator of John
Watson (WO).
- William Selby & his wife Martha
executors of John Purnell (WO).
Additional accounts.

Sheriff (SO) to summon (N) Hern (SO)
widow & executrix of Edward Hern (SO) to
prove his will & take LoA on his estate.

14 April. Thomas Aisquith (g, SM)
exhibited:
- will of Joshua Nelson.
- will of John Cheshire. Also, bond
of Pricilla Cheshire administratrix.
Sureties: Joseph Watson, Philemon
Cheshire. Date: 6 March 1746/7.
- will of Peter Johnson. Also, bond
of George Hayden administrator.
Sureties: Clement Hayden, Richard

Hayden. Date: 8 April 1747.
- inventory & LoD of John Tole.
- inventory & LoD of Hugh Hopewell.
- inventory of Andrew Hilton.
- accounts of Mazotin Furgoe administrator of Alexander Furgoe.
- accounts of Pricilla Burne administratrix of Michael Burne.
- accounts of Meveril Lock administrator of George Wallis.
- accounts of Notley Jordan & his wife Elisabeth administratrix of Luke Hopkins.
- accounts of John Wherrill administrator of John Branan.
- accounts of Isaac Pavett administrator of Joseph Pavett.

Sheriff (SM) to summon Meverell Lock (g, SM) to show cause why he does not deliver to John Tyson guardian of Sarah Nickolls (daughter of Thomas Nickolls (dec'd)) Negro James devised to her by her father.

15 April. Exhibited from PG:
- will of Elisabeth Waters, constituting Joseph Waters (AA) executor. Said executor was granted administration. Sureties: Gerrard Hopkins (AA), Samuel Waters (PG). Date: 15 April 1747.

32:71
- accounts of Stephen Lee who married Sarah Magruder executrix of Robert Magruder.

16 April. Ennalls Hooper (g, DO) exhibited:
- will of James Smith, constituting Joseph Brown executor. Said executor was granted administration. Sureties: Daniel Morris (p), Peter Adams (p). Date: 14 March 1746.
- will of Thomas Ennalls, constituting Ann Ennalls, Henry Ennalls, & Thomas Ennalls executors. Said executors were granted administration. Sureties: John Cail, Joseph Ennalls. Date: 11 February 1746.
- will of John Brown.
- will of Philadelphia Williams, constituting John Williams executor.

Said executor was granted administration. Sureties: John Fisher (p), John Hopkins (p). Date: 10 March 1746.

- will of Robert Sherwin, constituting Mary & Stephen Sherwin executors. Said executors were granted administration. Sureties: Daniel Sulivane (p), Peter Edmondson (p). Date: 11 March 1746.
- will of John Brannock. Also, bond of Frances Brannock administratrix. Sureties: Nehemiah Lecompt, Benjamin Woodward. Date: 11 March 1746.
- will of William Clifton, constituting Sarah Clifton & John Clifton executors. Said executors were granted administration. Sureties: John Marrott, Sr. (p), Thomas Williams, Sr. (p). Date: 12 March 1746.
- will of Henry Dean, constituting John Dean executor. Said executor was granted administration. Sureties: William Robinson (p), James Bright (p). Date: 13 March 1746.
- will of James Meloney. Also, bond of George Drewry administrator. Sureties: Robert Parkinson, William Standford, Jr. Date: 14 March 1746. Also, renunciation of Ezekiell Keene. Date: 27 February 1746.
- will of John Vickars. Also, bond of Sarah Vickars administratrix. Sureties: Thomas Wheeler, John Vickars. Date: 30 March 1747.
- bond of Thomas Nevett administrator of William Mills. Surety: Ebenezar White (g). Date: 11 March 1746.
- bond of Esther Carey administratrix of Dennis Carey. Sureties: William Edmondson, Edward Hardikin. Date: 13 March 1746.

32:72
- bond of Mary Rotten administratrix of Henry Rotten. Sureties: Ralf Smith (p), Samuel Ireland (p). Date: 1 December 1746.
- bond of James Edmondson administrator of Francis Owen. Sureties: John Hayward, Moses Poole. Date: 24 February 1746.

Court Session: 1747

- bond of Rachel Draper administratrix of William Draper. Sureties: Samuel Fountain (p), Joseph Couch (p). Date: 10 March 1746.
- bond of John McCollister & Patrick McCollister administrators of David McCollister. Sureties: Andrew McCollister (p), Titus Hubbert (p). Date: 13 January 1746.
- inventory of Daniel Hubbert.
- inventory of John Willey.
- additional inventory of William Cullen.
- inventory & LoD of Henry Smith.
- inventory of William Robinson.
- inventory of Christian McKormack.
- inventory & LoD of Thomas Phillips.

William Rogers (g, AA) exhibited:
- will of William Scandrell, Jr. Also, bond of Thomas Carradine (QA) acting executor. Sureties: William Coursey (QA), Thomas Emory (QA). Date: 15 April 1747. Also, renunciation of William Scandrel (father), recommending his son-in-law Thomas Carradine. Date: 21 February 1746.
- inventory of John Handling.
- accounts of John Tayman administrator of Joseph Tayman.

15 April. Mr. Walter Hanson (CH) to examine accounts of:
- Penelope Brown administratrix of John Brown (CH).
- Elisabeth Mchone administratrix of Robert Mchone (CH).
- Margret Chapman administratrix of John Chapman (CH).
- Anne Smoot & Thomas Smoot executors of Barton Smoot (CH).
- Mary Neale executrix of Benjamin Neale (CH).
- Sarah Hawkins administratrix of Thomas Hawkins (CH). Additional accounts.

32:73   Mr. Thomas White (BA) to examine accounts of:
- Ann Cadle administratrix of Benjamin Cadle (BA).

Court Session: 1747

Mr. Ennalls Hooper (DO) to examine
accounts of:
• Moses Poole & his wife Rosannah
  executrix & Thomas Stanford executor
  of Charles Stanford (DO).

Mr. Peter Dent (PG) to examine
additional accounts of:
• Josiah Beall & Lucy Beall executors
  of Virlinda Beall executrix of John
  Beall (PG).

18 April. Mr. Charles Hynson (KE) to
examine accounts of:
• Daniel Bryant administrator of Isaac
  Riley (KE).
• Hanse Hanson & his wife Margaret
  executrix of Glanvile Rolph (KE).
  Additional accounts.
• George Hall executor of Benjamin
  Jones (KE). Additional accounts.

Mr. Thomas Aisquith (SM) to examine
accounts of:
• Ann Cutler administratrix of William
  Cutler (SM).
• Benjamin Fenwick administrator of
  Cutbert Fenwick (SM).
• Elijah Waters executor of Thomas
  Waters (SM).
• Winifred Thomas administratrix of
  Mark Thomas (SM).
• Henry Lyon administrator of Thomas
  Morriss (SM).
• Joseph Jones executor of Mary Jones
  (SM).
• Mary Wall administratrix of Thomas
  Wall (SM).

Exhibited from KE:
• 3rd additional accounts of John
  Spencer & his wife Sarah
  administratrix of Hanse Hanson.

32:74   William Tilghman (g, QA) exhibited:
• will of John Long.
• will of Thomas Scotten.
• will of John Osborn.
• will of John Baggs.
• will of Richard Scotten,
  constituting Mary Scotten executrix.
  Also, widow's election. Said

executrix was granted administration. Sureties: Richard Smith (p), Thomas Bailey (p). Date: 26 March 1747.

- bond of Henrietta McDonald administratrix of Donald McDonald. Sureties: John Dempster (QA), Neille McNeille (KE). Date: 18 February 1746.
- bond of John Jackson administrator of Jonathan Seymeter. Sureties: John Emory, Nathan Wright. Date: 19 February 1746.
- bond of Margaret Richardson administratrix of William Richardson. Sureties: Thomas Meloyd (p), Thomas Adams (p). Date: 14 February 1746.
- bond of Alice Alliband administratrix of Thomas Alliband. Sureties: Abraham Williams, Nathaniel Downs. Date: 12 March 1746.
- bond of Jervis Spender (KE) administrator of Christopher Williams, during minority of his son Christopher Williams. Sureties: William Carmichall, John Meconnekin. Date: 26 February 1746.
- bond of William Dulany administrator of Michael Dulany. Sureties: William Durding (p), William Mayson (p). Date: 19 March 1746.
- bond of Margaret Banning administratrix of John Banning. Sureties: William Wheatley (p), John Wootters (p). Date: 25 March 1746/7.
- bond of Sarah Newnam administratrix of Joseph Newnam. Sureties: Humphry Wells (p), William Newnam (p). Date: 27 March 1747.
- bond of Richard Kemp & his wife Mary administrators of Henry Green. Sureties: Thomas Bailey (p), John Bird (p). Date: 9 April 1747.
- bond of Tabitha Persons executrix of Thomas Persons. Sureties: John Nabb (p), James Wrench (p). Date: 5 March 1746.

32:75 Also, renunciation of John Downes, Jr. (executor). Date: 5 March 1746.

- inventory of John Thompson.
- inventory of James Townsend.
- inventory & LoD of Trustram Thomas (Wye).
- inventory & LoD of Sarah Owens.
- inventory of Thomas Curtis.
- inventory of Jonathan Seymeter.
- inventory of John Wheatley, Jr.
- inventory of Stephen Sweatman.
- inventory of William Nevill, Jr.
- inventory & LoD of John Earle.
- inventory of William Farrell.
- additional inventory of Thomas Sevil.
- LoD on estate of John Carman.
- accounts of Thomas Lee executor of Richard Buckley.
- accounts of Sarah Newnam administratrix of Hercules Cooke.

22 April. Thomas Bullen (g, TA) exhibited:
- accounts of Cassandra White executrix of William White executor of John Barnyeatt.
- 2nd additional accounts of Cassandra White executrix of William White.
- will of John Chambers, constituting Rebecca Chambers executrix. Also, widow's election. Sureties: Thomas Porter (p, g), Jonathan Dobson (p). Date: 3 April 1747.
- bond of Bridget Ford administratrix of Thomas Ford. Sureties: Job Guest (p), James Cook (p), Samuel Passifield (p). Date: 18 March 1746.

32:76
- inventory & LoD of Philemon Porter.
- inventory of Henry Sworden.
- inventory of Rev. Daniel Maynadier.
- additional accounts of Abraham Clark & his wife Elisabeth administratrix of John Jones.
- accounts of Elisabeth Storey administratrix of Richard Storey.
- accounts of Jacob Hindman administrator of Robert Bettice.
- accounts of Rosanna Barwick executrix of William Barwick.

Mr. Thomas Bullen (TA) to examine accounts of:

- Daniel Maynadier administrator of Rev. Daniel Maynadier (TA).
- Richard Gurling Robinson & his wife Judith administratrix of John Harrison (TA).
- Stephen Stickbury & his wife Jane executrix of John Studham (TA).
- Elisabeth Louther administratrix of Robert Louther (TA).
- Mary Merchant administratrix of James Merchant (TA).
- William Martin executor & Thomas Loveday & his wife Grace executrix of Samuel Martin.

24 April. John Paca son of Aquilla Paca (BA, dec'd) vs. Peregrine Brown (BA) executor of Rachel Paca executrix of said dec'd. Sheriff (BA) to summon defendant to show cause why he does not pay plaintiff his portion of his father's estate.

22 April. Mary & Nicholas Johnson (PG) administrators of Peter Johnson (PG) were granted LoA on his estate. Appraisers: Capt. Thomas Prather, James Davies.

24 April. William Thornton (sheriff, AA) to summon Jemima Robinson (AA) executrix of Mordecai Hammond to take LoA on his estate. N.E.

32:77 25 April. Sheriff (QA) to summon Hannah Earle executrix of John Earle (QA) to render inventory.

28 April. John Tyson guardian to Sarah Nickolls vs. Meverell Lock (g, SM). Sheriff (SM) to summon defendant to show cause why he does not deliver to said Sarah, the Negro James devised to said Sarah by her father Thomas Nickolls.

29 April. Exhibited from AA:
- bond of Dr. George Steuart administrator of Mordecai Hammond. Sureties: Philip Thomas, Esq. (AA), Nicholas Maccubbin (merchant, Annapolis). Date: 29 April 1747.

30 April. Jacob Franklin & James Deal
to appraise estate of Abraham Simmons
(AA), not appraised by Jacob & John
Franklin.

1 May. Exhibited from AA:
• receipt of Abraham Parkerson from
   Edward Lusby, due from his father
   Abraham Parkinson. Witnesses:
   Ephraim Gover, Hary Camden, L.
   Thomas.

Capt. John Hunter agent for
representatives of Alice Andrews (AA)
vs. Samuel Smith (AA) & Francis Mapp
(AA) executors of said dec'd. Sheriff
(AA) to summon defendants to render
accounts.

2 May. Sheriff (DO) to summon Septimus
Noell (DO), Samuel Lecompte (DO), David
Peterkin (DO), & John Lecompte (DO)--all
witnesses to will of Hugh Eccleston
(DO)--to prove said will.

32:78   4 May. W.C. for Lawrence Macnemara &
his wife Elisabeth (CH) vs. Mary Ann
Atcherson executrix of John Atcherson.
Attachment rendered on defendant.

6 May. Exhibited from AA:
• accounts of Nicholas Besom & his
   wife Margaret (late Margaret Young)
   executrix of John Young.

Mr. Peter Dent (PG) to examine
additional accounts of:
• Presila Willson executrix of Thomas
   Willson (PG).

9 May. Mr. William Tilghman (QA) to
examine accounts of:
• Richard Dash & his wife Rebecca
   administrators of Thomas Civil (QA).

Mr. Nehemiah King (SO) to examine
accounts of:
• Isabella Dashiells executrix of
   William Dashiells (SO).
• Rachell Piper & Christopher Piper
   executors of Christopher Piper (SO).
• George Dashiell & George McClester

sureties for Margaret Blewer
executrix of James Blewer (SO).
- Matthew Wallace acting executor of
Richard Wallace (SO).

11 May. William Rogers (g, AA)
exhibited:
- bond of John Ross, Esq. (Annapolis,
AA) on estate of James Rawlins.
Date: 11 May 1747.
- inventory of Henry Wright.

7 May. Mr. Edward Dorsey on behalf of
Ebenezar Reyner & his wife Sarah (KE)
vs. estate of David Pirkins (KE).
Caveat against proving said will.

Court Session: 12 May 1747

32:79   Docket:
- Sheriff (PG) to summon Lingan Wilson
(PG) administrator of Joseph Wilson
(PG) to render inventory.
- Sheriff (PG) to summon James Wilson
(brother) & Henry Wright Wilson
(nephew) of Joseph Wilson (PG,
dec'd) to show cause why they refuse
to sign inventory as next of kin.
- Thomas Sligh & Henry Morgan sureties
on estate of Buckler Partridge (BA)
vs. Jane Partridge administratrix
of said dec'd. Sheriff (BA) to
render attachment to defendant to
render accounts. Accounts
exhibited. Discontinued.
- Thomas Clark on behalf of Margaret &
Susanna Clark minors & orphans of
Abraham Clark (CV) vs. John Griffen
(CV) administrator of said dec'd.
Sheriff (CV) to summon defendant to
render additional inventory with
additional chattel.
32:80 - Henry Hooper, Jr. administrator of
Rosannah Reed (DO) vs. Sarah Dodd
(DO). Sheriff (DO) to render
attachment to defendant to show
cause why she conceals estate of
dec'd. Struck off.
- Raymond Stapleford, Charles
Stapleford, & Thomas Stapleford
executors of Elisabeth Taylor (DO)
vs. Dorothy Gollothon (DO) &

Dorothy Loockerman (DO). Sheriff (DO) to render attachment to defendants to show cause why they conceal estate of dec'd.

- Sheriff (DO) to summon Thomas Morison & his wife widow of Philip Ellis (DO) to take LoA.
- S.B. for Baptist Barber & his wife Elisabeth (SM) vs. W.C. for Samuel & Richard Southern executors of John Johnson Southern. Libel, answer.
- Edward Dorsey procurator for executors of Godfrey Milner (BA) vs. Stephen Bordley procurator for Thomas White (g, BA). Plaintiffs: Bryan Philpot (merchant, London) & John Philpot (merchant, London) executors of Godfrey Milner (merchant, London) executor of Isaac Milner (merchant, London).

32:81   Text of libel. Said Isaac died in 1743, with a will constituting his brother Godfrey (London) executor. Said will was proved on 1 July 1743 before Edward Kinnaston (Doctor of Law, Master Keeper of Prerogative Court of Canterbury). Said Godfrey died, with a will proved on 2 August 1744 before said Kinnaston surrogate of John Bettesworth (Doctor of Law, Master Keeper of Prerogative Court of Canterbury).

32:82   Mentions: John Risteau (sheriff, BA).
Text of answer.

32:83   ...
32:84   Mentions: John Reynell.
32:85   ...
32:86   Before: John Hall, Samuel Owings. Exhibited 1st schedule. Bills of: Elias Legross on Isaac Milner, Jacob Giles on (N) Hyde, Daniel Scott on (N) Forward, Samuel Webster on Isaac Milner.
Exhibited 2nd schedule. Payments to: Thomas Sheredine, Darby Lux, Sarah Read, Phil. Hamond & John Galloway, Alex. Lawson, Alex. Black, William Dallam, John Paca, William Perkins, John Hall, Isaac Webster, John Forward, Rees Meredith, Lance Todd, Jr., Michael Gilbert.

Court Session: 12 May 1747

32:87   Exhibited 3rd schedule. Bills of exchange: Susannah Stokes, Thomas Bladen, Esq., Rees Meredith, John Hall, Lord Baltimore, Thomas Sheredine.
Exhibited 4th schedule. Received from: John Paca, Mary Walker, executors of Dr. George Walker, Michael Gilbert, Jacob Bull, Dr. Josias Middlemore.

32:88   Ruling: LoA on said estate revoked & left to remedy at law.
- Patrick Grey (BA) vs. Patrick Doran (AA) administrator of John Handling (AA). Sheriff (AA) to summon defendant to render inventory. Inventory exhibited.
- E.D. for Rachel Richardson (AA) vs. S.B. for Thomas Richardson surviving executor of Richard Richardson. Libel.
- Sheriff (SO) to summon (N) Hern (SO) widow & executrix of Edward Hern (SO) to prove said will.
- John Paca son of Aquila Paca (BA, dec'd) vs. Peregrine Brown (BA) executor of Rachel Paca executrix of said dec'd. Sam. Richardson (sheriff, BA) to summon defendant to show cause why he does not pay plaintiff his portion of his father's estate.

32:89   To be left off.
- Ja. Hollyday, Jr. (sheriff, QA) to summon Hannah Earle executrix of John Earle (QA) to render inventory. Inventory exhibited. Discontinued.
- John Tyson guardian to Sarah Nickolls vs. Meverell Lock (g, SM). Sheriff (SM) to summon defendant to show cause why he does not deliver to said Sarah, the Negro James devised to said Sarah by her father Thomas Nickolls. Libel.
- John Hunter agent for representatives of Alice Andrews (AA) vs. Samuel Smith (AA) & Francis Mapp (AA) executors of said dec'd. William Thornton (sheriff, AA) to summon defendants to render accounts. Accounts exhibited. Discontinued.

32:90 • Sheriff (DO) to summon Septimus
Noell (DO), Samuel Lecompte (DO),
David Peterkin (DO), & John Lecompte
(DO)--all witnesses to will of Hugh
Eccleston (DO)--to prove said will.

• W.C. for Lawrence Macnemara & his
wife Elisabeth (CH) vs. Mary Ann
Atcherson executrix of John
Atcherson. Samuel Hanson (sheriff,
CH) to summon defendant.

Court Session: 1747

<u>12 May</u>. Thomas Bullen (g, TA)
<u>exhibited</u>:
• bond of Margaret Coleman
administratrix of John Coleman.
Sureties: Josiah Coleman, Samuel
Hopkins. Date: 23 April 1747.

• bond of William Garey administrator
of Jane Garey. Sureties: Robert
Hall, John Kininmont. Date: 21
April 1747.

• bond of Robert Goldsborough
administrator of James Clayland.
Sureties: Nicholas Goldsborough,
William Finney. Date: 21 April
1747.

• bond of Samuel Kininmont
administrator dbn of Lewis Jones.
Sureties: William Garey, Philemon
Horney. Date: 14 April 1747.

• inventory & LoD of Samuel Dudley.

• inventory of Nicholas Lowe.

• additional inventory of Jonathan
Taylor.

• accounts of Christopher Spry
executor of Thomas Spry.

• accounts of Thomas Dudley
administrator of John Batcheldor.

• accounts of William Alexander
administrator of Thomas Alexander,
during minority of John Alexander.

• Eve Macdaniel administratrix of
Daniell Macdaniell.

• accounts of Thomas Bozman
administrator dbn of Jonathan
Taylor.

32:91 • accounts of Risdon Bozman surety for
Daniel McDaniel administrator of
Laughlin McDaniel.

Exhibited from PG:
- additional accounts of Charles Drury (AA) administrator of Nathan Selby.

13 May. Mr. Thomas Bullen (TA) to examine accounts of:
- Sarah Berry executrix of James Berry (TA).

Mr. Gabriel Parker (CV) to examine accounts of:
- Peter Hellen executor of Susannah Hellen (CV).
- Elisabeth Kent & Abs. Kent executors of Abs. Kent (CV). Additional accounts.

14 May. Gabriel Parker (g, CV) exhibited:
- will of James Cranford. Also, renunciation of executors. Also, bond of Elisabeth Cranford administratrix. Sureties: William Lyle, Thomas Rhodes. Date: 20 April 1747.
- inventory of Jesse Bourne.
- accounts of Sarah Scarff administratrix of Nicholas Scarff.
- accounts of James Dotson executor of James Freeman.

15 May. Nehemiah King (g, SO) exhibited:
- will of George Tull.
- will of Mary Wilson. Also, bond of Abraham Heath administrator. Sureties: James Hayman, Isaac Hayman. Date: 23 April 1747.
- will of George Wilson.
- bond of Tunstall Hack acting executor of John Tunstall. Sureties: Robert Jenkins Henry, Heber Whittingham, Henry Ballard. Date: 8 April 1747. Also, renunciation of Spencer Hack & William Arbuckel guardian to Spencer Hack. Date: 21 March 1746. Signed: William Arbuckle, Spencer Hack. Witness: Thomas Jones.
- inventory of John Horsey.
- inventory of Charles Revill.
- 2nd accounts of Samuel Collins

32:92

acting executor of Richard Chambers.
- accounts of Purnall Newbold administrator of Thomas Newbold.

Notice to Mr. William Tilghman (Deputy Commissary, QA) to prove inclosed will of Solomon Robinson & to notify John Robinson (heir-at-law).

18 May. Mr. Walter Hanson (CH) to examine additional accounts of:
- James Freeman & his wife Janet administratrix of Arthur Westman (CH).

19 May. MM Charles Ridgeley (justice, BA) & Samuel Owings (justice, BA) to take oath of John Tipton (BA) in relation to inventory of William Welsh (BA), appraised by said Tipton & William Wheeler.

William Rogers (g, AA) exhibited:
- will of John Gray, Sr., constituting Bridgett Gray & Samuel Gray executors. Also, widow's election. Said executors were granted administration. Sureties: Joshua Gray (p), John Gray (p). Date: 19 May 1747.
- bond of Ann Tongue administratrix of James Tongue. Sureties: Joseph Chew (p), William Tillard (p). Date: 14 May 1747.

32:93
- inventory of Morgan Jones.
- inventory of Mary Covel.

22 May. Exhibited from AA:
- additional accounts of Aaron Rawlings & William Rawlings executors of Aaron Rawlings.
- accounts of John Dowell & his wife Susanna administratrix of Morgan Jones.

Exhibited from QA:
- accounts of John Mumford administrator of John Mumford.

23 May. Walter Hanson (g, CH) exhibited:
- will of Archibald, Johnson

constituting Elinor Johnson & Joseph Johnson executors. Said executors were granted administration. Sureties: Lodwick Adams (p), John Patterson (p). Date: 15 May 1747.

- bond of Francis Elgin administrator of John Wise. Sureties: George Elgin, John Wathen. Date: 5 May 1746.
- bond of Jane Parnham & Francis Parnham administrators of John Parnham. Sureties: William Neale, Joseph Pile. Date: 19 March 1746.
- inventory of Jonathan Davis. /
- additional inventory of Francis Goodrick.
- accounts of Anne McDaniel executrix of Daniel McDaniel.
- accounts of Joseph Hanson Harrison executor of Stephen Evans.
- accounts of Mary Goodrick, Edward Goodrick, & Francis Goodrick acting executors of Francis Goodrick.
- accounts of James Muncaster executor of Richard King.

Charles Hynson (g, KE) exhibited:
- accounts of Hanse Hanson & his wife Margaret executrix of Glanvill Rolph.

27 May. Exhibited from QA:
- inventory of Robert Wilson.

30 May. Exhibited from PG:
- bond of Robert DeButts administrator of Joseph Jenings. Sureties: John Addison (g), Edward Sprigg (g). Date: 30 May 1747.

32:94 Luke Trotten & his wife Elisabeth executrix of Stephen Body one of sureties on estate of Thomas Dulany (BA) vs. Sarah Dorsey (BA) executrix of said Dulany. Sheriff (BA) to summon defendant to render full accounts.

Notice to Justices of BA: There is a considerable balance due to the estate of Thomas Dulany (BA), including a large sum due Dennis Dulany (son, minor). Stephen Body (BA, dec'd) was one of the

sureties; Luke Trotten & his wife
Elisabeth executrix of said Body cannot
be safe in giving security.

2 June. Exhibited from AA:
* accounts of Samuel Smith & Francis
  Mapp executors of Alice Andrews.

Exhibited from CE:
* accounts of John Macky, Esq. & his
  wife Araminta executrix of William
  Alexander, Esq.

Exhibited from AA:
* 2nd additional accounts of David
  Weems (g) surviving executor of
  William Lock.

Exhibited from BA:
* additional accounts of James Crow
  administrator of John Crow.

4 June. John Tootell (DO) & his wife
Rosannah vs. Thomas Woolford (DO) one
of executors of Roger Woolford (DO).
Libel. Sheriff (DO) to summon defendant
to render answer.

Exhibited from BA:
* accounts of Jane Partridge
  administratrix of Buckler Partridge
  administrator of Joseph Penhallow.

5 June. Exhibited from BA:
* accounts of Jane Partridge
  administratrix of Dr. Buckler
  Partridge.

32:95 6 June. Mr. Walter Hanson (CH) to
examine additional accounts of:
* Arthur Lee & his wife Ann
  administratrix of Robert Yates (CH).

8 June. Thomas White (g, BA) exhibited:
* will of William Barney. Also,
  widow's election.
* will of Francis Holland.
* will of Richard Deavor, constituting
  Mary Deavor executrix. Said
  executrix was granted
  administration. Sureties: Parker
  Hall, Richard Ruff. Date: 6 May

1747.
- will of Christopher DurbinShaw.
- bond of Thomas Burney (alias Thomas Presbury) executor of James Presbury. Sureties: William Bradford, James Maxwell. Date: 24 March 1746.
- bond of Mary Frisby administratrix dbn of Susanna Stokes. Sureties: Edward Wakeman, Winstone Smith. Date: 25 March 1747.
- bond of Jemima Jackson administratrix of Jacob Jackson. Sureties: James Maxwell, Benjamin Childs. Date: 2 June 1747.
- bond of Mary Frisby administratrix of Peregrine Frisby. Sureties: John Hall, John Hall (Swan Town). Date: 25 March 1747.
- bond of Avarilla Hall administratrix of Thomas Maccroy. Surety: Parker Hall. Date: 17 April 1747.
- inventory of Samuel Cooper.
- inventory of Geor Henry March.
- inventory & LoD of Rowland Vine.
- inventory of Edward Day.
- accounts of James Rigbie administrator of Samuel Cooper.
- accounts of Ann Cadle administratrix of Benjamin Cadle.

Petition of Stephen Bordley for Robert Carter & John Bugsy representatives of William Welsh (BA). Administrators of said estate: Judith Welsh, Thomas Carr, Thomas Ford. Date: 25 May 1747. Bond on said estate assigned to petitioners. Mentions: Charles Robinson who married the widow.

32:96 Mr. Thomas White (BA) to examine accounts of:
- Sarah Vine executrix of Rowland Vine (BA).
- Thomas Harrison administrator of John Chambers (BA).
- Johanna Smith & Thomas Smith executors of William Smith (BA).
- William Hollis executor of William Snellson (BA).
- Susanna Butler executrix of Henry Butler (BA). Additional accounts.

- Alexander Maccomas, Jr. & his wife
  Deborah administratrix of Thomas
  Deavor (BA). Additional accounts.

10 June. Exhibited from PG:
- will of Isaac Wells.

11 June. George Matthews (PG) executor
of Isaac Wells was granted LoA on his
estate. Sureties: Henry Ballinger (PG),
Daniel Matthews (PG). Appraisers:
William Tanyhill, Joseph Wells. Mr.
William Beatty (PG) to administer oath
to said George Matthews. Delivered to
Mr. Robert DeButts.

MM Caleb & Basil Dorsey to appraise
estate of William Fell (BA) in AA.

Exhibited from AA:
- accounts of Ephraim Gover (BA) &
  Philip Gover (BA) surviving
  executors of Samuel Gover.

Exhibited from PG:
- bond of Mary Parr executrix of John
  Parr. Sureties: Darby Ryan, Stephen
  Julien. Date: 11 June 1747.
  Appraisers: Mr. Thomas Beatty,
  James Crouch. Mr. William Beatty
  to administer oath.

17 June. John Thompson (g, CE)
exhibited:
- will of James Paul Heath. Also,
  renunciation of executors.

Benton Harris (g, WO) exhibited:
- will of Daniel Davis, constituting
  Elisabeth Davis executrix. Also,
  widow's election. Said executrix
  was granted administration.
  Sureties: James Smith, John Davis.
  Date: 4 June 1747j.
32:97 - will of Thomas Coffin, constituting
  Thomas Coffin executor. Said
  executor was granted administration.
  Sureties: William Woodcraft, John
  Coffin. Date: 3 June 1747.
- bond of Rebeckah Pirkins
  administratrix of Thomas Pirkins.
  Sureties: Daniel Coe, Alexander

Court Session: 1747

Linch. Date: 3 June 1747.
- bond of John Selby & Parker Selby executors of Parker Selby. Sureties: Joshua Mitchell, William Walton, Jr., Peter Claywell. Date: 18 April 1747. Also, renunciation of Mary Selby (widow), recommending the other executors. Date: 15 April 1747.
- accounts of Joshua Morss & his wife Mary administrators of John Burton.

18 June. Exhibited from BA:
- 3rd additional accounts of Joseph Lane acting executor of Samuel Maccubbin.

Mr. Gabriel Parker (CV) to examine accounts of:
- Young Parran administrator of Moses Parran (CV).

Exhibited from BA:
- inventory of John Parrish.

John Thompson (g, CE) exhibited:
- will of Edward Jackson.
- bond of Elisabeth Steal administratrix of John Steal. Sureties: Benjamin Starrat, Jarett Nelson. Date: 12 March 1746.
- bond of Agnes Maffett & William Maffett administrators of Samuel Maffett. Sureties: Michael Wallace, David Patterson. Date: 11 March 1746.
- bond of James Bayard administrator of John Milvill. Sureties: James Taylor, William Gent. Date: 27 March 1747.
- bond of Sabina Rumsey administratrix of Richard Evans. Sureties: Joshua George, John Baldwin. Date: 6 May 1747.
- bond of George Rock administrator of William Goddard. Sureties: William Bristow, Amos Fogg. Date: 12 March 1746.
32:98 - bond of Edward Furroner administrator of Thomas Stark. Sureties: David Rickets, Thomas Ryland. Date: 13 April 1747.

Page 57

Court Session: 1747

- bond of Catherine Wooleston administratrix of Richard Wooliston. Sureties: Cornelius Wooliston, Joseph Court. Date: 24 April 1747.
- bond of Elenor Wooliston administratrix of Richard Wooliston, Jr. Sureties: Cornelius Wooliston, Edward Armstrong. Date: 2 April 1747.
- bond of Rachel Smith administratrix of William Smith. Sureties: Richard Segwick, Benjamin Starrell. Date: 24 April 1747.
- inventory of Joseph Allman.
- inventory of Abraham Watson.
- inventory of William Bailey.
- inventory of Peter Jones.
- additional inventory of John Pennington, Sr.
- inventory of William Beck.
- inventory of Patrick McGrahan.
- inventory of Richard Wooliston, Jr.
- accounts of John Cockran & James Ogleby executors of John Ogleby.
- accounts of Ann Freeman administratrix of William Freeman.

Exhibited from TA:
- additional accounts of Robert Harwood acting executor of Mary Edmondson.

22 June. Charles Hynson (g, KE) exhibited:
- will of Butman Medford, constituting Sarah Medford executrix. Said executrix was granted administration. Sureties: George Medford, George Rasin. Date: 25 April 1747.
- will of Thomas Sanders, constituting Mary Sanders executrix. Said executrix was granted administration. Sureties: Jacob Caulk, John Clayton. Date: 6 March 1746.
- will of Michaell Miller. Also, bond of Samuel Miller administrator. Sureties: Ralph Page (g), Stephen Glanvill (g). Date: 18 April 1747. Also, renunciation of Ra. Page (executor). Date: 3 April 1747.

- will of George Douglass.
- will of Benjamin Inch.
- will of John Bean.
- bond of George Clark & his wife Mary administrators of Daniell Knock. Sureties: Hugh Mchard (cooper), Archibald Boyd (blacksmith). Date: 3 April 1747.
- bond of Margaret Boyer administratrix of William Boyer. Sureties: Solomon Semans, George Clayton. Date: 28 March 1747.

32:99
- bond of Thomas Humphry administrator of William Allen. Sureties: Daniel Hall (p), James Wilson (p). Date: 17 May 1747. Also, renunciation of Elisebath Allen (widow), recommending Thomas Oumphrie (greatest creditor). Date: 9 May 1747. Witnesses: John Watson, James Steed.
- bond of Sarah Dyer administratrix of Edward Dyer. Sureties: John Wallace (p), Samuel Mansfield (p). Date: 6 June 1745.
- bond of Margaret McClain administratrix of Neil McClain. Sureties: Mathew Deadman (p), Benjamin Palmer (p). Date: 19 March 1746.
- bond of Sarah Scott administratrix of Charles Scott. Sureties: John Stevenson (p), Thomas Pryer (p). Date: 28 March 1747.
- bond of Mary Granohan administratrix of Thomas Granohan. Sureties: Samuel Morris (p), John Dening (p). Date: 17 May 1747.
- bond of John Everitt administrator of Edward Davis. Sureties: Jeremiah Covinton (p), John Thornton (p). Date: 20 April 1747. Also, renunciation of Sarah Hendrakesen (sister). Date: 31 March 1747.
- bond of Elisabeth Boyer administratrix of James Boyer. Sureties: John Clayton (p), George Clayton (p). Date: 6 March 1746.
- bond of Elisabeth Wallace administratrix of John Wallace. Sureties: John Graham (p), William Keeting (p). Date: 11 April 1747.

- inventory of Nicholas Neil.
- inventory of Thomas Richardson.
- inventory of Neal McClean.
- inventory of Patrick Henratee.
- additional inventory of William Brown.
- inventory of John Tennant.
- inventory of James Gray.
- inventory of Maj. Ebenezar Blakistone.
- inventory of Thomas Sanders.
- inventory of James Boyer.
- inventory of Chrispin Buttler.
- accounts of Samuel Miller executor of Martha Miller.
- accounts of Isaac Crow administrator of William Crow.

32:100
- additional accounts of Isaac Freeman administrator of John Bennett.
- 2nd additional accounts of Elisabeth Ringgold administratrix dbn of William Buckham.

26 June. Peter Dent (g, PG) exhibited:
- will of Samuel Barker, constituting Mary Barker executrix. Said executrix was granted administration. Sureties: Thomas Athey (p), Walter Athey (p). Date: 12 June 1747.
- bond of Mary Downs administratrix of Henry Downs. Sureties: William Downs (p), William White (p). Date: 16 June 1747.
- bond of Elisabeth Massey administratrix of Henry Massey. Sureties: William Tyler (PG), John Hanson (g, CH). Date: 11 May 1747.
- inventory of Alexander Magruder.
- 2nd additional inventory of Thomas Jennings.
- inventory of William Masson.
- inventory of Bingle Page.
- inventory of George Woodhead.
- accounts of Susanna Magruder executrix of Alexander Magruder.
- accounts of Josiah & Lucy Beall executors of Virlinda Beall executrix of John Beall.
- additional accounts of Prisila Willson administratrix of Thomas Willson.

Court Session: 1747

- accounts of Andrew Gibbs administrator of Hanah Dent.
- 2nd additional accounts of Allen Bowie who married widow of Capt. William Finch.
- additional accounts of Anne Attkinson administratrix of John Attkinson.

William Tilghman (g, QA) exhibited:
- will of Charles Moor.
- will of Matthew Williams. Also, widow's election.
- will of John Baynard, constituting Thomas Baynard (DO) & John Casson (QA) executors. Said executors were granted administration. Sureties: Henry Casson, Henry Feddeman. Date: 9 April 1747.
- will of John Nevil. Also, bond of Solomon Seney & his wife Ann administrators, during minority of John Nevil. Sureties: Benjamin Whittington (p), James Roberts (p). Date: 11 June 1747.
- bond of Sarah Carter administratrix of John Carter. Sureties: Henry Carrow (p), Valentine Carter (p). Date: 16 April 1747.
- bond of Sarah Start administratrix of John Start. Sureties: Violet Primrose (p), Thomas Elliott Hutchings (p). Date: 23 April 1747.
- bond of Matthew Griffith administrator of Andrew Price, during minority of Thomas Price. Sureties: John Burk, Jr. (p), Christopher Wise (p), James Ayler (p). Date: 15 June 1747.
- 32:101 bond of Mary Silvester administratrix of John Silvester. Sureties: James Silvester (p), David Silvester (p). Date: 14 May 1747.
- bond of Elisabeth Whittington administratrix of Joseph Whittington. Sureties: Richard Gould (p), Benjamin Whittington (p). Date: 18 June 1747.
- bond of Mary Tippens administratrix of Edward Tippens. Sureties: Thomas Tippens (p), John Sparks (p). Date: 4 June 1747.

- bond of Martha Granger administratrix of Thomas Granger. Sureties: Thomas Tanner (p), Thomas Benton (p). Date: 21 May 1747.
- bond of Joseph Sudler administrator of Thomas Norman. Sureties: Charles Browne, James Harvey. Date: 11 June 1747. Also, renunciation of Sarah Norman (widow). Date: 21 May 1747.
- bond of Charles Birmingham executor of John Birmingham. Sureties: Thomas Sands (p), John Wicks (p). Date: 14 May 1747.
- inventory of Robert Norrest Wright.
- inventory & LoD of Michael Serjeant.
- inventory of Thomas Parsons.
- inventory of Thomas Trickey.
- inventory of William Richardson.
- inventory of Christopher Williams.
- inventory of John Douglass.
- inventory of Henry Green.
- inventory & LoD of Thomas Alliband.
- inventory of Richard Scotten.
- accounts of Sarah Hays administratrix of John Hays, Jr.

Mr. Charles Hynson (KE) to examine accounts of:
- Margaret McClain administratrix of Neil McClain (KE).
- Patrick Keran surviving administrator of Patrick Handraty (KE).
- Daniel Cunningham & his wife Hannah administratrix of William Smithers (KE).
- Beatrice Pearce executrix of Gideon Pearce, Jr. (KE).
- Samuel Wallace administrator of John Tennant (KE).
- Joseph Wicks & James Dunn administrators of Robert Dunn (KE).
- John Green administrator of Bowles Green (KE).
- Morgan Hurt & his wife Martha administratrix of William Browne (KE).
- Collin Farguson executor of Robert Dew (KE). Additional accounts.

27 June. Gabriel Parker (g, CV) exhibited:

- will of Richard Blake, constituting Susannah Blake executrix. Said executrix was granted administration. Sureties: Sutton Isaacke, James Heighe. Date: 22 May 1747.

32:102
- inventory of Abraham Card.
- inventory of William Dawkins, Jr.
- accounts of William Peirce administrator of Richard Peirce.
- accounts of John Wood administrator of William Wood.
- accounts of Betty Sedwick executrix of Benjamin Sedwick.

Mr. John Thompson (CE) to examine accounts of:
- Francis Carruthers & his wife Ann administratrix of Archibald Steel (CE).
- Elinor Wright & James Evans administrators of James Wright (CE).
- Michael Tully & his wife Rachel administratrix of Robert Croker (CE).
- Mary Pennington executrix of John Pennington, Jr. (CE).

30 June. Exhibited from QA:
- accounts of Dinah Bryan administratrix of John Bryan.

Mr. Walter Hanson (CH) to examine accounts of:
- Juliana Simpson executrix of Andrew Simpson (CH).
- Philip Terrill & his wife Elisabeth executrix of Samuel Burgess executor of John Craxon (CH).
- Hudson Wathen & John Wathen executors of John Wathen (CH).
- Robert Whythill & his wife Elisabeth administratrix of John Theobalds (CH). Additional accounts.
- Ignatius Gardner & James Middleton executors of Vincent Askin (CH). Additional accounts.

1 July. Mr. William Tilghman (QA) to examine accounts of:
- Bridget Primrose administratrix of William Primrose (QA).

- Vincent Price administrator of Timothy Lane (QA).
- James Daley executor of John Daley (QA).
- Rebecca Curtis administratrix of Thomas Curtis (QA).

4 July. Mr. Gabriel Parker (CV) to examine accounts of:
- Martha Brook administratrix of John Brook (CV).
- Elisabeth Griffin administratrix of John Griffin (CV).
- Robert How & his wife Elisabeth administratrix of William Harris (CV).
- Capel King administrator of Sarah Malden (CV). Additional accounts.
- James Russell administrator of Francis Drake (CV).
- Robert Connant & his wife Dorcas executrix of Jonah Whinfield (CV). Additional accounts.

32:103 10 July. Exhibited from QA:
- additional inventory & LoD of William Turbutt.

William Rogers (g, AA) exhibited:
- bond of George Steuart administrator of Alexander Rosenquest. Sureties: Walter Dulany (g, Annapolis). Date: 15 June 1747.
- bond of George Chocke administrator of William Hays. Sureties: Francis Crandall (p), Nicholas Norman (p). Date: 22 June 1747.
- inventory of Richard Smith.
- inventory of Capt. Joel Hutchison.
- inventory of Capt. John Wabby.
- accounts of Jeremiah Covell administrator of Mary Covell.

4 June. John Tootell (DO) & his wife Rosannah vs. John Woolford (SO) one of executors of Roger Woolford (DO). Sheriff (SO) to summon defendant to answer libel.

10 July. Executors of Samuel Young (CV) vs. Richard Young (AA) surviving executor of Col. Samuel Young (AA).

Court Session: 1747

Sheriff (AA) to summon defendant to
render final accounts.

Creditors of Philip Smith (merchant,
London) vs. William Chapman (AA) one of
administrators of said dec'd. Sheriff
(AA) to summon defendant to render final
accounts.

11 July. Mr. Nehemiah King (SO) to
examine accounts of:
- James Otley & his wife Sarah
  executrix of Robert Bowyer (SO).
- William Dashiell executor of Mathias
  Dashiell (SO).

Mr. Benton Harris (WO) to examine
accounts of:
- Charles Rackliff & his wife Comfort
  administratrix of Hugh Stevenson
  (WO).
- Warren Burross & his wife Prissilla
  administratrix of John Willey (WO).
- David Smith one of sureties for
  Martha Harvey administratrix of John
  Harvey (WO).

Mr. Thomas Bullen (TA) to examine
accounts of:
- Rachel Thompson administratrix of
  Thomas Thompson (TA).

32:104 Exhibited from CV:
- inventory of John Rousby, Esq. in
  SM. Also, accounts of Edward Lloyd,
  John Rousby, & Abraham Barnes
  executors.

Court Session: 14 July 1747

Docket:
- Sheriff (PG) to render attachment to
  Lingan Wilson (PG) administrator of
  Joseph Wilson (PG) to render
  inventory.
- Sheriff (PG) to summon James Wilson
  (brother) & Henry Wright Wilson
  (nephew) of Joseph Wilson (PG,
  dec'd) to show cause why they do not
  sign inventory as next of kin.
- Raymond Stapleford, Charles
  Stapleford, & Thomas Stapleford

executors of Elisabeth Taylor (DO)
vs. Dorothy Gollothon (DO) &
Dorothy Loockerman (DO). Sheriff
(DO) to render attachment to
defendants to show cause why they
conceal estate of dec'd.

Sheriff (SO) to summon Thomas
Morrison & his wife widow of Philip
Ellis (DO) to take LoA on his
estate.

- S.B. for Baptist Barber & his wife
Elisabeth (SM) vs. W.C. for Samuel &
Richard Southern executors of John
Johnson Southern. Libel, answer.

32:105 • Patrick Grey (BA) vs. Patrick Doran
(AA) administrator of John Handling
(AA). William Thornton (sheriff,
AA) to summon defendant to render
accounts.

- Edward Dorsey procurator for
Rachel Richardson (AA) vs.
Stephen Bordley, Esq. procurator
for Thomas Richardson surviving
executor of Richard Richardson.
Text of libel. Plaintiff is
spinster & only daughter of
Richard Richardson, Jr. (p, AA,
dec'd) who is one of sons of
Richard Richardson the elder
(AA, dec'd). Said Richard
Richardson the elder d. 1743,
leaving: widow, children: Mark
Richardson, Thomas Richardson,
Mary wife of Philip Dowell, Ann
wife of John Conner, Lydia wife
of Joseph Bickerton, Ann wife of
William Lewis, & the plaintiff.

32:106 Mentions: William Thornton
(sheriff,
AA).

32:107 Text of answer by Thomas
Richardson,
Jr. surviving executor.
Ruling: plaintiff.

- Sheriff (SO) to summon (N) Hern
widow & executrix of Edward Hern
(SO) to prove said will & take
LoA.

- Sheriff (DO) to summon Septimus
Noell (DO), Samuel Lecompte
(DO), David Peterkin (DO), &

Court Session: 14 July 1747

John Lecompte (DO) (all
witnesses to will of Hugh
Eccleston (DO)) to prove said
will.

- Luke Trotten & his wife
  Elisabeth executrix of Stephen
  Body one of sureties on estate
  of Thomas Dulany (BA) vs. Sarah
  Dulany (BA) executrix of said
  Dulany. Henry Morgan (sheriff,
  BA) to summon defendant to
  render final accounts.

32:108
- E.D. for John Tootell & his wife
  Rosannah (DO) vs. Thomas Woolford
  (DO) & John Woolford (SO) executors
  of Roger Woolford. Libel.
- Executors of Samuel Young (CV) vs.
  Richard Young (AA) surviving
  executor of Col. Samuel Young (AA).
  William Thornton (sheriff, AA) to
  summon defendant to render final
  accounts.
- Creditors of estate of Philip Smith
  (merchant, London) vs. William
  Chapman (AA) one of administrators
  of said dec'd. William Thornton
  (sheriff, AA) to summon defendant to
  render final accounts.

[Omitted from May Court, f. 90]
Confession of Mary Ann Atcherson, John
Hamell, & John Moore to judgement to
Laurence Macnamara & his wife Elisabeth.
Date: 11 May 1747. Signed (justices of
peace (CH)): Robert Hanson, Will.
Eilbeck.

Court Session: 1747

32:109 14 July. Thomas Aisquith (g, SM)
exhibited:
- will of John Perce, constituting Ann
  Perce & Benjamin Williams executors.
  Also, widow's election. Said
  executors were granted
  administration. Sureties: James
  Egerton, James Burne. Date: 11 May
  1747.
- will of Patrick Forest, constituting
  Frances Forest executrix. Also,
  widow's election. Said executrix
  was granted administration.

Sureties: Stephen Chilton, Edward
Hilard Hebb. Date: 25 May 1747.
- will of Daniel Clocker.
- will of John Biggs.
- inventory & LoD of John Abell, Sr.
- inventory & LoD of John Heard, Sr.
- inventory & LoD of Richard Dever.
- inventory & LoD of Thomas Notley
  Goldsmith.
- inventory & LoD of John Cheshire.
- inventory & LoD of Peter Johnson.
- inventory of Ann Joy.
- inventory & LoD of Mathew Herbert.
- additional inventory of Thomas
  Waters.
- additional inventory of Mary Jones.
- accounts of William Hambleton & his
  wife Mary administratrix of John
  Mollehone.
- accounts of Mary Sledmore
  administratrix of John Sledmore.
- accounts of Margret Graves
  administratrix of John Graves.
- accounts of Mary Phippard executrix
  of William Phippard.
- accounts of Thomas Simpson & his
  wife Mary executrix of John Fanning.
- accounts of Joseph Pile surviving
  executor of Henry Wharton.
- accounts of William Yates executor
  of William Bradburne.

15 July. Exhibited from AA:
- 2nd additional accounts of Dr.
  James Walker administrator of John
  Gardiner.

Mr. Ennalls Hooper (DO) to examine
accounts of:
- Eleanor Eccleston executrix of
  Thomas Eccleston (DO).

16 July. Exhibited from BA:
- bond of Sarah Gorsuch administratrix
  of Charles Gorsuch. Sureties: John
  Gorsuch (p), William Gorsuch (p).
  Date: 16 July 1747.

21 July. Walter Hanson (g, CH)
exhibited:
- bond of Perry Pattison & his wife
  Mary administratrix of Jacob Balye.

32:110 •

Sureties: Richard Griffith, John Ratcliff. Date: 3 June 1747.

bond of Perry Pattyson & his wife Mary administrators of Benjamin Banister. Sureties: Richard Griffis, John Pattison. Date: 20 May 1747.

• additional inventory of Sarah Fowke.
• inventory of John Wise.
• inventory of James Sayers.
• inventory of John Weathers.
• inventory of Edward Walker.
• inventory of Robert Sias.
• accounts of Margret Chapman administratrix of John Chapman.
• accounts of John Alexander & Gerrard Fowke administrators of Sarah Fowke.
• accounts of Penelope Brown administratrix of John Brown.
• accounts of Mary Chapman executrix of Richard Chapman.
• accounts of Ann Smoot & Thomas Smoot executors of Barton Smoot.
• accounts of Mary Neale executrix of Benjamin Neale.
• accounts of Jane Brent executrix of William Brent.

<u>25 July</u>. Peter Dent (g, PG) exhibited:
• will of James Pelley, constituting Jayne Pelley executrix. Said executrix was granted administration. Sureties: Francis Piles (g), Leonard Piles (g). Date: 25 June 1747.
• bond of Solomey Large administratrix of Philip Large. Sureties: Ninian Willitt (g), John Busey (g). Date: 24 June 1747.
• bond of Samuel Beall, Jr. administrator of Lucy Beall. Sureties: Joseph Beall (g), Isaac Brooke (g). Date: 29 June 1747.
• inventory of Henry Massey at his Quarter in Sugarlands.
• inventory of Nathaniel Hays. Also, accounts of Charles Hays administrator.
• accounts of Joseph Ryon executor of John Orchard.
• inventory of Elisabeth Waters.

Ebenezar Reyner (KE) & his wife Sarah vs. Rebecca Perkins (KE) & David Perkins (KE). Sheriff (KE) to summon defendants to render answer to libel.

27 July. Notice to Mrs. Mary Ann Hamilton (PG) widow of James Hamilton (taylor, PG). If she does not take LoA on his estate, LoA will be granted to Mr. William Beall.

32:111 Exhibited from DO:
- will of Hugh Eccleston.

Exhibited from PG:
- accounts of Stephen Julian & his wife Ann administratrix of William Hedges.
- will of Matthias Reasling. Appraisers: William Dern, Thomas Beatty. Mr. William Beatty to administer oath.

Exhibited from BA:
- inventory of Edward Perrigoe. Also, accounts of Avarilla Perigoe administratrix.
- inventory of Martha Bowen Also, accounts of Samuel Bowen administrator.

Exhibited from DO:
- accounts of Rev. Thomas Airey administrator of John Pitt.

Exhibited from BA:
- inventory of William Mattingly. Also, accounts of Constant Pelley (AA) executrix.

28 July. Exhibited from PG:
- bond of Henrica Beatty administratrix of John Beatty. Sureties: John Biggs, John Middagh. Date: 17 March 1746.

31 July. Exhibited from SM:
- accounts of Rachel Bussey (CV) executrix of Hezekiah Bussey.

Exhibited from BA:
- inventory of John Cockey.

Court Session: 1747

Mary Chappell vs. William Thornberry
(AA) & James Chappell (AA) executors of
James Chappell (CV). Sheriff (AA) to
summon defendants to take LoA.

1 August. Exhibited from DO:
* bond of Joseph Ennalls administrator
  of Julius Robinson (merchant, Island
  of Barbadoes). Sureties: Ashbury
  Sutton (merchant, Annapolis), Samuel
  Middleton (innholder, Annapolis).
  Date: 1 August 1747.

32:112   Mr. Ennalls Hooper (DO) to examine
accounts of:
* Col. Adam Muir administrator of
  Laurence Mason (DO), during minority
  of William Mason.

Exhibited from AA:
* accounts of William Cockey & Joshua
  Owings executors of John Cockey
  executor of Col. Thomas Cockey.

7 August. Exhibited from PG:
* bond of Philip Pindell administrator
  of Elisabeth Pindell. Sureties:
  Thomas Harwood (p), Thomas Pindell
  (p). Date: 7 August 1747.

8 August. Exhibited from BA:
* accounts of John Bailey
  administrator of Mary Smith.
* accounts of John Bailey
  administrator of Mary Smith
  executrix of William Smith.

John Smith Prather, Thomas Prather, &
Thomas Williams executors of Martha
Yoakley vs. Joseph Milburn Semmes & his
wife. Subpoena for costs.

Exhibited from QA:
* accounts of Charles Connor & his
  wife Mary administrators of Charles
  Connor.

10 August. Exhibited from PG:
* bond of John Prather administrator
  of Edward Prather. Sureties: Thomas
  Bull, Samuel Bull. Date: 10 August
  1747. Also, renunciation of Ann

Court Session: 1747

Prather (widow), recommending John
Prather (greatest creditor). Date:
8 August 1747. Witness: Suanah
Prather.

Thomas Aisquith (g, SM) exhibited:
- will of Richard Shirly. Also, bond
  of Grace Shirly administratrix.
  Sureties: Robert Greenwell, Thomas
  Norriss. Date: 15 July 1747.
- will of Isaac Walter. Also, bond of
  George Walter administrator.
  Sureties: Charles Beech, Roger
  Copsey. Date: 27 July 1747.
- bond of John Horn administrator of
  John Horn. Sureties: George
  Aisquith, Joseph Hopewell. Date: 1
  August 1747.
- bond of Joseph Hopewell
  administrator of Thomas Francis
  Hopewell. Sureties: George
  Aisquith, John Hopewell. Date: 28
  July 1747.
- accounts of Ann Cutler
  administratrix of William Cutler.
- accounts of Mary Watt administratrix
  of Thomas Watt.
- accounts of Elijah Waters executor
  of Thomas Waters.
- accounts of Henry Lyon administrator
  of Thomas Morriss.
- accounts of Benjamin Finwick
  administrator of Cuthbert Fenwick.
- accounts of Winefred Thomas
  administratrix of Mark Thomas.

11 August. Thomas Bullen (g, TA)
exhibited:
- will of John Alen Jones.
- will of Aaron Higgs, constituting
  Agnes Higgs executrix. Also,
  widow's election. Said executrix
  was granted administration.
  Sureties: Joseph Kininmont (p),
  Peter Calk (p). Date: 5 June 1747.
- bond of Edward Neall & Jonathan
  Neall administrators of Samuel
  Neall, during minority of Martha
  Neall (daughter). Sureties: Thomas
  Porter, Richard Turbutt. Date: 26
  May 1747.
- bond of Jane Feddeman administratrix

32:113

of Richard Feddeman. Sureties:
Joseph Parrott (g), Daniel Maynadier
(g). Date: 23 May 1747.
- additional inventory & LoD of Samuel
  Martin.
- inventory of Daniel Ward.
- inventory of Thomas Edwards.
- inventory of Thomas Ford.
- additional inventory of Rev. Daniel
  Maynadier.
- accounts of Mary Merchant
  administratrix of James Merchant.
- accounts of Richard Gurling Robinson
  & his wife Judith administratrix of
  John Harrison.
- accounts of Thomas Barnett & his
  wife Phebe administratrix of Richard
  Giles.
- accounts of William Martin executor
  & Thomas Loveday & his wife Grace
  executrix of Samuell Martin.
- accounts of Daniel Maynadier
  administrator of Rev. Daniel
  Maynadier.

12 August. Exhibited from AA:
- 2nd additional accounts of John
  Burle executor of Lancelott Todd.
- accounts of Elinor Ryon executrix of
  Dennis Ryon.

17 August. Mr. Nehemiah King (SO) to
examine accounts of:
- James Caldwell & his wife Rachel
  executrix & Christopher Piper
  executor of Christopher Piper (SO).

32:114 Nehemiah King (g, SO) exhibited:
- will of Robert Price, constituting
  Mary Price executrix. Said
  executrix was granted
  administration. Sureties: Robert
  Givan, George Hardy. Date: 17 June
  1747.
- will of Edward Hern, constituting
  Deborah Hern executrix. Said
  executrix was granted
  administration. Sureties: John
  White, Sr., Southey Whittington, Sr.
  Date: 11 July 1747.
- will of John Rickcords, constituting
  Ann Rickcords executrix. Said

executrix was granted administration. Sureties: Thomas Parramore, Joseph Callaway. Date: 8 August 1747.
- bond of Rachel Roach administratrix of Charles Roach. Sureties: Thomas Bannister, Nathaniel Horsey, Jr. Date: 1 July 1747.
- bond of Thomas Jones administrator of Nathaniel Jackson. Sureties: Heber Whittingham (g), Samuel Wilson (g). Date: 26 May 1747.
- bond of Joseph Ennolls (DO) administrator of Henry Wolter. Sureties: Thomas Hayward (SO), Thomas Wing (DO). Date: 19 June 1747.
- accounts of Isabella Dashiell executrix of William Dashiell.
- accounts of Matthew Wallace acting executor of Richard Wallace.

Mr. Gabriel Parker (CV) to examine additional accounts of:
- Peter Hellen, Jr. & his wife Penelope executrix of Ann Dawkins (CV).

Mr. Thomas Aisquith (SM) to examine accounts of:
- Mary Swann administratrix of James Swann (SM).
- William Sumner Billingsly executor of William Billingsly (SM).
- John Smoot executor of Eleanor Aston (SM).
- John Goldsmith, William Goldsmith, & Michel Goldsmith executors of Thomas Notley Goldsmith (SM).
- Elisabeth Nelson administratrix of Joshua Nelson (VA). [That part of estate in SM.]
- Samuel Sothorn & Richard Sothorn executors of John Johnson Sothorn (SM). 2nd additional accounts.

19 August. Exhibited from BA:
- bond of John Jones & John Logsdon administrators of John Wooley. Sureties: William Cockey (p), William Logsdon (p). Date: 19 August 1747. Also, renunciation of

32:115

Anne Wooley (widow), recommending her 2 sons-in-law John Jones & John Logsdon. Appraisers: Joseph Cromwell, Thomas Bond, John Hawkins.
- additional inventory of John Rattenbury.

20 August. Exhibited from CV:
- LOD on estate of Richard Lane. Also, additional accounts of Sarah Lane executrix.

22 August. Gabriel Parker (g, CV) exhibited:
- bond of Thomas Gray administrator of Jasper Floyd. Sureties: John Wood, John Millis. Date: 27 July 1747.
- inventory of James Cranford.
- additional accounts of Elisabeth Kent & Abs. Kent executors of Absolom Kent.
- accounts of Elisabeth Griffin administratrix of John Griffin.

26 August. William Rogers (g, AA) exhibited:
- will of Ruth Howard, constituting John Dorsey & Edward Dorsey executors. Said executors were granted administration. Sureties: Edward Dorsey (son of Edward), Ely Dorsey. Date: 12 August 1747.
- bond of John Evitts (joyner, Annapolis) administrator of Susanna Murray. Sureties: George Lingan (g, Annapolis), Thomas Fleming (blockmaker, Annapolis). Date: 27 July 1747.
- inventory of Suanna Murray.
- inventory of John Gray, Sr.
- accounts of Philip Jones administrator of Richard Smith.

Thomas Bullen (g, TA) exhibited:
- inventory of John Standley.
- inventory of Richard Feddeman.
- accounts of Sarah Berry executrix of James Berry.

27 August. Mr. Thomas Bullen (TA) to examine accounts of:
- Stephen Stickbury & his wife Jane

- executrix of John Studham (TA).
- Robert Goldsborough & his wife Mary Ann administratrix of John Robins (TA).
- Katherine Skinner executrix of Richard Skinner (TA).
- Philemon Hambleton executor & Feddeman Rolle & his wife Lydia executrix of John Sherwood (TA).
- Feddeman Rolle administrator of Francis Rolle.

Exhibited from TA:
- inventory of Col. John Sherwood.

Exhibited from BA:
- accounts of Philip Jones acting executor of John Rattenbury.

32:116 29 August. Peter Dent (g, PG) exhibited:
- bond of Anne Crook administratrix of John Crook. Sureties: Thomas Oston (p), Joseph Willson (p). Date: 5 August 1747.

31 August. Exhibited from PG:
- bond of Mary Johnson & Nicholas Johnson administrators of Peter Johnson. Sureties: Thomas Cherry, Daniel Ashcraft. Date: 11 April 1747.
- accounts of James Plummer administrator of Philemon Plummer.

Sewall Long & his wife Margaret one of daughters of Richard Acton (BA, dec'd) vs. Ann Acton (BA) widow of said dec'd. Sheriff (BA) to summon defendant to take LoA on his estate.

1 September. Exhibited from AA:
- accounts of Rebecca Winston executrix of John Powell.

5 September. Exhibited from BA:
- accounts of Elisabeth Parish executrix of John Parish.

Court Session: 8 September 1747

Docket:

- Sheriff (PG) to render attachment to Lingan Wilson (PG) administrator of Joseph Wilson (PG) to render inventory. Inventory exhibited.

32:117

- Sheriff (PG) to summon James Wilson (brother) & Henry Wright Wilson (nephew) to Joseph Wilson (PG, dec'd) to show cause why they do not sign inventory as next of kin. Inventory exhibited. Discontinued.

- Raymond Stapleford, Charles Stapleford, & Thomas Stapleford executors of Elisabeth Taylor (DO) vs. Dorothy Gollothon (DO) & Dorothy Loockerman (DO). Sheriff (DO) to render attachment to defendants to show cause why they conceal estate of dec'd.

- Sheriff (SO) to summon Thomas Morrisson & his wife widow of Philip Ellis (DO) to take LoA on his estate.

- S.B. for Baptist Barber & his wife Elisabeth (SM) vs. W.C. for Samuel & Richard Sothoron executors of John Johnson Sothoron. Libel, answer.

- Patrick Grey (BA) vs. Patrick Doran (AA) administrator of John Handling (AA). Sheriff (AA) to summon defendant to render accounts.

- Sheriff (SO) to summon (N) Hern (SO) widow & executrix of Edward Hern (SO) to prove said will & to take LoA.

32:118

- Sheriff (DO) to summon Septimus Noell (DO), Samuel Lecompte (DO), David Peterkin (DO), & John Lecompte (DO) to prove will of Hugh Eccleston (DO). Will proved. Discontinued.

  - Luke Trotten & his wife Elisabeth executrix of Stephen Body one of sureties on estate of Thomas Dulany (BA) vs. Sarah Dulany (BA) executrix of said dec'd. Henry Morgan (sheriff, BA) to render attachment to defendant to render full accounts. Accounts exhibited. Discontinued.

  - E.D. for John Tootell & his wife Rosannah (DO) vs. Thomas

Court Session: 8 September 1747

- Woolford (DO) & John Woolford (SO) executors of Roger Woolford. Libel.
- Executors of Samuel Young (CV) vs. Richard Young (AA) surviving executor of Col. Samuel Young (AA). William Thornton (sheriff, AA) to render attachment to defendant to render full accounts.
- Creditors on estate of Philip Smith (merchant, London) vs. William Chapman (AA) one of administrators of said dec'd. Sheriff (AA) to summon defendant to render final accounts. Additional accounts exhibited. Discontinued.

32:119
- Mary Chappell vs. William Thornbury (AA) & James Chappell (AA) executors of James Chappell (CV). William Thornton (sheriff, AA) to summon defendants to take LoA. Struck off.
- John Smith Prather, Thomas Prather, & Thomas Williams executors of Marth Yoakley vs. Joseph Milburne Semmes & his wife. Subpoena for costs. John Hepburn exhibited that Mr. John Smith Prather (PG) served the subpoena to Joseph Milburn Semms (CH) & his wife Rachell & that they refuse to pay costs.
- E.D. for Ebenezar Reyner & his wife Sarah (KE) vs. Rebecca Perkins & David Perkins. Libel.
- Sewall Long & his wife Margaret one of daughters of Richard Acton (BA, dec'd) vs. Ann Acton (BA) widow of said dec'd. Sheriff (BA) to summon defendant to take LoA on said estate.

Court Session: 1747

32:120 8 September. Exhibited from PG:
- inventory of Joseph Wilson.

Thomas White (g, BA) exhibited:
- nuncupative will of John Carlise. Also, bond of Daniel Deavor administrator. Sureties: Ford

Barns, Ford Barns, Jr. Date: 15
August 1747.
- will of Hollis Hanson.
- will of Archibald Rollo.
- bond of Cordelia Holland
administratrix dbn of Susanna
Holland. Sureties: James Phillips,
Talbot Risteau. Date: 4 April 1747.
- bond of Cordelia Holland executrix
of Francis Holland. Sureties: James
Phillips, Talbot Risteau. Date 4
April 1747.
- bond of Richard Dallam & Richard
Ruff administrators of Abraham
Wallis. Surety: Nicholas Ruxton
Gay. Date: 1 June 1747.
- bond of Joseph Henly administrator
of Thomas Farlow. Sureties: Edward
Morgan, William Rayl (or Raye).
Date: 1 August 1747.
- bond of Bithia Barns administratrix
of James Barns. Sureties: James
Loney, Amos Garrett. Date: 2 August
1747.
- bond of Mary Barney executrix of
William Barney. Sureties: Thomas
Sheredine, Absolom Barney. Date: 31
August 1747.
- bond of Esther Rutter executrix of
Thomas Rutter. Sureties: Richard
Rutter, Moses Rutter. Date: 31
August 1747.
- inventory of James Scarffe.
- inventory of Jacob Jackson.
- inventory of Mathew Fisher.
- inventory of Suanna Stokes.
- accounts of William Hollis executor
of William Snelson.
- accounts of Johannah Smith & Thomas
Smith executors of William Smith.
- accounts of Sarah Vine executrix of
Rowland Vine.
- additional accounts of Susanna
Butler executrix of Henry Butler.
- accounts of John Frazier
administrator of Matthew Fisher.
- additional accounts of Alexander
Maccomus, Jr. & his wife Deborah
administratrix of Thomas Deaver.

Exhibited from SM:
- additional accounts of Meverel Lock

administrator of George Wallis.

32:121 9 September. Benton Harris (g, WO)
exhibited:
- will of Abraham Outten, constituting
  Rhoda Outten executrix. Also,
  widow's election. Said executrix
  was granted administration.
  Sureties: Isaac Marshall, Joshua
  Sturgis. Date: 30 June 1747.
- inventory of Hampton Hopkins.
- inventory of Robert Watson.
- inventory of John Evans Linton.
- inventory of Tabitha Parker.
- inventory of Mathew Payn.
- inventory of Thomas Coffen.
- accounts of Alexander Buncle
  administrator of John Evans Linton.
- accounts of Warren Burrus & his wife
  Presilla administratrix of John
  Willey.
- accounts of David Smith one of
  sureties of Mary Harvey
  administratrix of John Harvey.

10 September. Exhibited from AA:
- additional accounts of MM Philip
  Smith & William Chapman
  administrators of Philip Smith
  (London).

11 September. Exhibited from BA:
- inventory & LoD of Capt. Daniel
  Bowly. Also, accounts of Elisabeth
  Bowly executrix.

MM Joseph Sudler & Marmaduke Goodwin to
appraise estate of Mr. John Bradford
(CE) in QA.

21 September. William Tilghman (g, QA)
exhibited:
- will of Benjamin Chairs. Also,
  widow's election.
- will of Nicholas Yoe, constituting
  Jane Yoe executrix. Said executrix
  was granted administration.
  Sureties: Caleb Esgate, Jr. (p),
  Alexander Lee (p). Date: 16 July
  1747.
- will of John Birmingham.
- will of John Chaires, constituting

Margaret Chaires executrix. Said executrix was granted administration. Sureties: Edward Browne (p), John Downs, Jr. (p). Date: 23 July 1747.

- will of John Eareckson, constituting Elisabeth Eareckson executrix. Also, widow's election. Said executrix was granted administration. Sureties: Robert Small (p), Jacob Carter (p). Date: 23 July 1747.
- bond of Mary Spears administratrix of Thomas Spears. Sureties: Andrew Belgrave (p), John Legg, Jr. (p). Date: 9 July 1747.
- bond of Samuel Osborn administrator of William Osborn. Sureties: John Stevens (p), Charles Connor (p). Date: 13 August 1747.
- bond of Henry Williams executor of Matthew Williams. Sureties: Abraham Williams (p), William Wrench (p). Date: 9 July 1747.
- additional inventory of Timothy Lane.
- inventory of John Birmingham.
- inventory of John Banning.
- inventory & LoD of John Nevil.
- inventory of Margaret Boon.

32:122
- accounts of Richard Leech & his wife Rebecca administrators of Thomas Civil.

28 September. Exhibited from AA:
- will of John Purdum.

1 October. Mr. Charles Hynson (KE) to examine accounts of:
- Ann Richardson administratrix of Thomas Richardson (KE).
- Mary Worrell executrix of Edward Worrell (KE).

Mr. William Tilghman (QA) to examine accounts of:
- Valentine Honey & his wife Sarah administratrix of George Sparks (QA).
- Margaret Richardson administratrix of John Thompson (QA).
- Jane McClean administratrix of

Daniel McClean (QA).
- Christopher Cross Ruth & his wife Rebecca executrix of Peter Countiss (QA).
- Jane Thomas & Benjamin Thomas executors of Trustram Thomas (QA).
- Daniel Ford & his wife Sarah administrators of James Maud (QA).
- Susanna Jennings administratrix of Bartholomew Jennings (QA).

5 October. Nehemiah King (g, SO) exhibited:
- will of John Caldwell, constituting Mary Caldwell executrix. Said executrix was granted administration. Sureties: William Davis, William Vennables. Date: 19 August 1747.
- will of George Phebuss, constituting Samuel Phebuss executor. Said executor was granted administration. Sureties: William Jones, Henry Wright. Date: 1 September 1747.
- bond of Elisabeth Tull executrix of George Tull. Sureties: William Stevens, Stephen Handy. Date: 1 September 1747.
- inventory of Robert Price.
- inventory of Ann Walker.
- inventory of William Harper. Also, accounts of Edward Harper executor.
- accounts of William Stevens administrator of John Hutchinson.
- accounts of William Dashiel executor of Matthias Dashiel.

6 October. William Tilghman (g, QA) exhibited:
- accounts of Rebecca Curtis administratrix of Thomas Curtis.
- accounts of Bridget Primrose administratrix of William Primrose.
- accounts of Vincent Price administrator of Timothy Lane.

8 October. Exhibited from PG:
- 3rd additional accounts of Andrew Scott & his wife Mary executrix of John Abington.

32:123 9 October. Peter Dent (g, PG)
exhibited:
- inventory of Henry Massey.
- inventory of Samuel Warring.
- inventory of Philip Large.

16 October. Joshua Caldwell guardian of
Samuel Caldwell one of executors of John
Caldwell (SO) vs. Mary Caldwell other
executor of said dec'd. Sheriff (SO) to
summon defendant to show cause why LoA
granted to her should not be revoked &
LoA granted to her & said Samuel
Caldwell.

17 October. William Cockey & Joshua
Owens executors of John Cockey (BA) vs.
Thomas Cockey (BA) & Thomas Boone (BA).
Sheriff (BA) to summon defendants to
show cause why they conceal estate of
dec'd.

19 October. Ennalls Hooper (g, DO)
exhibited:
- will of Samuel Bedford.
- will of Thomas Smith, constituting
  William Smith & John Stevens Smith
  executors. Said executors were
  granted administration. Sureties:
  Jarvis Langfitt (g), George Griffith
  (g). Date: 13 August 1747.
- will of Richard Wallace,
  constituting Bathula Wallace
  executrix. Said executrix was
  granted administration. Sureties:
  William Standford, Jr. (p), Henry
  Fisher (p). Date: 10 June 1747.
- will of Edward Wright, constituting
  Martha Wright executrix. Said
  executrix was granted
  administration. Sureties: William
  Kennerly, William Grantham. Date:
  12 August 1747.
- will of John Wingate, constituting
  Rachel Wingate executrix. Said
  executrix was granted
  administration. Sureties: Henry
  Travers, Sr. (g), Roger Hooper (g).
  Date: 12 August 1747.
- will of Edward Russam, constituting
  Edward Trippe executor. Said
  executor was granted administration.

Sureties: William Murray (g), Henry Ennalls. Sr. (g). Date: 17 July 1747.

- bond of Elisabeth Jones administratrix of Samuel Jones. Sureties: Abraham Jones (p), Ezekial Johnson (p). Date: 12 August 1747.
- bond of Anne Andrew administratrix of Richard Andrew. Sureties: Richard Andrew (g), George Andrew (g). Date: 8 June 1747.
- bond of Mary Todd administratrix of Michael Todd. Sureties: John Harper, James Safford. Date: 12 August 1747.
- Dorothy Gollorthon administratrix of William Gollorthon. Sureties: Thomas Stapleford (p), Peter Edmondson (p). Date: 10 June 1747.
- bond of Lucretia Eccleston executrix of Hugh Eccleston. Sureties: James Peterkin (g). Walter Stevens (g). Date: 12 August 1747.
- bond of Peter Edmondson administrator of John Brown. Sureties: Thomas McKeel, Joseph Cox Gray. Date: 18 July 1747.
- inventory of Robert Sherwin.
- inventory of James Foxson.
- inventory of William Clifton.
- additional inventory of John Pitt.
- inventory of Francis Owen.
- inventory of Dennis Carey.
- inventory of Henry Roten.
- additional inventory of George Williams.
- inventory of John Munday.
- inventory of Henry Dean.
- inventory of William Draper.
- inventory of Richard Andrew.
- inventory & LoD of Philadelphia Williams.
- inventory of John Brannock.
- inventory of William Roughten.
- inventory & LoD of John Vickars.
- inventory of Richard Wallace.
- inventory of James Maloney.
- inventory of Thomas Bramble.
- additional inventory of Elisabeth Taylor.
- inventory & LoD of James Smith.
- inventory of William Gollorthon.

32:124

- inventory of Thomas Ennalls.
- additional inventory of Lewis Griffith.
- additional inventory of Thomas Eccleston.
- inventory of Lewis Griffith.
- accounts of Patrick Stack & his wife Elisabeth administrators of Samuel Cole.
- accounts of John Hupper executor of Grace Hupper.
- accounts of Elinor Phillups administratrix of Thomas Phillips.
- accounts of Sarah Adams administratrix of Thomas Adams.
- accounts of Thomas Stanford executor of John Stanford.
- accounts of Rachel Sexton administratrix of Andrew Sexton.
- accounts of John Pollard, Jr. administrator of George Williams.
- accounts of James Edmondson administrator of Francis Owen.
- accounts of William Smith administrator of John Hodson Secundus
- accounts of Mary Smith administratrix of Henry Smith.
- accounts of Mary Whiteacre administratrix of Joseph Whiteacre.
- 2nd additional accounts of William Bartlet & his wife Margaret executors of William Harper.
- accounts of Margaret & Andrew Arnatt administrators of William Arnatt.
- 2nd additional accounts of John Pattison & Moses Lecompte & his wife Mary executors of St. Leeger Pattison.
- accounts of Phillis Clarkson executrix of Robert Clarkson.
- accounts of George Slacomb & his wife Frances executrix of Lewis Griffith.
- accounts of Thomas Whealer acting executor of Charles Whealer.
- accounts of Josias Moore administrator of John Jamison.
- additional accounts of Anne Coburn administratrix of Samuel Coburn.
- accounts of Anne Tregoe & William Tregoe administrators of William

Tregoe.
- accounts of James Safford administrator of Abram Safford.
- accounts of Joanna Allcock executrix of Burtonwood Allcock.
- accounts of Elisabeth & William Edmondson executors of William Edmondson.
- accounts of James Cullen administrator of William Cullen.
- accounts of Raymond & Thomas Staplefort executors of Elisabeth Taylor.
- accounts of William Harvey administrator of Richard Harvey.
- accounts of Elinor Eccleston & Hugh Eccleston executors of Thomas Eccleston.

Gabriel Parker (g, CV) exhibited:
- will of Sarah Smith, constituting Joseph Hall & Parker Young executors. Said executors were granted administration. Surety: William Holland. Date: 13 October 1747.
- inventory of Moses Parran.
- inventory of Richard Blake.
- accounts of Young Parran administrator of Moses Parran.
- additional accounts of Robert How & his wife Elisabeth administratrix of William Harris.
- accounts of Peter Hellen, Jr. & his wife Penelope executrix of Ann Dawkins.

32:125 20 October. John Thompson (g, CE) exhibited:
- will of John Young. Also, bond of Mary Young administratrix. Sureties: Amos Fogg, Simon Johnson, Jr. Date: 10 October 1747.
- bond of Henrieta Maria Elbarry & James Bayard administrators of Christopher Elbarry. Sureties: Peter Bayard (g), William (g). Date: 16 June 1747.
- bond of Henry Dobson administrator of George Bristow. Sureties: Thomas Ricketts, David Hamton. Date: 17 August 1747.

- bond of Sarah Jackson administratrix of Edward Jackson. Sureties: Richard Sedgwick, Henry Jackson. Date: 10 June 1747.
- bond of Thomas Money & Elisabeth Money administrators of William Chambers. Sureties: Robert Money, Jr., Matthew Bulley. Date: 24 August 1747.
- inventory & LoD of Samuel Maffitt.
- inventory of David Lawson.
- inventory & LoD of Hugh Walker.
- inventory of Edward Jackson.
- inventory of Richard Wooliston, Sr.
- additional accounts of John Baldwin & his wife Mary administratrix of Dom. Carroll.
- accounts of Mary Penington executrix of John Penington.
- accounts of Elinor Wright & James Evans executors of James Wright.
- accounts of Francis Carruthers & his wife Ann administratrix of Archibald Steel.
- accounts of Michael Tully & his wife Rachel administratrix of Robert Crocker.

21 October. Thomas Bullen (g, TA) exhibited:
- will of Margaret Ward, constituting Matthew Tilghman executor. Said executor was granted administration. Sureties: William Goldsborough (g), James Tilghman (g). Date: 6 October 1747.
- bond of Joseph Hicks, Jr. administrator of Charles Hicks. Sureties: Joseph Hicks, Anthony Lecompte. Date: 1 September 1747.
- additional inventory & LoD of John Robins.
- accounts of Stephen Stichbury & his wife Jane executrix of John Studham.
- accounts of Robert Goldsborough & his wife Mary Anne administratrix of John Robins.

22 October. Peter Dent (g, PG) exhibited:
- bond of Cave Magruder administratrix of James Magruder. Sureties: Osbern

Sprigg (g), Thomas King (g). Date:
7 October 1747.
- inventory of John Crook.
- inventory of Henry Downes.
- inventory of Samuel Barker.
- accounts of Martha Page administratrix of Bingley Page.
- accounts of Anne Crook administratrix of John Crook.

32:126 John Meconikin for Jannet Clayland niece of John Gibb (QA, dec'd) vs. estate of said dec'd. Caveat against granting LoA. 23 October. Said Meconikin withdrew his caveat & consented to proving said will.

22 October. Mr. Charles Hynson (KE) to examine accounts of:
- Mary Worrell executrix of Edward Worrell (KE).

Exhibited from QA:
- will of John Gibb.

23 October. Exhibited from QA:
- bond of James Massey, Sr. & John Hadley, Sr. executors of John Gibb. Sureties: William Elbert (p), James Casey (p), John Spry (p). Date: 22 October 1747.

Exhibited from PG:
- bond of David McCullock (merchant, BA) administrator of James McCaull. Sureties: John Wardrop (merchant, CV), Robert Swann (merchant, Annapolis, AA). Date: 23 October 1747. MM William Wilkinson (CH) & John Wilson (CH) to appraise said estate in CH.

24 October. Benton Harris (g, WO) exhibited:
- bond of Andrew Gray administrator of Jacob Gray. Sureties: John Massey, Ceasar Goodwin, Sr. Date: 16 September 1747.
- bond of Elisabeth Murray administratrix of Duncan Murray. Sureties: Alexander Buncle, Thomas Lambden. Date: 10 October 1747.

- inventory of Daniel Davis.
- inventory of William Turvill.
- additional inventory of William Davis.
- accounts of William Selby & his wife Martha executrix of John Purnell.
- accounts of Charles Rackliff & his wife Comfort administratrix of Hugh Stevenson.

26 October. Exhibited from AA:
- exemplifications of will & LoA from London on estate of Isaac Milner. Also, bond of John Gassaway administrator. Sureties: William Cotter (g), John Howard (g). Date: 26 October 1747.
- exemplifications of will & LoA from London on estate of Godfrey Milner. Also, bond of John Gassaway administrator. Sureties: William Cotter, John Howard. Date: 26 October 1747.

32:127 28 October. Exhibited from AA:
- will of John Galloway.
- will of John Purdum.
- additional accounts of William Cockey & Joshua Owings executors of John Cockey executor of Col. Thomas Cockey.

31 October. Catharine Prichard widow of Capt. John Prichard (PG) vs. Rebecca Tilley executrix of said dec'd. Sheriff (PG) to summon defendant to render inventory.

2 November. Walter Hanson (g, CH) exhibited:
- will of Matthew Compton, Sr.
- bond of Elisabeth Douglass administratrix of Benjamin Douglass. Sureties: Benjamin Douglass, John Hanson Youngest. Date: 3 September 1747.
- bond of Jane Mankin administratrix of Tubman Mankin. Sureties: John Brooks (p), Charles Baker (p). Date: 1 August 1747.
- inventory of James Dougal.
- inventory of Archibald Johnson.

- inventory of Benjamin Banister.
- inventory of Jacob Baley.
- inventory of Tubman Mankin.
- additional inventory of John Craxon.
- additional accounts of James Freeman & his wife Jane administratrix of Arthur Westman.
- accounts of Elisabeth Mckorn administratrix of Robert Mckorn.
- accounts of Juliana Simpson executrix of Andrew Simpson.
- accounts of Hudson Wathen & John Wathen executors of John Wathen.
- accounts of Phillip Terrill & his wife Elisabeth executrix of John Craxon.

Mr. Walter Hanson (CH) to examine accounts of:
- Susannah Waters administratrix of William Waters (CH).
- Philip Terrill & his wife Elisabeth executrix of Samuel Burgess (CH).
- James Middleton & Ignatius Gardner executors of Vincent Askin (CH). Additional accounts.
- Elisabeth Tarvin executrix of Richard Tarvin, Sr. (CH). 2nd additional accounts.
- Charles Bevans & his wife Anne administratrix of Thomas Jenkins (CH). 2nd additional accounts.

Exhibited from BA:
- inventory of William Fell in BA & at his Quarter in AA.

3 November. Exhibited from AA:
- accounts of Raymond Jones administrator of George Vennam.

MM Joseph Ogle & Joseph Wood to appraise estate of John Beatty (PG). Mr. Nathaniel Wickham to administer oath.

32:128 4 November. Exhibited from KE:
- will of Christopher Granger, constituting Ann Granger executrix. Said executrix was granted administration. Sureties: Samuel Wickes (p), Nathaniel Hynson (p). Date: 4 November 1747.

Court Session: 1747

James Ringgold & Alexander Williamson to appraise estate of Christopher Granger (KE).

William Cumming, Esq. vs. Francis Finn (PG) executor of Mary Ogden (CH). Sheriff (PG) to summon defendant to render inventory.

5 November. Mr. William Tilghman (QA) to examine accounts of:
• John Covington & Henry Covington executors of Henry Covington (QA).
• Susannah Jumpe acting executrix of William Jumpe (QA).

6 November. William Rogers (g, AA) exhibited:
• bond of Catharine Hudson (Annapolis) administratrix of William Hudson. Sureties: James Callahan (taylor, Annapolis), James Barnes (innholder, Annapolis). Date: 6 October 1747.
• bond of John Birckhead & Samuel Birckhead administrators of Matthew Birckhead. Sureties: Nehemiah Birckhead (p), Alexander Fraizer (p). Date: 27 October 1747.
• bond of Mary Purdum (AA) & John Purdum (PG) executors of John Purdum. Sureties: Thomas Hutchcraft (p, AA), William Gray (p, PG). Date: 28 September 1747.

7 November. Exhibited from QA:
• inventory of Elisabeth Clouds.
• additional accounts of Edward Tilghman executor of Maj. William Turbutt.

Thomas Aisquith (g, SM) exhibited:
• will of Clare Sherburn, constituting Nicholas Sherburn executor. Said executor was granted administration. Sureties: William Joseph, Charles Hodgkins. Date: 17 September.
• will of John Binks, constituting John Dossey executor. Said executor was granted administration. Sureties: Owen Guyther, Robert Hager. Date: 31 August 1747.
• will of Peter Oneal. Also, widow's

election.
- bond of William Flower administrator of Mary Dossey. Sureties: John Dossey, Robert Hager. Date: 21 September 1747.

32:129
- bond of Francis Mitchell administrator of Luke Cecill. Sureties: William Harrison, Peter Mugg. Date: 7 August 1747.
- inventory of Edward Austin.
- inventory & LoD of Patrick Forrest.
- accounts of Luke Marrall & his wife Mary administratrix of Nicholas Fardrey.
- accounts of Tekela Joy administratrix of Enock Joy.
- accounts of James Walls administrator dbn of Timothy Tole.

Mr. Peter Dent (PG) to examine accounts of:
- Martha Page administratrix of Bingly Page (PG).
- Blanford Bevine acting executor of Dr. John Kirkwood (PG).
- Humphry Ball & his wife Elisabeth executrix of Thomas Jennings (PG). Additional accounts.

Mr. Thomas Bullen (TA) to examine accounts of:
- William Oxenham & his wife Mary administratrix of Daniel Ward (TA).
- Rachel Thompson administratrix of Thomas Thompson (TA).
- Sarah Santee executrix of Nathaniel Santee (TA).

Exhibited from AA, as receipts for their filial portions:
- received of Thomas Cheney, legacy from Susannah Brown. Date: 20 June 1747. Signed: Richard Cheney. Witnesses: Otho French, John Hopper.
- received of Thomas Cheney, legacy from Susannah Brown. Date: 20 June 1747. Signed: Lewis Cheney. Witnesses: Otho French, John Hopper.
- received of Thomas Cheney, his wife's portion from Susannah Brown. Date: 7 October 1746. Signed: William Phelp, Jr. Witness: Samuell

Court Session: 1747

Day.
- received of Thomas Cheney, his wife's portion from Susannah Brown. Date: 7 October 1746. Signed: Richard Rickets. Witnesses: Jonathon Ta<unreadable>, Richard Seele.

Court Session: 10 November 1747

32:130 Docket:
- Sheriff (PG) to render attachment to Lingan Wilson (PG) administrator of Joseph Wilson (PG) to render inventory.
- Raymond Stapleford, Charles Stapleford, & Thomas Stapleford executors of Elisabeth Taylor (DO) vs. Dorothy Gollothon (DO) & Dorothy Loockerman (DO). Sheriff (DO) to render attachment to defendants to show cause why they conceal estate of dec'd.
- Sheriff (SO) to summon Thomas Morrison & his wife widow of Philip Ellis (DO) to take LoA.
- S.B. for Baptist Barber & his wife Elisabeth (SM) vs. W.C. for Samuel & Richard Sothoron executors of John Johnson Sothoron. Libel, answer.
- Patrick Grey (BA) vs. Patrick Doran (AA) administrator of John Handling (AA). Sheriff (AA) to summon defendant to render accounts.
- Sheriff (DO) to summon (N) Hern (SO) widow & executrix of Edward Hern (SO) to prove said will & to take LoA. Will proved & LoA were granted. Discontinued.

32:131
- E.D. for John Tootell & his wife Rosannah (DO) vs. Thomas Woolford & John Woolford executors of Roger Woolford. Libel.
- Executors of Samuel Young (CV) vs. Richard Young (AA) surviving executor of Col. Samuel Young (AA). William Thornton (sheriff, AA) to render attachment to defendant to render final accounts.
  - Richard Young deposed before Ezekiel Gillis (JP, AA) that there are some papers of his

father's which he believes to be deposited in the hands of Mr. David Arnold & Mr. Mackey (of New Castle).

- John Smith Prather, Thomas Prather, & Thomas Williams executors of Martha Yoakley vs. Joseph Milburn Semmes & his wife. Attachment to be rendered to defendant for costs.

- E.D. for Ebenezar Reymer & his wife Sarah (KE) vs. Daniel Dulany for Rebecca Perkins & David Perkins. Libel. James Ringgold, Jr. (sheriff, KE) to summon defendant to render answer. MM John Gresham & Daniel Cheston to take answer of defendant.

32:132 - Sewall Long & his wife Margaret one of daughters of Richard Acton (BA, dec'd) vs. Ann Acton (BA) widow of said dec'd. Sheriff (BA) to summon defendant to show cause why she does not take LoA on his estate.

- Joshua Caldwell guardian for Samuel Caldwell one of executors of John Caldwell (SO) vs. Mary Caldwell other executor of said dec'd. Sheriff (SO) to summon defendant to show cause why LoA granted to her should not be revoked & LoA granted to said defendant & said Samuel.

- William Cockey & Joshua Owing executors of John Cockey (BA) vs. Thomas Cockey (BA) & Thomas Boone (BA). Henry Morgan (sheriff, BA) to summon defendants to show cause why they conceal estate of said dec'd.

- Catharine Prichard widow of Capt. John Prichard (PG) vs. Rebecca Tilley executrix of said dec'd. Osborn Sprigg (sheriff, PG) to summon defendant to render full inventory. Continuance was granted.

- William Cumming, Esq. vs. Francis Finn (PG) executor of Mary Ogden (CH). Osborn Sprigg (sheriff, PG) to summon defendant to render inventory.

32:133 10 November. Mr. Thomas White (BA) to examine additional accounts of:
- Winstone Smith & his wife Susanna executrix of George Stokes (BA).
- Joshua Hardisty & his wife Kezia executrix of John Taylor (BA).
- Cordelia Holland executrix of Francis Holland administrator dbn of Susanna Holland (BA).

11 November. Mr. John Thompson (CE) to examine accounts of:
- James Porter & Nathaniel Owing acting executors of Alexander Owing (CE).
- Mary Jones administratrix of Peter Jones (CE).
- Charles Bullard & his wife Mary administratrix of John Belarmine (CE).
- John Lawson administrator of David Lawson (CE).
- William Mackie & Samuel Walker executors of Hugh Walker (CE).
- George Rock & his wife Mary administratrix of Robert Storey (CE).
- Francis Maybury executor of James Irwin (CE).
- Elisabeth Walson administratrix of Abraham Walson (CE).
- Sarah Jackson administratrix of Edward Jackson (CE).
- John Baldwin & his wife Mary administratrix of Dominick Carroll (CE). 2nd additional accounts.
- Francis Carruthers & his wife Ann administratrix of Archibald Steel (CE). Additional accounts.

Exhibited from AA:
- additional accounts of John Dowell & his wife Susanna administratrix of Morgan Jones.

12 November. Exhibited from PG:
- bond of Richard Holland administrator dbn of Thomas Holland. Surety: Samuel Waters (p). Date: 12 November 1747.
- accounts of William West administrator of John Magee.

Thomas Bullen (g, TA) exhibited:
- will of Thomas Gully, constituting Rachel Gully executrix. Also, widow's election. Said executrix was granted administration. Sureties: Richard Gibson, Solomon Harwood. Date: 27 October 1747.
- bond of Mary Parratt administratrix of William Parratt. Sureties: William Richardson, Peter Commerford. Date: 5 November 1747.
- bond of Hannah Dobson administratrix of Isaac Dobson. Sureties: Thomas Loveday, Edward Neall. Date: 1 November 1747.

13 November. Exhibited from PG:
- accounts of Richard Holland acting executor of Margaret Holland.

Exhibited from AA:
- accounts of Charles Connant executor of James Mackclanan.

32:134 Mr. Thomas Bullen (TA) to examine accounts of:
- Thomas Powell & his wife Mary executrix & Richard Dudley executor of Samuel Dudley (TA).
- William Herrington & his wife Rachel administratrix of Thomas Thompson (TA).

Exhibited from KE:
- 4th additional accounts of John Spencer who married Sarah Hanson widow & administratrix of Hans Hanson.

16 November. Exhibited from PG:
- inventory of Mordecai Coleman.

21 November. Mr. Nehemiah King (SO) to examine accounts of:
- Elgett Hitch who married Elisabeth Handy executrix of Ebenezar Handy (SO).
- Mary Price executrix of Robert Price (SO).
- James Lucas executor of Ann Walker (SO).

Mr. Benton Harris (WO) to examine
accounts of:
- Mary Allen executrix of Francis
  Allen (WO).
- Elisabeth Hill administratrix of
  Hutten Hill (WO).

23 November. Exhibited from PG:
- additional inventory of William
  Hedges.

Exhibited from BA:
- bond of Joseph Taylor administrator
  dbn of John Cole. Sureties: William
  Barney (p, BA), Thomas Williamson
  (g, Annapolis). Date: 23 November
  1747.

24 November. Gabriel Parker (g, CV)
exhibited:
- will of Thomas Hunt, constituting
  Elisabeth Hunt executrix. Said
  executrix was granted
  administration. Sureties: Job Hunt,
  Nicholas Swormstedt. Date: 14
  November 1747.
- will of Everard Taylor, constituting
  Sarah Taylor executrix. Said
  executrix was granted
  administration. Sureties: Charles
  Clagett, John Johnson, Jr. Date: 6
  November 1747.
- bond of Hugh Mcquire administrator
  of William Attishe (shoemaker).
  Sureties: Samuel Harrison, John
  Norfolk. Date: 10 November 1747.

Peter Dent (g, PG) exhibited:
- will of Joseph Hatton, constituting
  Lucy Hatton executrix. Said
  executrix was granted
  administration. Sureties: John
  Hawkins, Jr. (g), Luke Marbury (g).
  Date: 14 November 1747.

32:135 30 November. Exhibited from BA:
- LoD on estate of John Cockey.
- inventory & LoD of John Wooley.
  Also, accounts of John Jones & John
  Logsdon administrators.
- accounts of William Cockey & Joshua
  Owings executors of Capt. John

Court Session: 1747

Cockey.

Mr. Thomas Aisquith (SM) to examine
accounts of:
- William Joseph & his wife Elisabeth
  executrix of Charles Ganyott (SM).

Mr. John Thompson (CE) to examine
accounts of:
- Col. Thomas Colvill executor of
  Solomon Hodgson (CE).
- Teresa Alman & Dr. Hugh Matthews
  administrators of Joseph Alman (CE).
- Rebecca Wye administratrix of
  William Wye (CE).
- Margaret Reynolds administratrix of
  Thomas Reynolds (CE).
- Nicholas Hyland executor of William
  Becke (CE).

William Rogers (g, AA) exhibited:
- will of John Franklin, constituting
  Isabel Franklin executrix. Also,
  widow's election. Said executrix
  was granted administration.
  Sureties: Joseph Chew (p), Richard
  Franklin (p). Date: 11 November
  1747.
- bond of Samuel Galloway executor of
  John Galloway. Sureties: Joseph
  Cowman (g), Jerom Plummer (g).
  Date: 4 November 1747.

2 December. Exhibited from AA:
- 2nd additional accounts of William
  Hollyday & his wife Mary
  administratrix of Mark Richardson.

4 December. Thomas White (g, BA)
exhibited:
- will of Robert Hollyday,
  constituting Charles Ridgely
  executor. Also, widow's election.
  Said executor was granted
  administration. Sureties: Lyde
  Goodwin, John Ridgely. Date: 3
  October 1747.
- will of George Hitchcock. Also,
  bond of John Tye acting executor.
  Sureties: Henry Satyr, John Cooke.
  Date: 11 November 1747. Also,
  renunciation of Mary Hitchcoke,

Page 98

recommending John Ty. Witnesses: Robert Gilbert, John Cook.

- bond of Ann Acton executrix of Richard Acton. Sureties: Henry Lewis, Daniel Ragon. Date: 1 October 1747.
- bond of Sarah Groves administratrix of William Groves. Sureties: James Maxwell, Henry Brereton. Date: 6 November 1747.

32:136
- bond of William Smith administrator of Samuel Gallion. Surety: Nicholas Ruxton Gay. Date: 21 September 1747.
- inventory of David Thomas.
- additional inventory of Susanna Holland.
- additional inventory of George Stokes.

5 December. Exhibited from AA:
- will of Dr. Samuel Stringer, constituting Lydia Stringer executrix. Said executrix was granted administration. Sureties: Richard Warfield, Sr. (g), Alexander Warfield (g, son of Richard). Date: 5 December 1747.

7 December. Peter Dent (g, PG) exhibited:
- will of Anna Maria Lee.
- will of John Pibon, Sr., constituting Jacob Piburn & Benjamin Piburn executors. Said executors were granted administration. Sureties: Elias Ashman (p), William Marshall (p). Date: 5 November 1747.
- will of John Smoot, constituting Mary Smoot executrix. Said executrix was granted administration. Sureties: John Crampkin (p), James Harrison (p). Date: 25 November 1747.
- bond of Mary Ann Hamilton administratrix of James Hamilton. Sureties: Thomas Catteratt (p), Michel Yourn (p). Date: 26 August 1747.
- bond of John Dawson administrator of John Morrison. Sureties: Edward

Stonestreet (g), George Dawson (g).
Date: 26 August 1747.
- inventory of James Pelley.
- LoD on estate of Ann Miller.
- accounts of John West executor of Benjamin West.

8 December. Gabriel Parker (g, CV)
exhibited:
- bond of Elisabeth Pardo administratrix of Barrington Pardo. Sureties: Martin Driver, John Greeves, Jr. Date: 28 November 1747.
- bond of Isabella Barton administratrix of John Barton. Sureties: Henry Chew, Francis Hollingshead. Date: 5 December 1747.
- bond of Jane Hollingshead administratrix of Margaret Davis. Sureties: Nicholas Swormstedt, Thomas Rhodes. Date: 28 November 1747.
- accounts of Peter Hellen executor of Susannah Hellen.

9 December. John Bull acting executor of Sarah Ruff vs. Richard Ruff (BA) & Daniel Ruff (BA) executors of Richard Ruff (BA). Sheriff (BA) to summon defendants to render inventory.

15 December. Exhibited from BA:
- will of John Crockett.

32:137 Exhibited from CV:
- 2nd additional accounts of Lewis Griffith & John Griffith executors of Samuel Griffith.

16 December. Thomas Bullen (g, TA)
exhibited:
- deposition of Edward Nedels, age 51, that he was sent for to write will of Bartholomew Greenwood (dec'd). Said Greenwood lived near Jordon's Branch in TA. Said Greenwood devised to his 2 daughters Eleanor & Elisabeth Greenwood. Date: 13 November 1747.

Court Session: 1747

William Tilghman (g, QA) exhibited:
- will of Lawrence Hall, constituting John Hall & William Hall executors. Said executors were granted administration. Sureties: John Faulkner, Burton Francis. Date: 15 October 1747.
- will of Thomas Hynson Wright.
- will of George Jackson, constituting Benjamin Jackson executor. Said executor was granted administration. Sureties: Francis Jackson (p), John Seth (p), William Harrington (p). Date: 28 November 1747.
- will of Thomas Needles.
- will of Arthur Emory.
- bond of Susanna Keld administratrix of Thomas Keld. Sureties: John Plummer (p, TA), John Keld (p, TA). Date: 1 October 1747.
- bond of Mary Kemp administratrix of William Kemp. Sureties: George Smith (p), Thomas Bailey, Jr. (p). Date: 16 October 1747.
- bond of Mary Chaires executrix of Benjamin Chaires. Sureties: Joseph Chaires (p), William Austin (p). Date: 23 November 1747.
- bond of Martha Story administratrix of Charles Story. Sureties: John Parker (p), William Bailey (p). Date: 25 November 1747.
- bond of Mirimi Browne administratrix of Edward Browne, Jr. Sureties: Edward Browne (p), Daniel Wilcox (p). Date: 26 November 1747.
- accounts of Christopher Cross Ruth & his wife Rebecca executrix of Peter Countiss.
- accounts of Anthony Hadder & his wife Mary administratrix of Ishmael Devenish.

32:138 Thomas Bullen (g, TA) exhibited:
- will of Hannah Dickenson.
- will of Sarah Loveday.
- will of John Wales.
- inventory & LoD of Richard Skinner.
- inventory & LoD of Richard Eubanks.
- inventory of Charles Hicks.
- inventory of Samuel Neall.
- inventory of Alexander Macotter.

- accounts of Katherine Skinner executrix of Richard Skinner.
- accounts of Feddeman Rolle administrator of Francis Rolle.

17 December. Exhibited from BA:
- additional accounts of Sarah Dulany executrix of Thomas Dulany.

2 January. Exhibited from BA:
- bond of Mary Crockett executrix of John Crockett. Sureties: Joseph Richardson (g, AA), Philip Hopkins (g, AA). Date: 2 January 1747.

8 January. Exhibited from BA:
- inventory of Richard Acton, Sr.

Exhibited from AA:
- additional accounts of John Batson administrator of Richard Randall.

Charles Hynson (g, KE) exhibited:
- will of Francis Barney, constituting James Corse & Ebenezar Pearkins executors. Said executors were granted administration. Sureties: George Rasin (p), Thomas Parkins (p). Date: 18 September 1747.
- will of James Corse, constituting James Corse executor. Said executor was granted administration. Sureties: John Corse (p), Henry Bodien (p). Date: 27 July 1747.
- will of William Trew.
- will of Ambrose Howard.
- nuncupative will of William Bower.
- bond of Issabell Denning administratrix of George Denning. Sureties: Nicholas Smith (p), William Smith (p). Date: 23 May 1747.
- bond of Jane Browne administratrix of John Brown. Sureties: William Hynson (g), William Granger (g). Date: 18 August 1747.
- bond of Mary Powell administratrix of Bryan Powell. Sureties: Daniel Bryan (g), William McClain (g). Date: 5 December 1747.
- bond of Thomas Parke (hatter) administrator of Thomas Parke.

Court Session: 1747

Sureties: Thomas Ringgold (g),
William Ringgold (g). Date: 17
August 1747.

- bond of Jacob Glenn executor of
  Jacob Glenn. Sureties: Hanse Hanson
  (p), Michael Hackett (p). Date: 29
  August 1747.
- inventory of James Greenwood.
- inventory & LoD of John Wallace.
- inventory & LoD of Michael Miller.
- inventory of Edward Davis.
- inventory of Charles Scott.
- inventory of William Boyer.
- inventory of George Denning.
- additional inventory of Bowles
  Green.
- inventory of Edward Dyer.
- inventory of Butman Medford.
- inventory & LoD of Jacob Glenn.
- additional accounts of Colin
  Farguson executor of Robert Due.
- additional accounts of George Hall
  executor of Benjamin Jones.
- accounts of Patrick Keran surviving
  administrator of Patrick Handraty.
- accounts of John Green administrator
  of Bowles Green.
- accounts of Morgan Hurt & his wife
  Martha administratrix of William
  Brown.

32:139

24 December. William Grantham & his
wife Sarah vs. William Kennerly (p, DO)
surviving executor of Joshua Kennerly
(DO, blacksmith). Sheriff (DO) to
summon defendant to render answer to
libel.

Court Session: 12 January 1747

Docket:
- G. Sprigg (sheriff, PG) to render
  attachment to Lingan Wilson (PG)
  administrator of Joseph Wilson (PG)
  to render accounts. Accounts
  exhibited. Discontinued.
- Raymond Stapleford, Charles
  Stapleford, & Thomas Stapleford
  executors of Elisabeth Taylor (DO)
  vs. Dorothy Gollothon (DO) &
  Dorothy Lookerman (DO). Sheriff
  (DO) to summon defendants to show

Page 103

cause why they conceal estate of
dec'd.

- Stephen Bordley, Esq. procurator for
Baptist Baker (g, SM) & his wife
Elisabeth vs. William Cumming, Esq.
procurator for Samuel & Richard
Sothoron executors of John Johnson
Sothoron.
Text of libel.

32:140   Plaintiff is widow of said dec'd.
Said dec'd made his will,
constituting his brothers Samuel
Southern & Richard Southern
executors. Mentions: John Donaldson
(father of plaintiff Elisabeth),

32:141   plaintiff as Rachel, Gilbert Ireland
(sheriff, SM).
Text of answer.

32:142   Mentions: Negro Nell (woman), Negro
Joe (boy), negroes belonging to
Henry Southern (son of dec'd) given
to him by his grandmother Mrs.
Dryden Forbes, dec'd married a
daughter of Col. Henry Peregrine
Jowles,

32:143   children of 2nd wife of said dec'd,
Mary Rose (dec'd was administrator
of her estate), Benjamin (brother of
whole blood who died since dec'd),
John Burch (brother of half blood),

32:144   Parson Donaldson (father of
plaintiff Elisabeth).
- Susanna Donaldson, age 21,
deposed on 4 March 1744/5 before
James Swann. Mentions: Mrs.
Dryden Forbes, Mrs. Rebeccah
Jowles.
- Leonard Clark, age 37, deposed
on 4 March 1744/5 before James
Swann.

32:145   - John Briscoe, John Briscoe, age
24, deposed on
4 March 1744/5 before James
Swann.
- Leonard Clark, age 37, deposed
on 5 March 1744/5 before James
Swann.
- John Burch, age 21, deposed on 5
March 1744/5 before James Swann.
Mentions: Henry Greenfield
Sothoron (son of dec'd).
- Leonard Clark, age 37, deposed

on 25 March 1745 before John
Chesley. Mentions: Henry
Greenfield Sothoron (son of
dec'd) & his mother Mary
Sothoron.

32:146 Ruling: dismissed.

- Patrick Grey (BA) vs. Patrick Doran
  (AA) administrator of John Handling
  (AA). William Thornton (sheriff,
  AA) to render attachment to
  defendant.
- E.D. for John Tootle & his wife
  Rosannah (DO) vs. Thomas Woolford
  (DO) & John Woolford (SO) executors
  of Roger Woolford. Libel.

32:147 - Executors of Samuel Young (CV) vs.
  Richard Young (AA) surviving
  executor of Col. Samuel Young (AA).
  Sheriff (AA) to render attachment to
  defendant to render final accounts.
- E.D. for Ebenezar Reyner & his wife
  Sarah (KE) vs. G.D. for Rebecca
  Perkins & David Perkins. Libel.
- Roger Boyce (sheriff, BA) to render
  attachment to Ann Acton (BA) to take
  LoA on estate of her husband Richard
  Acton (BA). LoA taken; inventory
  exhibited. Discontinued.
- Joshua Caldwell guardian to Samuel
  Caldwell one of executors of John
  Caldwell (SO) vs. Mary Caldwell
  other executor of said dec'd.
  Sheriff (SO) to summon defendant to
  show cause why LoA granted to her on
  said estate should not be revoked &
  LoA granted to her & said Samuel.
  To be left off.
- William Cockey & Joshua Owings
  executors of John Cockey (BA) vs.
  Thomas Cockey (BA) & Thomas Boone
  (BA). Roger Boyce (sheriff, BA) to
  render attachment to defendants to
  show cause why they conceal estate
  of dec'd. Both deposed.

32:148 Discontinued.

- Catharine Prichard widow of Capt.
  John Prichard (PG) vs. Rebecca
  Tilley executrix of said dec'd.
  Sheriff (PG) to summon defendant to
  render full inventory. Said Tilley
  exhibited that there is a suit in
  chancery between her & Richard

Court Session: 12 January 1747

- Snowden. Discontinued.
- Osborn Sprigg (sheriff, PG) to summon Francis Finn (PG) executor of Mary Ogden (CH) to render inventory. Said Finn exhibited that Nehemiah Ogden has prevented her from exhibiting an inventory. Discontinued.
- John Butt acting executor of Sarah Ruff vs. Richard Ruff (BA) & Daniel Ruff (BA) executors of Richard Ruff (BA). Sheriff (BA) to summon defendants to render inventory.
- D.D. for William Grantham & his wife Sarah (DO) vs. William Kennerly only surviving executor of Joshua Kennerly. Libel.

Court Session: 1747

32:149   9 January. Exhibited from PG:
- will of Thomas Fowler.

13 January. Exhibited from PG:
- accounts of Lingan Wilson administrator of Joseph Wilson.

Exhibited from AA:
- accounts of Lewis Stinchcombe executor of Henry Wright.

16 January. Exhibited from AA:
- Richard Young (AA) deposed on 16 January 1747 before Thomas Jennings, that he requested his nephew Samuel Budd to got to Mrs. Araminta Mackey (New Castle) for some papers regarding the division of the estate of Samuel Young, Esq. (dec'd).

30 January. Exhibited from BA:
- bond of William Cockey administrator of John Cockey, Jr. Sureties: Joshua Owings (p), George Ashman (p). Date: 13 January 1747. Appraisers: Col. William Hammond, Capt. Robert North.

2 February. Thomas Aisquith (g, SM) exhibited:
- bond of Elisabeth Blackman administratrix of Thomas Blackman.

Page 106

Court Session: 1747

Sureties: John Godard, Ignatius
Chambeling. Date: 26 October 1747.
- bond of William Looker administrator
of LIndsy Opie. Sureties: John
Williams, John Curlett. Date: 4
November 1747.
- inventory & LoD of Richard Shirley.
- inventory & LoD of Isaac Walters.
- inventory of John Horn.
- accounts of Mary Swann
administratrix of James Swann.
- accounts of Elisabeth Nelson
administratrix of Joshua Nelson.
- accounts of William Sumner
Billingsley executor of William
Billingsley.
- 2nd additional accounts of Samuel
Southoron & Richard Southoron
executors of John Johnson Southoron.
- accounts of John Smoote executor of
Elinor Aston.
- accounts of Richard Ford & his wife
Ann executrix of Edward Aprice.
- accounts of John Goldsmith, William
Goldsmith, & Michel Goldsmith
executors of Thomas Notley
Goldsmith.

32:150 Exhibited from PG:
- inventory of Eleanor Hilleary.
- inventory of Peter Johnson.

5 February. Mr. Charles Hynson (KE) to
examine accounts of:
- Thomas Barkley & his wife Isabella
executrix of Richard Wethered (KE).

Exhibited from BA:
- inventory of John Cole. Also,
accounts of Jonathan Taylor
administrator dbn.
- LoD on estate of William Fell.

4 February. Exhibited from BA:
- will of Edward Fottrell. Also,
renunciation of executors.

10 February. Mr. Thomas Aisquith (SM)
to examine accounts of:
- Lazarus Ross & his wife Mary
administratrix of John Railey (SM).
- Elisabeth Rule, Edward Hillard Hebb,

& William Hebb, Jr. executors of
Thomas Hebb (SM).

Exhibited from AA:
- inventory & LoD of John Wooden.
Also, accounts of Solomon Wooden
executor.

5 February. Exhibited from BA:
- accounts of Sarah Fell & Joseph
Taylor executors of William Fell.

12 February. Mr. Thomas White (BA) to
examine accounts of:
- Cordelia Holland executrix of
Francis Holland (BA).
- Mary Frisby administratrix dbn of
Susanna Stokes (BA).
- Thomas Burney (alias Thomas
Presbury) executor of James Presbury
(BA).

William Tilghman (g, QA) exhibited:
- inventory & LoD of Joseph Newman.
- inventory of John Hart.
- inventory of Thomas Spears.
- inventory & LoD of Thomas Norman.
- inventory of John Baynard.
- inventory of John Eareckson.
- inventory of John Chaires.
- additional inventory of Peter
Countiss.
- inventory of John Carter.
- inventory & LoD of Nicholas Yoe.
- inventory & LoD of William Osborn.
- inventory of Matthew Williams.
- inventory of James Silvester.
- inventory of Thomas Granger.

32:151 24 February. Mr. Benton Harris (WO) to
examine accounts of:
- Samuel Parker administrator of Leah
Parker (WO).
- George Parker executor of Tabitha
Parker (WO).
- Rebeckah & William Ennis executors
of William Ennis (WO).
- Sarah Johnson administratrix of
Leonard Johnson (WO).

Mr. William Tilghman (QA) to examine
accounts of:

- Robert Hawkins & his wife Hanah executrix of John Earle (QA).
- Rebecca Williams administratrix of John White (QA).
- Jonathan Evans surviving executor of John Evans (QA).
- Anne Thomas administratrix of Trust. Thomas (QA).

Mr. Charles Hynson (KE) to examine accounts of:
- Sarah Blakiston administratrix of Ebenezar Blakiston (KE).
- Samuel Wallis administrator of John Tennant (KE).
- Sarah Scott administratrix of Charles Scott (KE).
- John Green administrator of Bowles Green (KE). Additional accounts.

Mr. Peter Dent (PG) to examine accounts of:
- George Beckwith & Basil Beckwith administrators of Anne Miller (PG).
- Mary Cramphin executrix of Henry Cramphin (PG).

27 February. Mr. Thomas Bullen (TA) to examine accounts of:
- Edward Neall & Jonathan Neall administrators of Samuel Neall, during the minority of Martha Neall (daughter) administrator of Francis Neall (TA).

Appointment of Mr. James Calder as Deputy Commissary (KE) in the room of Mr. Charles Hynson (KE).

10 February. Exhibited:
- receipt of Elisabeth Battee of Solomon Wooden executor of her father John Wooden (AA), Negro Bess (woman). Date: 21 January 1747/8. Witness: J. Battee.

32:152 3 March. Nehemiah King (SO) exhibited:
- will of Francis White, constituting Mary White & Thomas White executors. Also, widow's election. Said executors were granted administration. Sureties: Edward

Roberts, Samuel Jones. Date: 26 September 1747.
- will of Robert Magraw.
- will of James Train, constituting William Smith & Day Scott executors. Said executors were granted administration. Sureties: Col. George Dashiell, John White (merchant). Date: 25 January 1747.
- will of Thomas Dixon, constituting Sarah Dixon & Isaac Dixon executors. Said executors were granted administration. Sureties: Outerbridge Horsey, William Smith. Date: 24 February 1747.
- bond of Mary Surman administratrix of John Surman. Sureties: Joseph Cotman, Sr., Robert Chambers. Date: 9 January 1747.
- inventory of George Phebus.
- inventory of Edward Hern.
- additional inventory of Christopher Piper.
- inventory of John Rickords.
- inventory of Charles Roach.
- inventory & LoD of George Tull.
- inventory of John Hand.
- inventory of Francis White.
- accounts of James Ottley & his wife Sarah executrix of Robert Bowyer.
- accounts of Rachell Piper (alias Rachell Caldwell) & Christopher Piper executors of Christopher Piper.
- accounts of Margrett Harris administratrix of Philip Harris.

5 March. Exhibited from PG:
- inventory of Isaac Wells. Also, accounts of George Matthews executor.

23 January. [See f. 149.] John Hammond Dorsey (BA) & his wife Frances vs. Walter Tolley (BA) executor of James Tolley (BA). Sheriff (BA) to summon defendant to render answer to libel.

Court Session: 8 March 1747

32:153 Docket:
- Raymond Stapleford, Charles

Court Session: 8 March 1747

Stapleford, & Thomas Stapleford
executors of Elisabeth Taylor (DO)
vs. Dorothy Gollothon (DO) &
Dorothy Loockerman (DO). Sheriff
(DO) to render attachment to
defendants to show cause why they
conceal estate of dec'd.

- Patrick Grey (BA) vs. Patrick Doran
(AA) administrator of John Handling
(AA). Sheriff (AA) to render
attachment to defendant to render
accounts. Richard Burdus (g,
coroner, AA) to render attachment to
sheriff (AA) for his contempt.
- E.D. for John Tootel & his wife
Rosannah (DO) vs. Thomas Woolford &
John Woolford executors of Roger
Woolford. Libel.
- Executors of Samuel Young (CV) vs.
Richard Young (AA) surviving
executor of Col. Samuel Young (AA).
Sheriff (AA) to render attachment to
defendant to render final accounts.
Consideration given for said
Richard's infirmities.

32:154
- E.D. for Ebenezar Reyner & his wife
Sarah (KE) vs. D.D. for Rebecca
Perkins & David Perkins. Libel,
answer.
- John Bull acting executor of Sarah
Ruff vs. Richard Ruff (BA) & Daniel
Ruff (BA) executors of Richard Ruff
(BA). Sheriff (BA) to summon
defendants to render inventory.
Inventory exhibited. Discontinued.
- D.D. for William Grantham & his wife
Sarah (DO) vs. William Kennerly
only surviving executor of Joshua
Kennerly. Libel.
- S.B. for John Hammond Dorsey & his
wife Frances (BA) vs. Daniel
Dulany, Jr., Esq. for Walter Tolley
executor of James Tolley. Libel.
Roger Boyce (sheriff, BA) to summon
defendant.

Court Session: 1747

10 March. Exhibited from PG:
- additional inventory of Nathan
Selby. Also, 2nd additional
accounts of Charles Drury

administrator.

11 March. Thomas White (g, BA)
exhibited:
- will of Sarah Ruff, constituting
  John Bull executor. Said executor
  was granted administration.
  Sureties: George Bradford, James
  Amos. Date: 19 November 1747.
- will of Comfort Dorsey constituting
  John Hammond Dorsey executor. Said
  executor was granted administration.
  Sureties: Talbot Risteau, James
  Richard. Date: 23 January 1747.
- will of Leonard Wheeler,
  constituting Thomas Wheeler & Ann
  Wheeler executors. Also, widow's
  election. Said executors were
  granted administration. Sureties:
  Thomas Bond, Nicholas Ruxton Gay.
  Date: 30 January 1747.
- will of William Denton.
- bond of William Dobbins
  administrator of Neil Lemmon.
  Sureties: Robert Dobbins, Robert
  Stevenson. Date: 7 March 1747.
- bond of Lawrence Watson
  administrator of Edward Nowland.
  Sureties: John Ensor, Jr., Moses
  Rutter. Date: 7 January 1747.
- bond of Cornelius Steward
  administrator of James Low.
  Sureties: John Murra (p), Arthur
  Brownly (p). Date 5 March 1747.
- bond of Nathan Rigbie administrator
  of Robert Woodford. Surety:
  Nicholas Ruxton Gay. Date 3
  February 1747.
- inventory & LoD of Isaac
  Butterworth.
- inventory & LoD of George Hitchcock.
- inventory & LoD of Richard Ruff.
- inventory & LoD of Thomas Rutter.
- inventory of John Huggins.
- inventory of Nicholas Coleman.
- additional accounts of Winstone
  Smith & his wife Susanna executrix
  of George Stokes.
- additional accounts of Joshua
  Hardisty & his wife Kezia executrix
  of John Taylor.

32:155

12 March. William Tilghman (g, QA)
exhibited:

- will of John Swift, constituting
  Gideon Swift executor. Said
  executor was granted administration.
  Sureties: James Hobbs, Humphrey
  Wells, Jr. Date: 24 December 1747.
- will of William Burroughs.
- will of Mary Ann Hopper.
- will of William Jarman, constituting
  Penelope Jarman executrix. Said
  executrix was granted
  administration. Sureties: Richard
  Costin (p), John Folkner (p). Date:
  18 February 1747.
- bond of James Emory surviving
  executor of Arthur Emory. Sureties:
  John Emory, Jr. (p), Thomas Emory
  (p). Date: 11 December 1747.
- bond of William Starkey
  administrator of Edward Starkey.
  Sureties: William Andrew (p),
  Benjamin Boone (p). Date 11
  December 1747. Also, renunciation
  of Susannah Starkey (widow). Date:
  10 December 1747. Witness: Benjamin
  Boon.
- bond of Tabitha Nevitt
  administratrix of William Nevitt.
  Sureties: Thomas Dockery (p),
  Hancock Jones (p). Date: 3 March
  1747.
- bond of Daniel Newman & William
  Newman administrators dbn of Joseph
  Newman, during the minority of
  Boxley Newman. Sureties: Richard
  Gould (p), Thomas Jackson (p).
  Date: 21 January 1747.
- bond of Katherine Sharp
  administratrix of James Sharp.
  Sureties: George Bell (p, QA),
  William Oxenham (p, TA). Date: 14
  January 1747.
- bond of Nathan Samuel Turbutt Wright
  & Thomas Wright executors of Thomas
  Hynson Wright. Sureties: Charles
  Downs, William Coursey, Nathan
  Wright, Matthew Dockery. Date: 31
  December 1747.
- bond of Thomas Roe, Jr.
  administrator dbn of Charles Story.
  Sureties: William Wheatly, George

Ford.   Date: 31 December 1747.

- bond of Solomon Seney & his wife Ann
  acting executrix of John Nevil.
  Sureties: John Collins (p), Benjamin
  Whittington (p).   Date: 10 February
  1747.

32:156
- inventory & LoD of Lawrence Hall.
- inventory of Andrew Price, Jr.
- inventory of Edward Tippens.
- inventory of John Gibbs.
- inventory of Thomas Keld.
- inventory of Edward Starkey.
- accounts of Valentine Honey & his
  wife Sarah administratrix of George
  Sparks.
- accounts of Margaret Richardson
  administratrix of John Thompson.
- accounts of Susanna Jennings
  administratrix of Bartholomew
  Jennings.
- accounts of John Covington & Henry
  Covington executors of Henry
  Covington.
- accounts of John Jackson
  administrator of Jonathan Scymeter.

14 March.   Thomas Bullen (g, TA)
exhibited:
- will of Benjamin Seney.
- will of Thomas Bounton, constituting
  Rebeckah Bounton executrix.   Also,
  widow's election.   Said executrix
  was granted administration.
  Sureties: William Gerke (p), Thomas
  Neighbours (p).   Date: 1 January
  1747.
- will of John Angley, constituting
  Thomas Helsby executor.   Said
  executor was granted administration.
  Sureties: Adam Brown (p), Hezekiah
  Macotter (p).   Date: 15 January
  1747.
- will of Andrew Orem.
- will of Isable Taylor.
- will of William Mackey, constituting
  Rachel Mackey executrix.   Also,
  widow's election.   Said executrix
  was granted administration.
  Sureties: James Chaplin (p), Francis
  Chaplin (p).   Date: 29 February
  1747.
- will of Richard Hall.   Also,

renunciation of 1 executor. Also,
bond of Thomas Baynard acting
executor. Sureties: John Nicholson
(p), Michael Meloney (p). Date: 8
March 1747.

- will of Thomas Hutchins,
constituting Priscilla Hutchins
executrix. Said executrix was
granted administration. Sureties:
Benjamin Silvester (p), Thomas
Matthews (p). Date: 8 March 1747.
- bond of Peter Commerford
administrator of William Parratt.
Sureties: Robert Harwood (g),
William Finney (g). Date: 23
February 1747.
- bond of Solomon Yewell (QA) & his
wife Mary administratrix of John
Seaders. Sureties: David
Fitzpatrick, George Noble. Date: 4
March 1747.
- bond of Alice Williamson
administratrix of John Williamson.
Sureties: Francis Pickering (p,
Wye), Nathaniel Conner (p). Date: 8
March 1747.
- accounts of William Oxenham & his
wife Mary administratrix of Daniel
Ward.
- deposition of Mary Hicks, age 22,
wife of Giles Hicks (p, TA) that she
often heard her mother Sarah
Broadaway (TA, dec'd) say that she
(said Sarah) was at the house of
Sarah Greenwood widow of Bartholomew
Greenwood (TA). Date: 7 March 1747.

32:157 15 March. Thomas Aisquith (g, SM)
exhibited:
- will of Henry Bacon, constituting
Ann Bacon executrix. Said executrix
was granted administration.
Sureties: James Pike, Cornelius
Manning. Date: 20 February 1747.
- bond of Sarah Mackey administratrix
of Stephen Mackey. Sureties: Robert
Hager, Astin Sanford Smoot. Date:
14 January 1747.
- bond of Mary Dugliss administratrix
of Thomas Dugliss. Sureties: Robert
Purtle, Henry Armstrong. Date: 3
February 1747.

- inventory of Thomas Francis Hopewell.
- inventory & LoD of Thomas Blackman.
- inventory & LoD of John Binks.
- inventory of Mary Dossey.

21 March. Richard Blackstone administrator of Thomas Blackstone (London) vs. Elisabeth Stallings (CV). Sheriff (CV) to summon defendant to show cause why she conceals estate of dec'd.

Court Session: 1748

26 March. Gabriel Parker (g, CV) exhibited:
- will of Jane Pattison, constituting John Gray executor. Said executor was granted administration. Sureties: John Bond, William Sharples. Date: 2 February 1747/8.
- will of John King, constituting Sarah King executrix. Said executrix was granted administration. Sureties: Richard Stallings, William Hickman. Date: 26 February 1747/8.
- bond of Sarah Deavour administratrix of William Deavour. Sureties: William Williams, John Freeman. Date: 23 February 1747/8.
- inventory of Marg. Davis.
- inventory of John Barton.
- inventory of Thomas Hunt.
- inventory of William Deavour.

Exhibited from PG:
- will of Joseph Erwin. Also, bond of William Erwin acting executor. Sureties: John Jones (farmer), Hugh Gilliland (farmer). Date: 26 March 1748. Also, renunciation of James Sharp, recommending Robert Erwin (now coming to age). Date: 19 March 1748. Witnesses: James Davies, Richard Chapman.

32:158 28 March. Walter Hanson (g, CH) exhibited:
- will of Stephen Mankin, constituting Matthew Breeding executor. Said executor was granted administration.

Page 116

Court Session: 1748

Sureties: Andrew Munroe (p), James Gray (p).

- will of John Courts, constituting William Courts, John Martin (Westmoreland Co. VA), & Charles Jones executors. Said executors were granted administration. Sureties: Thomas Hungerford (g), Edward Ford (g), Charles Bruce (g), James Plant (g). Date: 29 January 1747.
- bond of Charles Jones administrator of Ishua Wilson. Sureties: Joseph Gwinn, Samuel Middleton. Date: 22 February 1747.
- inventory of Benjamin Douglass, Jr.
- accounts of Jemima Sea administratrix of Robert Sea.
- additional accounts of James Middleton & Ignatius Gardner executors of Vincent Askin.
- 2nd additional accounts of Anne Beavan acting administratrix of Thomas Jenkins.

30 March. Exhibited from SO:
- accounts of James Lucas (WO) executor of Ann Walker.

31 March. Mr. Thomas White (BA) to examine accounts of:
- Henry Green & his wife Elisabeth acting executrix of David Thomas (BA).
- Richard Ruff & Daniel Ruff executors of Richard Ruff (BA).

4 April. Nehemiah King (g, SO) exhibited:
- will of Samuel Dorman.
- will of William Cox, constituting Mary Cox executrix. Said executrix was granted administration. Sureties: John Milbourn, Charles Dickeson. Date: 17 March 1747/8.
- inventory & LoD of John Caldwell.
- inventory of John Surman.

Thomas Bullen (g, TA) exhibited:
- bond of Sarah Carroll administratrix of Denton Carroll. Sureties: Joseph Hopkins (p), Robert Spencer (p).

Court Session: 1748

Date: 30 March 1748.
- inventory of Henry Colston.
- inventory of William Mackey.
- deposition of Richard Rowlingson (schoolmaster), age 29, that he went to the house of William Mackey (St. Peter's Parish) to write his will. Mentions (son of dec'd): Hezekiah, Philip, Robert.

32:159 Date: 16 March 1747.

Exhibited from QA:
- accounts of William Starkey administrator of Edward Starkey.

5 April. Mr. Nehemiah King (SO) to examine accounts of:
- Elisabeth Tull executrix of George Tull (SO).
- George Dashiels & George McClester for Margaret Blewer executrix of James Blewer (SO).
- Debborah Hern executrix of Edward Hern (SO).
- William Draper & his wife Alce executrix of Thomas Winder (SO).
- Henry Lowes administrator of Obid Wollston (SO).
- Elgett Hitch & his wife Elisabeth executrix of Ebenezar Handy (SO).
- Mary Price executrix of Robert Price (SO).
- Rose Costin administratrix of Isaac Costin (SO). Additional accounts.
- Thomas Browne administrator of David Browne (SO).

9 April. Exhibited from AA:
- additional inventory of Matthew Elliott.

Mr. Thomas Aisquith (SM) to examine accounts of:
- Joseph Jones executor of Mary Jones (SM).
- John Dossey executor of John Binks (SM).
- Elinor Gardiner administratrix of Clement Gardiner (SM).

Mr. Walter Hanson (CH) to examine accounts of:

- Susanna Waters administratrix of William Waters (CH).
- Robert Whythill surviving administrator of John Theobalds (CH).
- Aaron Nalley & his wife Elisabeth administratrix of Henry Brawner (CH).
- Sarah Hawkins administratrix of Thomas Hawkins (CH). Additional accounts.
- Mary Hamersly administratrix of Francis Hamersly (CH).

Mr. Thomas Bullen (TA) to examine accounts of:
- Thomas Powell & his wife Mary executrix of Richard Dudley executor of Samuel Dudley (TA).
- Robert Goldsborough administrator of James Clayland (TA).
- William Roberts & his wife Sarah executrix of Nathaniel Santee (TA).
- Tamson Eubanks executrix of Richard Eubanks (TA).

32:160 11 April. Benton Harris (g, WO) exhibited:
- will of Henry Smock.
- transcript of will of William Fassitt from PA.
- will of James Mumphord.
- will of William Whale, constituting Mary Whale executrix. Said executrix was granted administration. Sureties: Lambert Fassitt, William Franklin. Date: 22 February 1747.
- will of James Martin, constituting Mary Martin executrix. Said executrix was granted administration. Sureties: John Martin, Henry Ayres. Date: 12 February 1747.
- bond of Mary Coffin administratrix of Thomas Coffin, Sr. Sureties: Philip Parker, Thomas Wildgoose. Date: 30 March 1748.
- bond of Elisabeth Bredell administratrix of James Stephen Bredell. Sureties: Joseph Gray, Samuel Powell. Date: 3 November

1747.

- bond of Mary Coffin administratrix of Thomas Coffin. Sureties: William Woodcraft, Thomas Wildgoose. Date: 20 February 1747.
- bond of James Smith administrator of John Langston. Sureties: David Smith, Charles Thompson. Date: 3 February 1747. Also, renunciation of Mary Langston, recommending her son James Smith. Date: 6 October 1747.
- bond of Rouse Fassitt administrator of James Ingoe. Sureties: Bartholomew Banan, John Greer. Date: 2 February 1747. Also, renunciation of Sarah Ingoe (widow), recommending Rous Fassitt (greatest creditor). Date: 18 January 1747/8. Witnesses: Bartholomew Bainum, John Greer.
- inventory of Thomas Purkins.
- inventory of Parker Selby.
- inventory of George Truitt.
- additional inventory of Hutten Hill.
- inventory & LoD of Jacob Gray. Also, renunciation of Isbell Grey (widow), recommending her son Andrew Gray. Date: 16 September 1747. Witness: Jacob Gray.
- accounts of John Teague administrator of John Watson.
- accounts of Elisabeth Hill administratrix of Hutten Hill.

32:161 Mr. Benton Harris (WO) to examine accounts of:
- John Campbell administrator of William Simpson (WO).
- Rackliff Pointer administrator of Turvill Pointer (WO).

12 April. Mr. James Calder (KE) to examine accounts of:
- Joseph Wickes & James Dunn administrators of Robert Dunn (KE).

15 April. Mr. William Tilghman (QA) to examine accounts of:
- Jane McClean administratrix of Daniel McClean (QA).
- Jane Thomas & Benjamin Thomas

executors of Trustram Thomas
(Tully's Neck, QA).
* Daniel Ford & his wife Sarah
administrators of James Maud (QA).
* Thomas Davis & Tabitha Davis
administrators of Thomas Parsons
(QA).

John Thompson (g, CE) exhibited:
* will of William Knight.

6 May. Peter Dent (g, PG) exhibited:
* will of Rebecca Riley, constituting
Hugh & Pharo Riley executors. Said
executors were granted
administration. Sureties: Nathaniel
Beal (g), William Feild (g). Date:
8 April 1748.
* will of Peter Brightwell.
* bond of James Wardrop & Hancock Lee
administrators of Elisabeth Lee.
Sureties: John Hepburn (g), John
Cooke (g). Date: 21 April 1748.
* inventory of Joseph Hatton.

Court Session: 10 May 1748

32:162 Docket:
* Raymond Stapleford, Charles
Stapleford, & Thomas Stapleford
executors of Elisabeth Taylor (DO)
vs. Dorothy Gollothon (DO) &
Dorothy Loockerman (DO). Enn.
Hooper (sheriff, DO) to render
attachment to defendants to show
cause why they conceal estate of
dec'd.
  - Dorothy Gollothon deposed on 12
    May 1748.
  - Dorothy Loockerman deposed on 12
    May 1748.
Discontinued.
32:163 * Patrick Grey (BA) vs. Patrick Doran
(AA) administrator of John Handling
(AA). Sheriff (AA) to render
attachment to defendant to render
accounts.
* Richard Burdus (g, coroner, AA) to
render attachment to William Thorton
(sheriff, AA) for his contempt.
Philip Jones (other coroner, AA) to
render attachment to said sheriff.

Court Session: 10 May 1748

- Edward Dorsey, Esq. procurator for John Tootel & his wife Rosannah (DO) vs. Thomas Woolford & John Woolford executors of Roger Woolford. Sheriff (DO) to summon said Thomas. Sheriff (SO) to summon said John.
- Executors of Samuel Young (CV) vs. Richard Young (AA) surviving executor of Col. Samuel Young (AA). Sheriff (AA) to render attachment to defendant to render final accounts.
- E.D. for Ebenezar Reyner & his wife Sarah (KE) vs. D.D. for Rebecca Perkins & David Perkins. Libel, answer.
- **32:164** • Daniel Dulany, Esq. for William Grantham & his wife Sarah (DO) vs. William Kennerly only surviving executor of Joshua Kennerly. Libel.
- J.B. for John Hammond Dorsey & his wife Frances (BA) vs. D.D. for Walter Tolley executor of James Tolley. Libel.
- Richard Blackstone administrator of Thomas Blackstone (London) vs. Elisabeth Stallings (CV). Daniel Rawlings (sheriff, CV) to summon defendant to show cause why she conceals estate of dec'd.
  - Said Stallings deposed. Discontinued.

Court Session: 1748

11 May. William Tilghman (g, QA) exhibited:
- will of Nathaniel Downes, constituting George Bennett executor. Said executor was granted administration. Sureties: Nathaniel Tucker (p), John Nab (p). Date: 31 March 1748.
- will of Richard Key, constituting Mary Key executrix. Said executrix was granted administration. Sureties: John Jackson (surgeon), Matthew Dockery (innholder). Date: 10 March 1747.
- will of Robert Jarman, constituting Mary Ann Jarman executrix. Said executrix was granted administration. Sureties: John Hall

(p), William Meeds (p). Date: 22 March 1747.

- will of James Roberts. Also, bond of Benjamin Roberts acting executor. Sureties: Solomon Seney (p), William Wharton (p). Date 24 March 1747.
- will of Richard Chance.
- will of James Cook.
- will of James Hollyday, Esq.
- will of Margaret Berry.
- will of William Wrench.
- bond of Sarah Emory administratrix of William Emory. Sureties: James Emory (p), John Downs (p). Date: 18 March 1747.
- bond of Mary Moody administratrix of James Moody. Sureties: Stephen Yoe (p), Aaron Yoe (p). Date: 22 March 1747.
- bond of Mary Powell administratrix of Richard Powell. Sureties: Daniel Willcocks (p), Thomas Powell (p). Date: 22 March 1747.

32:165
- bond of Hannah Burroughs (QA) & Thomas Burroughs (KE) executors of William Burroughs. Sureties: John Scotton (p), Thomas Nicholson (p). Date: 21 April 1748.
- inventory of Arthur Emory.
- inventory & LoD of Charles Story.
- inventory of Edward Brown (son of Edward).
- additional inventory of Matthew Williams.
- additional inventory of Patrick Fowler.
- accounts of Thomas Meradith executor of Sarah Owens.

Peter Dent (g, PG) exhibited:
- will of Joseph Lovejoy.
- bond of Winifred Lewis administratrix of John Lewis. Sureties: Edward Lanham (p), Anthony Simmes (p). Date: 2 May 1748.
- bond of Anne Brightwell executrix of Peter Brightwell. Sureties: Joseph Letchworth (p), Thomas Grimes (p). Date: 7 May 1748.
- bond of Anne Beavin administratrix of Henry Beavin. Sureties: Blanford Beavin, Richard Beavin. Date: 7 May

1748.
- bond of Jane Gray administratrix of Robert Gray. Sureties: <torn>ford Beavin (p), William Miles (p). Date: 7 May 1748.
- inventory of Lucy Beal.

Thomas Bul<torn> (TA) exhibited:
- nuncupative will of Mary Younger.
- will of John Nayler.
- will of Samuel Sharp, constituting <torn> Sharp executrix. Said executrix was granted administration. Sureties: William Dickinson, William Troth. Date: 12 April 1748.
- will of James Coben. Also, bond of <torn> Coben executor. Sureties: Samuel Bartlett, Russell Armstrong. Date: 6 May 1748.
- will of Peter Pinkstone.
- inventory of Thomas Bounton.
- inventory of William Parratt.
- inventory of Thomas Clark.

13 May. Mr. Gabriel Parker (CV) to examine accounts of:
- Dorcas Dawkins executrix of William Dawkins, Jr. (CV).
- Thomas Ireland, Jr. administrator of Jesse Bourne (CV).

14 May. Exhibited from PG:
- will of John Henn, constituting John Middagh & William Barrack executors. Said executors were granted administration. Sureties: Peter Barrack, <torn>iel Henn. Date: <torn> April 1748.
- bond of Barbara Reasling & Johannes Middagh executors of Matthias Reasling. Sureties: Jacob Stoner (p), Stephen Ramsheige (p). Date: 13 June 1747.
- bond of Anna Kersner administratrix of John George Kersner. Sureties: Peter Rench (farmer), Jonathan Hagar (blacksmith). Date: 20 April 1748.

32:166
- inventory & LoD of John Beatty.
- inventory & LoD of Andrew Hedges.
- inventory of Matthias Reasling.

Court Session: 1748

16 May. Thomas Aisquith (g, SM)
exhibited:
- will of Francis Ratcliff. Also,
  widow's election.
- will of William Cannaday Forrest.
- will of Sarah Mackey.
- will of Edward Baxter. Also,
  widow's election.
- will of Rev. John Donaldson,
  constituting Elisabeth Donaldson
  executrix. Also, widow's election.
  Said executrix was granted
  administration. Sureties: James
  Mills, Richard Cooke. Date: 6 April
  1748.
- will of Thomas Payn, constituting
  Elisabeth Payn executrix. Also,
  widow's election. Said executrix
  was granted administration.
  Sureties: John Taylor, Joseph
  Fitzjeffery. Date: 19 April 1748.
- will of Richard Daintry,
  constituting Edward Passons
  executor. Said executor was granted
  administration. Sureties: Timothy
  Barnhouse, Francis Hillton. Date:
  28 April 1748.
- will of Bassil Cooper, constituting
  William Looker executor. Said
  executor was granted administration.
  Sureties: Joseph Hopewell, George
  Aisquith. Date: 2 May 1748.
- bond of Asten Sanford Smoot
  administrator dbn of Stephen Mackey.
  Sureties: Robert Hager, Thomas
  Bissco. Date: 21 March 1747/8.
- bond of George Thompson, Jr.
  administrator of Ignatius Knott.
  Sureties: Thomas Thompson, John
  Medley Thompson. Date: 3 May 1748.
- bond of Ann Norriss administratrix
  of John Norriss. Sureties: Mark
  Norriss, Luke Heard. Date: 9 March
  1747.
- bond of Mary Sissell administratrix
  of Matthew Sissell. Sureties:
  George Tearin, Thomas Edwards.
  Date: 20 April 1748.
- bond of Elisabeth Hayden
  administratrix of Francis Hayden.
  Sureties: James Thompson, Thomas
  Thompson. Date: 20 April 1748.

- bond of Thomas Russell administrator of Ezekel Greentree. Sureties: Luke Russell, Alexander Forguson. Date: 30 March 1748.
- bond of John Manning administrator of Robert Thomas. Sureties: Stourt. Edwards, Clement Medley. Date: 5 April 1748.
- inventory of Luke Cissell.
- inventory & LoD of John Pearce.
- inventory & LoD of Linsy Opey.
- inventory of John Norriss.
- additional inventory of Peter Johnson.
- accounts of Joseph Alvey executrix of Margaret Alvey.

18 May. Exhibited from QA:
- additional inventory of Patrick Robertson.

Exhibited from SO:
- accounts of Matthias Gale acting executor of Col. Levin Gale.

Exhibited from PG:
- inventory of James Hamilton.

32:167 Gabriel Parker (g, CV) exhibited:
- will of Francis Hutchins, constituting Littleton Waters executor. Said executor was granted administration. Sureties: Thomas Ireland, Jr., William Ireland. Date: 4 May 1748.
- bond of Ann Day administratrix of Robert Day. Sureties: Samuel Robertson, John Birkhead. Date: 23 April 1748.
- bond of Thomas Reynolds administrator of William Everrest. Surety: William Wyle. Date: 20 April 1748.
- inventory of William Allistree.
- inventory of Jesper Floyd.
- accounts of James Russell administrator of Francis Drake.
- accounts of Hugh McGuire administrator of William Allistree.

19 May. Exhibited from PG:
- inventory of James McCaull.

Court Session: 1748

20 May. Exhibited from BA:
• will of Elisabeth Parish.

Exhibited from CV:
• accounts of Sabritt Sollars & his
  wife Mary administratrix of Thomas
  Tongue.

23 May. Francis Day was granted LoA on
estate of Stephen Higgens, as greatest
creditor. Mentions: Mary Higgens
(widow).

Mr. Thomas Aisquith (SM) to examine
accounts of:
• James Heard executor of John Heard
  (SM).

25 May. John Thompson (g, CE)
exhibited:
• nuncupative will of John Husband.
  Also, bond of Joshua Meakins & his
  wife Elisabeth administrators.
  Sureties: Michell Ruley, William
  Price. Date: 11 March 1747/8.
• will of William Douglas.
• will of John Ward. Also, bond of
  Mary Ward, Peregrine Ward, & Henry
  Ward administrators. Sureties:
  Thomas Davis, John Cooper. Date: 30
  March 1748.
• will of Alphonso Cosden. Also, bond
  of Benjamin Terry administrator.
  Sureties: Thomas Ryland, David
  Ricketts. Date: 4 April 1748.
• will of John Ritchey. Also, bond of
  James Ritchey administrator.
  Sureties: Robert Ritchey, Thomas
  Killgore. Date: 7 April 1748.
32:168 • will of Mary Canady. Also, bond of
  Thomas Cooch administrator.
  Sureties: William Price, James
  Boulding. Date: 10 May 1748.
• will of Richard Boulding. Also,
  bond of William Price administrator.
  Sureties: James Boulding, Martin
  Alexander. Date: 10 May 1748.
• will of John Stump. Also, bond of
  John Stump administrator. Sureties:
  Benjamin Chew, Nathan Baker. Date:
  19 November 1747.
• bond of Joseph Penington

administrator of Allen McClain. Sureties: David Ricketts, John Chambers, Jr. Date: 19 October 1747.

- bond of Adam Dobson administrator of Richard Dobson. Sureties: Zebulon Hollingsworth, Thomas Booth. Date: 8 April 1748.
- bond of John Roberts administrators of Jonathan Hynds. Sureties: John Roberts, Jr., Edward Morgan. Date: 1 April 1748.
- bond of Thomas Ellot administrator of Thomas Jordan. Sureties: Cornelius Brady, John Stump. Date: 11 March 1747/8.
- bond of Peter Bayard administrator of James Hill. Sureties: John Baldwin, James McLachlan. Date: 22 February 1747.
- bond of Elianor Porter administratrix of Robert Porter. Sureties: Richard Sedgwick, Andrew McAdow. Date: 12 May 1748.
- bond of John Cooker administrator of Mark Dunn. Sureties: Peregrine Ward, William Ellis. Date: 30 March 1748.
- bond of John Jackson administrator of Mary Douglass. Sureties: William Ellis, William Pearce. Date: 20 February 1747.
- bond of Elisabeth Barnaby & James Bayard administrators of John Barnaby. Sureties: Joseph Hodgson, William Gent. Date: 13 May 1748.
- bond of John Jackson administrator of Archibald Douglass. Sureties: William Ellis, Arthur Ellis. Date: 29 February 1748.
- bond of Thomas Rickets & John Rickets administrators of John Gray. Sureties: John Jones, David Leech. Date: 8 April 1748.
- inventory & LoD of George Bristow.
- inventory of Margaret Patterson.
- inventory & LoD of William Smith.
- inventory & LoD of Thomas Stark.
- inventory & LoD of John Stump.
- inventory of John Steel.
- accounts of Samuel Walker & William Mackey executor of Hugh Walker.

- accounts of James Porter & Nathaniel Ewing executors of Alexander Ewing.
- accounts of Elisabeth Watson executrix of Abram Watson.
- accounts of Sarah Jackson administratrix of Edward Jackson.
- accounts of Mary Jones administratrix of Peter Jones.
- accounts of Terressa Alman & Dr. Hugh Mathews administrators of Joseph Alman.

32:169 James Calder (g, KE) for Charles Hynson exhibited:
- will of Anne Richardson, constituting William Rasin executor. Said executor was granted administration. Sureties: John Tilden (g), Abraham Rasin (g). Date: 13 February 1747.
- bond of William Murray administrator of James Punney. Sureties: James Smith (g), Beddinfield Hands (g). Date: 30 January 1747. Also, renunciation of Thomas Punney (brother) & John Punney (brother) recommending Dr. William Murray (greatest creditor). Date: 30 July 1747.
- bond of Susannah Douglass executrix of George Douglass. Sureties: Joseph Douglass (g, KE), Archibald Douglass (g, CE). Date: 13 March 1746.
- bond of James Arono administrator of Thomas Wells. Sureties: John Whaley (p), William Whaley (p). Date: 12 December 1747.
- inventory of William Thomas.

James Calder (g, KE) exhibited:
- will of Col. Charles Hynson, constituting Francina Hynson executrix. Said executrix was granted administration. Sureties: Matthias Harris (g), William Hynson (g). Date: 3 May 1748.
- will of William Powell.
- will of Hannah Hoker, constituting Henry Hoker executor. Said executor was granted administration. Sureties: William Trew (p), Joseph

Garnett (sadler). Date: 9 May 1748.
- bond of Arthur Miller administrator of Isaac Jameson. Sureties: Joseph Garnett (sadler), John McCraken (tailor). Date: 2 May 1748.
- bond of John Gresham & Ralph Page administrators of Elisabeth Thorp. Sureties: Benjamin Rickard, Phillip Taylor. Date: 12 April 1748.
- bond of Phillip Taylor administrator of Thomas Farmer. Sureties: Benjamin Meeks (p), John Cooper (p). Date: 9 April 1748.
- bond of James Tibbitt administrator of Richard Tibbitt. Sureties: Thomas Maslin (p), Thomas Unick (p). Also, renunciation of Samuel Tibbitt (brother), recommending his brother James Tibbitt. Date: 2 April 1748.
- bond of Henry Truelock administrator of Henry Truelock. Sureties: William Jones (p), William Reason (p). Date: 2 May 1748.
- inventory of Maj. John Brown.

32:170 13 May. Richard Blackstone administrator of Thomas Blackstone (CV) vs. Philip Young (mariner, CV). Daniel Rawlings (sheriff, CV) to summon defendant to show cause why he conceals estate of dec'd. No such person. Discontinued. N.B. There is a Philemon Young.

25 May. Nicholas Clouds administrator of Sarah Price (QA) vs. Benjamin Kirby (QA). Sheriff (QA) to summon defendant to show cause why he conceals estate of dec'd.

Ennalls Hooper (g, DO) exhibited:
- will of Col. Adam Muir.

Mr. James Calder (KE) to examine accounts of:
- Samuel Wallace administrator of John Tennant (KE).
- John Garrett & his wife Sarah administratrix of Ebenezar Blackiston (KE).
- Thomas Barkley & his wife Isabella executrix of Richard Wethered (KE).

Exhibited from BA:
* inventory of William Barney. Also,
  accounts of Mary Barney executrix.

27 May. Exhibited from DO:
* bond of Thomas Muir executor of Adam
  Muir. Sureties: Robert Jenkins
  Henry, Esq. (SO), John Henry (WO).
  Date: 27 May 1748. Appraisers:
  Capt. Charles Dickinson (DO), Mr.
  William Potts (DO), Capt. John
  Tribe (WO), Mr. Robert Allan (WO).

28 May. Exhibited from AA:
* accounts of Philip Thomas, Esq.
  administrator of Samuel Chew, Jr.

32:171 Thomas Bullen (g, TA) exhibited:
* will of John Lowe, constituting Mary
  Lowe & James Lowe executors. Also,
  widow's election. Said executors
  were granted administration.
  Sureties: William Webb Haddaway,
  Robert Sands. Date: 17 May 1748.
* inventory of Isaac Dobson, Jr.
* inventory & LoD of John Chambers.
* additional accounts of Jacob
  Bromwell administrator of Jacob
  Cole.

Exhibited from BA:
* additional inventory of Capt. John
  Cockey. Also, additional accounts
  of William Cockey & Joshua Owings
  executors.

31 May. Walter Hanson (g, CH)
exhibited:
* will of James Gow.
* bond of John Muschett administrator
  of Thomas Lamphier. Sureties: John
  Cunninghame (g), Collin Mitchell
  (g). Date: 7 March 1747.
* bond of Robert Yates administrator
  of Ann Wyeth. Sureties: Thomas
  Brooke (g), Henry Thompson (g).
  Date: 10 March 1747.
* bond of Margret Ridge administratrix
  of Henry Ridge. Sureties: Thomas
  Brooke, Richard Speake. Date: 18
  May 1748.
* bond of Jane Freeman administratrix

of James Freeman. Sureties:
Ledstone Smallwood, John Hamill.
Date: 31 March 1748.

- inventory of Joshua Willson.
- inventory of Stephen Mankin.
- inventory of John Parnham.
- accounts of Francis Elgine administrator of John Wise.
- accounts of Aaron Nalley & his wife Elisabeth administratrix of Henry Brawner.
- accounts of Perry Pattison & his wife Mary administratrix of Benjamin Banister.
- accounts of Perry Pattison & his wife Mary administratrix of Jacob Bayley.
- accounts of Timothy McCan administrator of John Weathers.

1 June. Exhibited from PG:
- will of John James, constituting Margaret James executrix. Said executrix was granted administration. Sureties: Joseph Ogle (p), John Justice (p). Date: 1 June 1748.

32:172   Mr. Peter Dent (PG) to examine accounts of:

- Blanford Beavin acting executor of Dr. John Kirkwood (PG).
- George Beckwith & Basill Beckwith administrators of Anne Miller (PG).
- Mary Cramphin executrix of Henry Cramphin (PG).
- Humphry Batt & his wife Elisabeth executrix of Thomas Jenings (PG). Additional accounts.
- Cathrine Williams executrix of Joseph Williams (PG).
- Elisabeth Massey administratrix of Henry Massey (PG).
- John Busey executor of Sarah Busey (PG).

2 June. Mr. Walter Hanson (CH) to examine accounts of:
- Mary Willson executrix of Alexander Willson (CH).

Court Session: 1748

Mr. Thomas Aisquith (SM) to examine accounts of:
- Susanna Lorton administratrix of John Lorton (SM).
- Joseph Hopewell administrator of Thomas Francis Hopewell (SM).
- Grace Harbert executrix of Matthew Harbert (SM).
- Pricilla Chesher administratrix of John Chesher (SM).
- John Horn administrator of John Horn (SM).

Exhibited from PG:
- inventory of Jane Edmonston.

Mr. Gabriel Parker (CV) to examine accounts of:
- Susannah Blake executrix of Richard Blake (CV).

Exhibited from CV:
- additional accounts of Richard Johns (CV) & Samuel Johns (KE, DE) executors of Isaac Johns.

Richard Blackstone administrator of Thomas Blackstone (London) vs. Philemon Young (mariner, CV). Sheriff (CV) to summon defendant to show cause why he conceals estate of dec'd. Said Young deposed. Discontinued.

32:173 Exhibited from SO:
- petition of John Clifton, Abraham Dickeson who married Rachel Clifton (daughter of Michael Clifton (SO, dec'd)), & Edward Dickeson who married Sarah Clifton (daughter of Michael Clifton (SO, dec'd)). Said Michael died on 1 May 1718, leaving 4 children: John, Rachel, Sarah, George. George is since dec'd. Their mother Sarah is still alive & has since married James Otley (Accomac Co. VA). Said Sarah (mother) had LoA & exhibited an inventory, but no accounts. Distribution granted to: widow (1/3rd); residue to children now living & representatives as such dec'd.

Page 133

Exhibited from TA:
- accounts of Edward Neall & Jonathan Neall administrators of Samuel Neall administrator of Francis Neall, during minority of Martha Neall (daughter).

9 June. Exhibited from PG:
- will of John Charlton, constituting Thomas Charlton & Henry Charlton executors. Also, widow's election. Said executors were granted administration. Sureties: Arthur Charlton (p), George Bond (p). Date: 8 April 1748.
- will of Edward Charlton, constituting Thomas Charlton & Henry Charlton executors. Said executors were granted administration. Sureties: Arthur Charlton (p), George Bond (p). Date: 8 April 1748.
- will of Andrew Hedges. Also, bond of Joseph Hedges acting executor. Sureties: Stephen Julian (farmer), Peter Stull (farmer). Date: 2 May 1748.
- inventory of John <torn>.

32:174 Mr. Thomas Bullen (TA) to examine accounts of:
- David Hall & his wife Sarah executrix of Thomas Clark (TA).
- William Sharp executor of Solomon Birckhead (TA). Additional accounts.
- David Hall & his wife Sarah administratrix of John Guy Williams (TA). 3rd additional accounts.

10 June. Mr. Thomas White (BA) to examine accounts of:
- Sarah Groves administratrix of William Groves (BA).

Mr. William Tilghman (QA) to examine accounts of:
- Susanna Jumpe acting executrix of William Jumpe (QA).
- Alice Alliband administratrix of Thomas Alliband (QA).

Court Session: 1748

Mr. Nehemiah King (SO) to examine accounts of:
- Rachell Roach administratrix of Charles Roach (SO).

Exhibited from CV:
- additional accounts of Edward Loyd (TA), John Rousby (CV), & Abraham Barnes (SM) executors of John Rousby, Esq.

11 June. Mr. Richard Burdus (Annapolis) vs. estate of Stephen Higgins (AA). Caveat against LoA being granted to Francis Day.

13 June. Mr. Benton Harris (WO) to examine accounts of:
- John Campbell administrator of William Simpson (WO).
- William Toadvine administrator of John Blewett (WO).
- George Johnson & his wife Ann administratrix of William Jarman (WO).
- Sarah Johnson administratrix of Leonard Johnson (WO).
- David Smith one of sureties for Martha Harvey administratrix of John Harvey (WO). Additional accounts.
- Lucretia Claywell & Peter Claywell executors of Peter Claywell (WO). Additional accounts.
- William Lathinghouse & his wife Mary administratrix of William Smith (WO). Additional accounts.
- William Selby & his wife Martha executrix of John Purnell (WO). 2nd additional accounts.

14 June. Exhibited from AA:
- additional accounts of Rebecca Winston (late Rebecca Powell) executrix of John Powell.

32:175 15 June. Exhibited from BA:
- additional inventory & LoD of Edward Day. Also, accounts of John Day executor.

16 June. Exhibited from QA:
- accounts of Joseph Sudler

Page 135

administrator of Thomas Norman.
* accounts of Matthew Griffith administrator dbn of Andrew Price, during minority of Thomas Price (son of said Andrew).

Exhibited from AA:
* will of Jane Galloway.
* will of Thomas Bordley.

Mr. Thomas Bullen (TA) to examine additional accounts of:
* Peter Calk & his wife Ann administratrix of John Davis (TA).

Capt. John West vs. Joseph Lane (AA) executor of Samuel Maccubbin, Jr. (BA). Sheriff (AA) to summon defendant to render final accounts.

28 June. Exhibited from QA:
* accounts of Patrick Robertson & Alexander Robertson executors of Patrick Robertson.

Exhibited from AA:
* LoD on estate of Thomas Rowles. Also, accounts of Sarah Rowles executrix.

29 June. Exhibited from QA:
* additional inventory & LoD of John Earle.

30 June. Exhibited from QA:
* accounts of Robert Hawkins & his wife Hannah executrix of John Earle.

Mr. James Calder (KE) to examine accounts of:
* Samuel Murphy & his wife Mary executrix of Nathaniel MacClanahan (KE).

1 July. Sheriff (CH) to summon James Mankin (CH) to show cause why LoA on estate of Charles Sandford (CH) should not be granted to Margret Morton (CH) as greatest creditor.

32:176 2 July. Mr. Thomas White (BA) to examine accounts of:

Court Session: 1748

- Jemima Jackson administratrix of Jacob Jackson (BA).
- Patience Stinchcomb administratrix of Nathaniel Stinchcomb (BA).

4 July. Exhibited from BA:
- inventory & LoD of Solomon Sheild.

Exhibited from TA:
- additional inventory & LoD of Francis Neall, Sr.

Exhibited from SO:
- inventory & LoD of Richard Brereton.

William Rogers (g, AA) exhibited:
- will of John Galloway.
- will of John Wooding, constituting Solomon Wooding executor. Said executor was granted administration. Sureties: Robert Davis (p), John Glover (p). Date: 12 December 1747.
- will of John Watts. Also, renunciation of executors. Also, bond of Joseph Cowman administrator. Surety: James Dick (merchant, AA). Date: 13 January 1747.
- will of Joshua Dorsey, constituting Anne Dorsey, Henry Dorsey, & Philemon Dorsey executors. Also, widow's election. Said executors were granted administration. Sureties: Henry Howard (p), Nicholas Dorsey (p), Joshua Dorsey, Jr. (p). Date: 6 February 1747.
- will of Mary Burley.
- will of Francis Mapp. Also, bond of Samuel Smith, Jr. administrator. Sureties: Samuel Lockwood (p), James Welsh (p). Date: 26 March 1748. Also, renunciation of Ezekiel Gilliss (executor). Date: 8 March 1747/8.
- will of Thomas Thackerill.
- will of John Cheshire, constituting Mary Cheshire & Stephen West, Sr. executors. Said executors were granted administration. Sureties: Nicholas Norman, William Chapman, Jr. Date: 11 March 1747.
- will of Hannah Linstead.
- will of Samuel Smith. Also, bond of

Elisabeth Smith acting executrix. Sureties: Samuel Smith (g, AA), John Smith (g, CE). Date: 3 June 1748. Also, renunciation of Samuel Smith (son, executor), recommending his mother Elisabeth Smith (executrix). Date: 2 June 1748. Witness: Richard Burdus.

- will of Mary Tepedo.
- bond of Elinor Budd administratrix of Henry Budd. Surety: Joseph Wright. Date: 4 April 1748.
- bond of Thomas Lusby administrator of Thomas Lusby. Sureties: Samuel Howard, Thomas Williamson. Date: 9 April 1748.
- bond of John Howard (son of Benjamin) administrator of Catherine Howard. Sureties: Caleb Dorsey (g), Thomas Hughes (g). Date: 10 March 1747.
- bond of Oneal Robertson administrator of Richard Linstead. Sureties: Mark Johnson, Edward Mattox. Date: 10 May 1758.
- bond of George Gordon (PG) administrator of John Ramsay. Surety: Robert Swann (merchant). Date: 21 January 1747.
- bond of Ruth Todd administratrix of John Todd. Sureties: John Dorsey, Jr. (p), Ely Dorsey (p). Date: 10 February 1747.
- inventory of John Purdum.
- inventory of Philip Norwood.
- inventory of Mordecai Hammond.
- inventory of John Ramsay.
- inventory of Dr. Samuel Stringer.
- inventory of John Dorsey, Sr.
- inventory of John Watts.

5 July. Appointment of Mr. William Young as Deputy Commissary (BA).

8 July. Exhibited from BA:
- bond of Charles Carroll (physician, Annapolis) administrator of Dennis Dunn. Sureties: Charles Carroll, Jr. (g, Annapolis), Thomas Williamson (innholder, Annapolis). Date: 8 July 1748.

Court Session: 1748

11 July. Benton Harris (g, WO)
exhibited:
- will of Peter Dolby, constituting
  John Dolby executor. Said executor
  was granted administration.
  Sureties: Daniel Boyce, Thomas
  Walter. Date: 8 April 1748.

32:178
- will of John Massey.
- bond of James Linsey & his wife
  Margrett administrators of John
  Read. Sureties: Joshua Mitchell,
  John Atkinson. Date: 10 June 1748.
- inventory of Abraham Outten.
- inventory & LoD of James Stephen
  Bredell.
- inventory of Thomas Coffin, Jr.
- accounts of Rebecka Ennis & William
  Ennis executors of William Ennis.
- accounts of Rackleff Pointer
  administrator of Turvil Pointer.
- accounts of George Parker executor
  of Tabitha Parker.
- accounts of Samuel Parker
  administrator of Leah Parker.
- accounts of John Campbell
  administrator of William Simpson.

Court Session: 12 July 1748

Docket:
- Patrick Grey (BA) vs. Patrick Doran
  (AA) administrator of John Handling
  (AA). Sheriff (AA) to render
  attachment to defendant to render
  accounts. Richard Burdus (g,
  coroner, AA) to render attachment to
  sheriff (AA) for his contempt.

32:179
  Sheriff (AA) appeared & agreed to
  purge the contempt. Discontinued.
- E.D. for John Tootell & his wife
  Rosannah (DO) vs. Stephen Bordley,
  Esq. for Thomas Woolford & John
  Woolford executors of Roger
  Woolford. Libel. Enn. Hooper
  (sheriff, DO) to summon said Thomas.
  Sheriff (SO) makes no return. Said
  Thomas filed answer.
- Executors of Samuel Young (CV) vs.
  Richard Young (AA) surviving
  executor of Col. Samuel Young (AA).
  Sheriff (AA) to render attachment to
  defendant to render final accounts.

Page 139

- E.D. for Ebenezar Reyner & his wife Sarah (KE) vs. D.D., Jr. for Rebecca Perkins & David Perkins. Libel, answer, general replication.

32:180

- D.D., Jr. for William Grantham & his wife Sarah (DO) vs. Stephen Bordley, Esq. for William Kennerly only surviving executor of Joshua Kennerly. Libel. Enn. Hooper (sheriff, DO) to summon defendant.
- S.B. for John Hammond Dorsey & his wife Frances (BA) vs. Daniel Dulany, Jr. for Walter Tolley executor of James Tolley. Libel. Roger Boyce (sheriff, BA) to summon defendant.
- Nicholas Clouds administrator of Sarah Price (QA) vs. Benjamin Kirby (QA). Sheriff (QA) to summon defendant to show cause why he refuses to pay plaintiff effects of said dec'd.
- Capt. John West vs. Joseph Lane (AA) executors of Samuel Maccubbin, Jr. (BA). William Thornton (sheriff, AA) to summon defendant to render final accounts.

Court Session: 1748

32:181 14 July. Thomas White (g, BA) exhibited:

- will of Zachariah Gray, constituting Rebecca Gray executrix. Said executrix was granted administration. Sureties: Thomas Sligh, Zachariah Gray, Peter Dowell. Date: 5 May 1748.
- will of Joshua Allinder, constituting Mary Allinder executrix. Said executrix was granted administration. Sureties: Thomas Allender, Joseph Allinder. Date: 15 April 1748. Also, renunciation of Thomas Ellet executor, recommending Mary Allinder (executrix). Date: 14 April 1748. Witnesses: Benjamin Chew, Nath. Broughton.
- will of John Aughard. Also, bond of Benjamin Goodin acting executor. Surety: Nicholas Ruxton Gay. Date:

Court Session: 1748

8 June 1748. Also, renunciation of William Ress (executor of John Varghwart).

- will of George Elliot, constituting Darby Hernly executor. Said executor was granted administration. Sureties: James Moore, William Wright. Date: 18 June 1748.
- bond of Thomas Sligh administrator of Thomas Mitchell. Sureties: Isaac Risteau, Nathan Nichollson. Date: 11 March 1747.
- bond of Thomas Sligh administrator of Philip Carback. Sureties: Isaac Risteau, Nathan Nicholson. Date: 11 March 1747.
- bond of Elisabeth Sheilds administratrix of Solomon Sheilds. Sureties: John Macconikin, William Barney. Date: 18 March 1747.
- bond of William Denton & John Denton executors of William Denton. Sureties: Thomas Jarman, John Parks. Date: 5 April 1748.
- bond of Ann Beck administratrix of Matthew Beck. Sureties: John White, Joseph Smith. Date: 5 April 1748.
- bond of Sophia Demmitt administratrix of Thomas Demmitt. Sureties: Tobias Stansbury, Danby Buckler Partridge. Date: 5 May 1748.
- bond of Benjamin Ingram administrator of Mary Ingram. Sureties: John Buck, Abraham Wright. Date: 7 June 1748.
- bond of Elisabeth Hillen administratrix of Solomon Hillen. Sureties: Walter Tolley, Isaac Risteau. Date: 29 April 1748.
- 32:182 bond of Margret Williams & Ford Barnes administrators of John Williams. Sureties: Thomas Mitchell, Jonathan Jones. Date: 30 April 1748.
- inventory of William Groves.
- inventory of John Carlisle.
- accounts of Mary Frisby administratrix dbn of Susanna Stokes.
- accounts of Daniel Deavor administrator of John Carlisle.

Court Session: 1748

15 July. John Thompson (g, CE)
exhibited:

- will of Richard Rutter. Also,
renunciation of 1 executor. Also,
bond of Moses Rutter & Mary Rutter
administrators. Sureties: Thomas
Rickets, John Jones. Date: 8 April
1748.
- will of John McKnitt. Also, bond of
Elisabeth McKnitt administratrix.
Sureties: Manassah Loage, Peter
Boushel. Date: 31 March 1748.
- will of John Ryland. Also, bond of
Rebecca Ryland administratrix.
Sureties: John Holland, John Ryland.
Date: 11 April 1748.
- will of James Armstrong. Also, bond
of Martha Armstrong administratrix.
Sureties: Archibald Armstrong,
Robert Ritchey. Date: 4 April 1748.
- will of James Foster. Also, bond of
Elisabeth Foster administratrix.
Sureties: James Boulding, William
Price. Date: 10 May 1748.
- bond of Sarah Johnson administratrix
of Bartholomew Johnson. Sureties:
John Buchanan, Bartholomew Johnson.
Date: 19 May 1748.
- bond of James Porter & John
Williamson administrators of Samuel
Archibald. Sureties: John
KirkPatrick, Jared Nilson. Date: 14
June 1748.
- bond of Robert Bell administrator of
Matthew Bonner. Sureties: James
Gossey, John Gossey. Date: 16 May
1748.
- bond of Jane Carr administrator of
William Carr. Sureties: John
Buchanan, Bartholomew Johnson.
Date: 19 May 1748.
- bond of Samuel Hill administrator of
James McFaden. Sureties: George
Lawson, James Mackey. Date: 30 May
1748.
- bond of James Bayard administrator
of Charles Bowen. Sureties: John
Baldwin, Joseph Hodgson. Date: 16
May 1748.
- bond of Robert Blackbourn & Robert
Stephenson administrators of
Briceson Blackbourn. Sureties:

Thomas Archer, Alexander McConnell.
Date: 15 June 1748.
- bond of Elisabeth Browne
administratrix of John Browne.
Sureties: James Brookes, Caleb
Cartman. Date: 9 July 1748.
- inventory of Richard Evans.
- inventory of Thomas Jordon.
- inventory of Col. John Ward.
- inventory of John McKnitt.
- inventory of Mark Dunn.

32:183 16 July. Mr. William Tilghman (QA) to
examine additional accounts of:
- Nicholas Glen & his wife Mary
administratrix of Robert Jones (QA).

18 July. Exhibited from QA:
- 2nd additional inventory of John
Earle. Also, additional accounts of
Robert Hawkins & his wife Hannah
executrix.

19 July. Exhibited from AA:
- accounts of Mary Elliott
administratrix of Matthew Elliott.

23 July. Exhibited from PG:
- inventory of Rebecca Riley.

25 July. William Tilghman (g, QA)
exhibited:
- nuncupative will of John Irons.
Also, bond of Hesther Money
executrix. Sureties: John Cheshire,
Thomas Nelson. Date: 19 May 1748.
- will of Joseph Branthwaite.
- bond of Rosanna Hollingsworth
administratrix of Isaac
Hollingsworth. Sureties: William
Mounseir, Thomas Parara. Date: 16
June 1748.
- bond of Mary Taylor administratrix
of John Taylor. Sureties: William
Baxter (p), Thomas Benton (p).
Date: 3 June 1748.
- bond of Elisabeth Andrew
administratrix of William Andrew.
Sureties: Peter Rich (innholder,
DO), William Harrington (p, QA).
Date: 9 June 1748.
- bond of William Harrington

administrator of John Norman.
Sureties: Henry Downes (p, QA),
Peter Rich (innholder, DO). Date: 9
June 1748.

- bond of Susanna Clough
administratrix of Nathaniel Clough.
Sureties: Jacob Boon (p, QA), Samuel
Atwell (p, TA). Date: 2 June 1748.
- bond of Jemima Andrew administratrix
of James Andrew. Sureties: Jacob
Boon (p), John Willson (p). Date: 2
June 1748.
- bond of Nathanael Satterfield
administrator of Joseph Satterfield.
Sureties: William Satterfield (p),
Nathanael Satterfield, Jr. (p).
Date: 2 June 1748.
- bond of John Cheshire administrator
of Margaret Berry, during minority
of William Matthews. Sureties:
Nathaniel Tucker (p), Thomas Nelson
(p). Date: 19 May 1748.

32:184 • bond of Nicholas Clouds
administrator of Sarah Price, during
minority of Mary Evans. Sureties:
Henry Jacobs (p), John Hall (p).
Date: 6 May 1748.

- bond of Daniel Walker administrator
of John Walker, during minority of
John Walker. Sureties: Stephen Yoe
(p), John Davis, Jr. (p). Date: 15
June 1748. Also, renunciation of
Sarah Walker (widow). Date: 14 May
1748. Witness: Henry Williams.
- inventory of William Nevill.
- inventory of Richard Keys.
- additional inventory of Trustram
Thomas.
- inventory & LoD of Richard Powell.
- inventory of James Moody.
- inventory of Thomas Hynson Wright.
- accounts of Ann Thomas executrix of
Trustram Thomas (Wye).

16 July. John Dunn who married Mary
daughter of William Smith (CE) vs.
William Currier & his wife Rachel (CE)
administratrix of said dec'd. Sheriff
(CE) to summon defendant to render
additional inventory.

Court Session: 1748

27 July. W.C. for Laurence Macnemara &
his wife Elisabeth (CH) vs. Mary Ann
Atcherson, John Hamill, & John Moore.
Attachment rendered to defendants to
satisfy things issued on supersedeas. 1
August. Thomas Bullen (g, TA)
exhibited:

- will of Thomas Eaton, constituting
  Anderton Eaton & Peter Eaton
  executors. Said executors were
  granted administration. Sureties:
  Joseph Hicks (p), William Ridgway
  (p). Date: 17 June 1748.
- will of Edward Elliott, constituting
  Edward Elliott executor. Said
  executor was granted administration.
  Sureties: Joseph Hopkins (p), Robert
  Spencer (p). Date: 9 June 1748.
- will of William Sinkler. Also,
  widow's election. Also,
  renunciation of 1 executor. Also,
  bond of Sarah Sinkler acting
  executrix. Sureties: John Robinson
  (p), John Wilson, Jr. (p). Date: 11
  June 1748.
- bond of Margaret Hardakin
  administratrix of Matthew Hardakin.
  Sureties: William Alexander (p),
  Walter Jenkins (p). Date: 17 June
  1748.
- inventory of Richard Hall.
- inventory & LoD of James Clayland.
- inventory of Denton Carroll.

32:185 - 3rd additional inventory & LoD of
  John Guy Williams.
- LoD on estate of Thomas Clarak.
- accounts of Robert Goldsborough
  administrator of James Clayland.
- additional accounts of William Sharp
  executor of Solomon Birckhead.

2 August. Exhibited from BA:
- bond of William Young as Deputy
  Commissary (BA). Sureties: William
  Dallam (p), William Smith (p).
  Date: 5 July 1748.

Exhibited from QA:
- additional accounts of Matthew
  Griffith administrator dbn of Andrew
  Price, during minority of Thomas
  Price (son of said Andrew).

Court Session: 1748

8 August. Exhibited from CH:
- accounts of Robert Whythill who married widow & administratrix of John Theobalds.

Exhibited from QA:
- additional accounts of Susanna Elliott executrix of John Elliott.

Exhibited from KE:
- accounts of Richard Gresham executor & James Ringgold & his wife Sarah executrix of William Thomas.

Petition of William Cumming, Esq. for Mr. John Urquhart (SM). John Graves, Jr. (SM) died indebted to petitioner. His widow took LoA. Bond on said estate assigned to petitioner.

32:186 Thomas Aisquith (g, SM) exhibited:
- will of John Medley, constituting Sarah Medley & Clement Medley executors. Also, widow's election. Said executors were granted administration. Sureties: Stephen Chelton, John Manning. Date: 5 April 1748.
- will of John Teppet, constituting Elisabeth Teppet executrix. Also, widow's election. Said executrix was granted administration. Sureties: John Maddox, Edman Boulen. Date: 5 July 1748.
- will of John Graves, constituting Elenor Graves & Ann Graves executrices. Said executrices were granted administration. Sureties: George Graves, Thomas Standage. Date: 5 July 1748.
- bond of Tersia Mickell administratrix of William Mickell. Sureties: James Thompson, John Mickell. Date: 5 July 1748.
- bond of William Knott administrator of John Knott. Sureties: Edward Field, John Toon. Date: 13 June 1748.
- inventory & LoD of Matthew Cissell.
- inventory & LoD of Richard Daintry.
- inventory of Robert Thomas.
- inventory & LoD of Stephen Mackey.

- accounts of John Dossey executor of John Binks.
- accounts of Lazarus Voss & his wife Mary administratrix of John Railey.
- accounts of Elenor Gardiner administratrix of Clement Gardiner.

9 August. Exhibited from PG:
- 3rd additional accounts of Charles Drury (AA) administrator of Nathan Selby.

William Young (g, BA) exhibited:
- will of Thomas Davis.
- bond of Samuel Jones administrator of John Jones. Sureties: Dr. William Lyon, John Hunt. Date: 3 August 1748.
- bond of Nicholas Ruxton Gay administrator of James Maxwell. Sureties: John Paca, Isaac Risteau. Date: 4 August 1748.
- inventory of John Frederick.
- inventory & LoD of Richard Deaver.

William Rogers (g, AA) exhibited:
- additional inventory of Ferdindo Battee.

12 August. Exhibited from BA:
- 4th additional accounts of Joseph Lane (AA) acting executor of Samuel Maccubbin, Jr.

32:187 Exhibited from QA:
- accounts of Elisabeth Earickson executrix of John Earickson.

15 August. Rev. Mr. John Urquhart creditor to estate of John Graves (SM) vs. Margaret Graves (SM) administratrix of said dec'd. Sheriff (SM) to summon defendant to render final accounts.

Rev. Mr. John Urquhart creditor to estate of John Graves (SM) vs. George Graves (SM). Sheriff (SM) to summon defendant to show cause why he conceals estate of dec'd.

Mr. Gabriel Parker (CV) to examine accounts of:

- Mary Card administratrix of Abraham Card (CV).
- Margaret Perrie administratrix of Samuel Perrie (CH).

Exhibited from CE:
- additional accounts of Col. Thomas Colvill administrator of Maj. John Copson.
- accounts of Col. Thomas Colvill executor of Solomon Hodgson.

Exhibited from AA:
- accounts of Elisabeth Battee & Samuel Battee executors of Ferdindo Battee.

Exhibited from BA:
- inventory of Dennis Dunn.

Walter Hanson (g, CH) exhibited:
- nuncupative will of Edward Kellet. Also, bond of James Muncaster administrator. Sureties: Hugh Perrie, Simon Smith. Date: 20 June 1748.
- will of John Maddox.
- bond of Jane Baden administratrix of Daniel Baden. Sureties: Francis Semmes, William Cooksey. Date: 28 May 1748.
- bond of James Mankin administrator of Cornelius Sandford. Sureties: Peter Harrout, John Brooks. Date: 12 August 1748.
- inventory of Anne Wyeth.
- inventory & additional inventory of Thomas Lamphier.
- inventory of James Freeman.
- additional accounts of Sarah Hawkins administratrix of Thomas Hawkins.
- accounts of Susanna Waters administratrix of William Waters.

32:188 16 August. Mr. Ennalls Hooper (DO) to examine accounts of:
- William Smith & John Stevens Smith executors of Thomas Smith (DO).

19 August. Gabriel Parker (g, CV) exhibited:
- inventory of Barrington Pardoe.

Court Session: 1748

- inventory of Robert Day.
- inventory of John King.
- accounts of Thomas Ireland, Jr. administrator of Jesse Bourne.
- accounts of Thomas Ireland, Jr. administrator of William Sumner.
- accounts of Thomas Ireland, Jr. administrator of Thomas Cranford.
- accounts of Martha Brooke administratrix of John Brooke.
- accounts of Capel King administrator of Sarah Maulden.

22 August. Peter Dent (g, PG)
exhibited:
- will of James Downing, constituting Anne Downing executrix. Also, widow's election. Said executrix was granted administration. Sureties: Henry Acton (p, CH), Smallwood Coghill (p, PG). Date: 13 June 1748.
- bond of Anne Davis administratrix of Walter Davis. Sureties: John Veatch (p), John Jacobs (p). Date: 29 June 1748.
- bond of Cathrine Condon administratrix of Richard Condon. Sureties: William Davis (p), John Bayne (p). Date: 29 June 1748.
- bond of Mary Cramphin administratrix of Basil Cramphin. Sureties: Thomas Gaton (p), John Riggs. (p). Date: 12 July 1748.
- inventory of Henry Cramphin.
- inventory of John Smoot.
- accounts of Andrew Gibbs administrator of William Mason.
- accounts of John Busey executor of Sarah Busey.
- additional accounts of Humphry Ball & his wife Elisabeth executrix of Thomas Jennings.
- accounts of Mary Cramphin executrix of Henry Cramphin.
- accounts of Solomy Large administratrix of Philip Large.
- accounts of George Beckwith & Basil Beckwith administrators of Anne Miller.
- accounts of Blanford Beavin acting executor of Dr. John Kirkwood.

- additional accounts of Andrew Gibbs executor of Hanah Deale.
- accounts of Elisabeth Massey administratrix of Henry Massey.
- accounts of Elisabeth Davison administratrix of John Davison.
- accounts of Cathrine Williams executrix of Joseph Williams.

Exhibited from PG:
- additional accounts of Thomas Bowie executor of James Bowie.

32:189 24 August. Exhibited from PG:
- additional accounts of George Matthews executor of Isaac Wells.

26 August. Richard Bennett, Esq. vs. estate of Mr. Samuel Hyde (merchant, London). Caveat against granting LoA.

Joseph Griffin vs. William Smith & John Stevens Smith executors of Thomas Smith (DO). Caveat against passing accounts.

27 August. Nehemiah King (g, SO) exhibited:
- will of Solomon Hitch, constituting Solomon Hitch executor. Said executor was granted administration. Sureties: Elgett Hitch, Thomas Ackworth. Date: 5 April 1748.
- will of Ann Samons.
- will of Nathaniel Horsey. Also, bond of Outerbridge Horsey acting executor. Sureties: Benjamin Lankford, William Smith. Date: 25 June 1748. Also, renunciation of William Coulbourn, recommending Outerbridge Horsey. Date: 23 June 1748.
- bond of Isbel Covington administratrix of Abraham Covington. Sureties: Daniel Jones, Thomas Mitchell. Date: 9 June 1748.
- bond of Sarah Holbrook & Thomas Holbrook administrators of Thomas Holbrook. Sureties: William Stoughton, David Polk. Date: 17 March 1747/8.
- bond of Clement Bayley administrator of Simon Burn (mariner). Sureties:

Robert Jenckins Henry, Heber
Whittingham. Date: 24 June 1748.

- bond of Joseph Weatherly
administrator of William Weatherly.
Sureties: Leavin Hitch, Robert
Hardy. Date: 22 June 1748. Also,
renunciation of Thomas Acworth,
Patience Weatherly, Mary Weatherly,
& Eliah Weatherly, recommending
Joseph Weatherly. Date: 20 June
1748.
- bond of Solomon Long administrator
of Wonney McClemmey. Sureties:
Whittington King, James Furnis.
Date: 13 July 1748.
- bond of Isaac Sirman administrator
of William Sirman Sureties: George
Bennitt, William Wright. Date: 25
June 1748.

32:190

- bond of Martha Wilson administratrix
of Samuel Wilson. Sureties: David
Wilson, Henry Waggaman. Date: 6
July 1748.
- inventory of Mary Wilson.
- inventory of Nathaniel Jackson.
- inventory & LoD of Thomas Dixon.
- inventory of William Cox.
- inventory of Solomon Hitch.
- inventory of John Gale.
- inventory & LoD of Thomas Holbrook.
- additional inventory & LoD of David
Browne.
- inventory of William Surman.
- accounts of Elisabeth Tull executrix
of George Tull.
- accounts of Susanna Phillips
administratrix of John Phillips.
- accounts of George Dashiel & George
McClester sureties for Margaret
Blewer (dec'd) executrix of James
Blewer.
- accounts of Deborah Hern executrix
of Edward Hern.
- additional accounts of Roase Coastin
administratrix of Isaac Costin.
- accounts of Mary Price executrix of
Robert Price.
- accounts of William Draper & his
wife Alice executrix of Thomas
Winder.
- accounts of Elget Hitch & his wife
Elisabeth executrix of Ebenezar

Handy.

- accounts of Thomas Browne administrator of David Browne.
- accounts of Isaac Moore administrator of Mary Sterling.

29 August. Exhibited from KE:
- bond of James Calder as Deputy Commissary (KE). Sureties: James Smith (g), William Murray (chyrurgeon). Date: 27 February 1747.

William Ryon (PG) & his wife Ann & Kessiah Bowen (spinster, PG) vs. Thomas Dorsett executor of John Bowen (PG). Sheriff (PG) to summon defendant to render answer to libel.

30 August. Ennalls Hooper (g, DO) exhibited:
- will of Edward Granger, constituting Price Ward & William Granger executors. Said executors were granted administration. Sureties: William Littleton, Thomas Nutter. Date: 5 December 1747.
- will of James Pattison.
- will of Cornelius Realey. Also, bond of John Oldfield acting executor. Sureties: John Smith (p), John Willobey (p). Date: 9 March 1747.
- will of John Dehorty, constituting Catherine Dehorty & George Dehorty executors. Said executors were granted administration. Sureties: Mathew Driver, William Smith, Sr. Date: 15 June 1747.

32:191 • will of Thomas Cannon, constituting Catherine Cannon executrix. Said executrix was granted administration. Sureties: William Clarkson, William Willson. Date: 15 June 1748.
- will of John Miller, constituting Dorethy Miller & John Hatfield executors. Said executors were granted administration. Sureties: Benjamin Woodward (p), William Jones (p). Date: 27 June 1748.
- will of Charles Robson.

- will of Mary Fish, constituting Henry Withgot executor. Said executor was granted administration. Sureties: William Jones (p), Mark Littleton (p). Date 26 May 1748.
- will of James Billings, constituting Ann Billings executrix. Also, widow's election. Said executrix was granted administration. Sureties: John Henry (g), Thomas Nevett (g). Date: 7 December 1747.
- bond of William Edmondson, Jr. administrator of Esther Edmondson. Sureties: Daniel Sulivane (g), Peter Edmondson (g). Date: 12 April 1748.
- bond of Sarah Meddis administratrix of Godfrey Meddis. Sureties: John Polland, Jr. (p), James Tregoe (p). Date: 15 June 1748.
- bond of Joseph Ennalls administrator of William Burn. Surety: William Smith (g). Date: 24 November 1747.
- bond of Miriam Harrington administratrix of Richard Harrington. Sureties: Peter Rich (p), John Thompson (p). Date: 9 August 1748.
- bond of William Layton administrator of William Layton. Sureties: Richard Layton (p). Nicholas Layton (p). Date: 11 August 1748.
- bond of William Littleton administrator of Comfort Wheelton. Sureties: Daniel Sulivane, Joseph Ennalls. Date: 5 December 1748.
- bond of Daniel Sulivane administrator of Peter Taylor. Sureties: John Anderton (g), John Rix (g). Date: 26 October 1747.
- bond of Richard Soward administrator of John Soward. Sureties: Arthur Whiteley (p), Samuel Hubbert (p). Date: 9 March 1747.
- bond of Elisabeth Fooks administratrix of James Fooks. Sureties: John Caill (g), Thomas Stewart (g). Date: 14 April 1748.
- bond of Joseph Ennalls administrator of James Evans. Sureties: John Hicks, Moses Poole. Date: 1 March 1747.
- bond of Rosannah Lewis

Court Session: 1748

administratrix of John Lewis.
Sureties: Peter Grimes (p),
Archabald Grimes (p). Date: 16 June
1748
- bond of Raymond Staplefort executor
of George Staplefort. Sureties:
George Griffith (p), Lewis Griffith
(p). Date: 10 August 1747.

32:192 • bond of John Stewart, Jr.
administrator of Thomas Cook.
Sureties: James Hooper (g), Thomas
Stewart (g). Date: 19 June 1748.
- bond of Mary Perray administratrix
of Ricahrd Perray. Sureties: John
Nicolls, Jr. (p), William Grainger
(p). Date: 9 March 1747.
- inventory of Edward Wright.
- additional inventory of Robert
Sherwin.
- inventory of John Brown.
- inventory of Richard Perray.
- inventory of James Billings.
- inventory & LoD of Thomas Smith.

4 September. John Medley & his wife
Frances vs. John Smith (SM)
administrator of Richard Smith (SM).
Sheriff (SM) to summon defendant to
render answer to libel.

8 September. Exhibited from BA:
- additional accounts of Philip Jones
acting executor of John Rattenbury.
- additional accounts of Mary Barney
executrix of William Barney.

30 August. Ennalls Hooper (g, DO)
exhibited:
- inventory & LoD of Edward Grainger.
- inventory of Edward Russum.
- inventory & LoD of Samuel Jones.
- inventory of John Wingate.
- inventory of James Pattison.
- inventory of Comfort Whealton.
- inventory of Michael Todd.
- inventory of Mary Fish.
- inventory of David McCollister.

8 September. Exhibited from PG:
- inventory, additional inventory, &
LoD of John Henn.

Court Session: 1748

Exhibited from AA:
- accounts of Bridget Gray & Samuel Gray executors of John Gray, Sr.

Exhibited from KE:
- bond of Samuel Galloway (g, AA) administrator dbn of Richard Lux. Sureties: Richard Franklin, William Coale. Date: 16 June 1748.

Exhibited from AA:
- LoD on estate of James Wilson.

32:193 9 September. William Tilghman (g, QA) exhibited:
- will of John Bennett.
- will of Timothy Webb. Also, widow's election.
- will of William Wilson, constituting Ann Wilson executrix. Also, widow's election. Said executrix was granted administration. Sureties: Robert Lloyd (g), John Clayland (p). Date: 23 August 1748.
- will of Thomas Fisher. Also, widow's election. Also, bond of Esther Fisher administratrix. Sureties: William Fisher (p), Benjamin Sylvester (p). Date: 4 August 1748.
- will of Cornelius Comegys. Also, bond of Mary Comegys administratrix. Sureties: John Harris (p), Thomas Sands (p). Date: 17 August 1748. Also, renunciation of C. Comegys (executor/executrix) & E. Comegys (executor/executrix). Date: 26 May 1748. Witnesses: V. Benton, William Pryor.
- will of Thomas Chaires.
- will of Cornelius Riddle.
- will of Littleton Ward.
- will of John Brown, constituting Sarah Brown executrix. Said executrix was granted administration. Sureties: John Downes, Jr. (p), William Elbert (p). Date: 29 August 1748.
- bond of Sarah Lindsey administratrix of Patrick Lindsey. Sureties: Henry Burt (p), William Wheeler (p). Date: 4 August 1748.

- bond of James Berwick & John Roe
  administrators of Richard Leech.
  Sureties: John Covington (p), Thomas
  Thomas (p). Date: 4 August 1748.
- bond of Sarah Chapman administratrix
  of Daniel Chapman. Sureties: John
  Sallaway (p), Henry Taylor (p).
  Date: 29 July 1748.
- bond of Amy Sprawl administratrix of
  Jeremiah Sprawl. Sureties: Emanuel
  Swift (p), Richard Swift (p). Date:
  28 July 1748.
- bond of Martha Cohee administratrix
  of James Cohee. Sureties: David
  Herrington (p), Zorobabel Wells (p).
  Date: 27 July 1748.
- bond of Caleb Esgate administrator
  of Caleb Esgate. Sureties: Gideon
  Swift (p), Zorobabel Wells (p).
  Also, renunciation of Dorthy
  Esgatte. Date: 26 July 1748.
  Witnesses: Zorobabel Wells, John
  Posterd.

32:194
- bond of Davenport Wells
  administrator of Sarah Newman.
  Sureties: Caleb Esgate (p), Charles
  Birmingham (p). Date: 21 July 1748.
- bond of Esther Boon administratrix
  of Benjamin Boon. Sureties: Abraham
  Boon (p), Benjamin Sutton
  (innholder). Date: 26 July 1748.
- bond of Elisabeth Beton
  administratrix of Thomas Beton.
  Sureties: John Nab (p), James Wrench
  (p). Date: 2 September 1748.
- inventory of Joseph Newman.
- inventory of William Emory.
- inventory & LoD of Nathaniel Downes.
- additional inventory of Solomon
  Clayton.
- inventory of James Roberts.
- inventory of Joseph Whittington.
- additional LoD on estate of John
  Carman.
- inventory of William Kemp.
- inventory of William Burroughs.
- inventory of William Jarman.
- inventory of Joseph Satterfield.
- additional inventory of William
  Jumpe.
- inventory of Job Naman.
- inventory of John Taylor.

Court Session: 1748

- inventory of William Andrews.
- inventory & LoD of James Andrews.
- additional inventory of William Nevill.
- additional inventory & LoD of Richard Keys.
- accounts of Daniel Ford & his wife Sarah administrators of James Maud.

10 September. Appointment of Mr. John Darnall as Deputy Commissary (FR).

12 September. Exhibited from PG:
- will of Mary Offutt, constituting Nathaniel Offutt executor. Said executor was granted administration. Sureties: Enoch Magruder, Richard Burgess. Date: 11 September 1748.

William Rogers (g, AA) exhibited:
- will of William Phelps, constituting Rachel Phelps executrix. Said executrix was granted administration. Sureties: William Phelps (p), Richard Phelps (p). Date: 20 August 1748.
- will of Charles Peirpoint. Also, renunciation of Sidney Peirpoint, recommending his/her son Joseph Peirpoint.
- bond of Francis Day administrator of Stephen Higgins. Sureties: Nicholas St. Lawrence (p), William Kirkland (p). Date: 9 August 1748.
- bond of Amos Sympson administrator of Amos Sympson. Sureties: Henry Griffith (p), Joseph White (p). Date: 15 August 1748.

32:195
- inventory of Thomas Lusby, Jr.
- inventory of William Hudson.
- inventory of Richard Linstead.
- accounts of John Evitts administrator of Susanna Murray.
- accounts of Thomas King executor of James Wilson.

Court Session: 13 September 1748

Docket:
- Sheriff (AA) to summon Patrick Doran (AA) administrator of John Handling (AA) to render accounts.

Court Session: 13 September 1748

- E.D. for John Tootell & his wife
  Rosannah (DO) vs. S.B. for Thomas
  Woolford & John Woolford executors
  of Roger Woolford. Libel, answer by
  Thomas Woolford.
- Executors of Samuel Young (CV) vs.
  Richard Young (AA) surviving
  executor of Col. Samuel Young (AA).
  Sheriff (AA) to render attachment to
  defendant to render final accounts.

32:196 • Edward Dorsey, Esq. procurator for
  Ebenezar Reyner, Jr. (p) & his wife
  Sarah (KE) vs. Daniel Dulany, Jr.
  Esq. procurator for Rebecca Perkins
  & David Perkins.
  Text of libel. Plaintiff is
  daughter of David Perkins (KE,
  dec'd), who died leaving wife
  Rebecca Perkins, son David Perkins
  (p), daughter said plaintiff. Copy
  of will, with legacies to: wife
  Rebekah plantation, daughter Sarah
  land in New Castle Co. PA, son
  David.

32:197 Mentions: James Ringgold, Jr.
  (sheriff, KE).
  - Edward Piner (KE) deposed that
    said Rebecca is weak & infirm.
    Date: 10 November 1747. Before:
    Robert Gordon.
  MM John Gresham (KE) & Daniel
  Cheston (KE) to take her testimony.

32:198 Text of answer. Said David died on
  6 April 1747.

32:199 Said David & Rebecca are Quakers.
  Text of general replication.

32:200 Ruling: defendants.
- D.D., Jr. for William Grantham & his
  wife Sarah (DO) vs. S.B. for William
  Kennerly only surviving executor of
  Joshua Kennerly. Libel, answer.
- S.B. for John Hammond Dorsey & his
  wife Frances (BA) vs. D.D., Jr. for
  Walter Tolley executor of James
  Tolley. Libel, answer.
- Nicholas Clouds administrator of
  Sarah Price (QA) vs. Benjamin Kirby
  (QA). Sheriff (QA) to summon
  defendant to show cause why he
  refuses to deliver to plaintiff
  effects of said dec'd.
- Capt. John West vs. Joseph Lane

Court Session: 13 September 1748

(AA) executor of Samuel Maccubbin, Jr. (BA). Sheriff (AA) to summon defendant to render full accounts. Final accounts exhibited. Discontinued.

- John Dunn who married Mary daughter of William Smith (CE) vs. William Currier & his wife Rachel (CE) administratrix of said dec'd. Sheriff (CE) to summon defendant to render additional inventory. LoD exhibited. Discontinued.

32:201
- W.C. for Laurence Macnemara & his wife Elisabeth (CH) vs. Mary Ann Atcherson, John Hamill, & John Moore. Sheriff (CH) to render attachment to defendants on supersedeas to satisfy judgement.

- Rev. Mr. John Urquhart creditor to estate of John Graves (SM) vs. George Graves (SM). Sheriff (SM) to summon defendant to show cause why he conceals estate of dec'd.

- Rev. Mr. John Urquhart creditor to estate of John Graves (SM) vs. Margaret Graves (SM) administratrix of said dec'd. Sheriff (SM) to summon defendant to render full accounts.

- E.D. for William Ryan & his wife Ann & Kesiah Bowen (PG) vs. Thomas Dorset executor of John Bowen. Libel.

- W.C. for John Medley & his wife Frances (SM) vs. John Smith administrator of Richard Smith. Libel.

Court Session: 1748

14 September. Exhibited from CE:
- LoD on estate of William Smith. Also, accounts of William Currier & his wife Rachel administratrix.

16 September. Exhibited from BA:
- LoD on estate of Francis Holland.

32:202 23 September. William Tilghman (g, QA) exhibited:
- accounts of Susanna Jumpe acting executrix of William Jumpe.

Court Session: 1748

- accounts of Allice Alliband administratrix of Thomas Alliband.

24 September. William Young (g, BA) exhibited:
- will of Joseph Thomas. Also, widow's election.
- bond of Ann Wood administratrix of William Wood. Sureties: Richard Jones, John Denton. Date: 26 August 1748.
- bond of Joseph Hopkins administrator of John Coulston. Surety: Nathan Rigbie. Date: 7 September 1748.
- bond of Richard Coop administrator of Solomon Stansbury. Sureties: Henry Hughs, William Kitely. Date: 12 August 1748.
- inventory & additional inventory of Samuel Griffith.
- inventory of Comfort Dorsey.

27 September. Exhibited from BA:
- inventory of Charles Gorsuch.

30 September. Thomas White (g, late Deputy Commissary (BA)) exhibited:
- will of Benjamin Bowen, constituting Edward Bowen & Elisabeth Baxter executors. Said executors were granted administration. Sureties: Robert Green, Abraham Eaglestone. Date: 1 July 1748.
- bond of Roger Donahue administrator of William Graves. Sureties: James Preston, William Clement. Date: 23 June 1748. Also, renunciation of Sarah Gravs (widow). Date: 18 June 1748. Witness: Thomas Wheeler.
- bond of Mary Henderson (AA) administratrix of Mary Frisby. Sureties: John Hall, Jr., John Paca, Jr. Date: 15 July 1748. Also, renunciation of Henretter Holland (sister), recommending Mrs. Mary Henderson. Date: 15 June 1748. Witness: John Hall, Jr.
- bond of Mary Henderson administratrix of Susannah Stokes. Sureties: John Hall, Jr., John Paca, Jr. Date: 15 June 1748.
- bond of Mary Henderson (AA)

administratrix of Peregrine Frisby.
Sureties: John Hall, Jr., John Paca,
Jr. Date: 15 June 1748.
- inventory of Robert Woolford.
- inventory of James Presbury.
- accounts of Henry Green & his wife
Elisabeth acting executrix of David
Thomas.
- Nathan Rigbie administrator of
Robert Woodford.

32:203 - accounts of Patience Stinchcomb
executrix of Nathaniel Stinchcomb.
- accounts of Jemima Jackson
administratrix of Jacob Jackson.
- accounts of Sarah Groves
administratrix of William Groves.

3 October. Thomas Bullen (g, TA)
exhibited:
- will of William Hopkins,
constituting Thomas Robarts
executor. Said executor was granted
administration. Sureties: Francis
Pickerin (p, Wye), Francis Armstrong
(p). Date: 2 August 1748.
- will of Isaac Rew. Also, widow's
election. Also, bond of Mary Rew
administratrix. Sureties: Samuel
Morgan (p), John Cuckoe (p). Date:
19 August 1748.
- bond of Elisabeth Williams
administratrix of William Williams.
Sureties: James Wilson (p), Isaac
Williams (p). Date: 1 September
1748.
- bond of Anne Vickers administratrix
of William Vickers. Sureties: Jacob
Loockerman (p), Samuel Broadaway
(p). Date: 6 August 1748.
- bond of Elisabeth Clayland
administratrix of Lambert Clayland.
Sureties: Isaac Dobson (p), Joseph
Turner (p). Date: 5 August 1748.
- inventory of Thomas Eaton.
- inventory of Thomas Hutchins.
- inventory of James Coben.
- accounts of John Connor & his wife
Bridget administrators of Thomas
Ford.
- 3rd additional accounts of David
Hall & his wife Sarah administratrix
of John Guy Williams.

- accounts of Peter Calk & his wife
  Ann administratrix of John Davis.

Benton Harris (WO) exhibited:
- will of Peter Johnson.
- will of Charles Townsend.
- will of James Oneal. Also, widow's
  election. Also, bond of Rachel
  Oneal administratrix. Sureties:
  Francis Lancake, John Oneal. Date:
  21 August 1748.
- bond of John Massey acting executor
  of John Massey. Sureties: Ebenezar
  Evens, John Campbell. Date: 2
  August 1748.
- inventory & LoD of Peter Dolby.
- inventory & LoD of John Read.
- inventory of William Whaley.
- accounts of George Johnson & his
  wife Ann administratrix of William
  Jarman.
- 2nd additional accounts of William
  Selby & his wife Martha executrix of
  John Purnell.
- accounts of William Todvine
  administrator of John Blewitt.
- accounts of David Smith one of
  sureties of Martha Harvey
  administratrix of John Harvey.
- accounts of Sarah Johnson
  administratrix of Leonard Johnson.
- additional accounts of Lucretia
  Claywell executrix of Peter
  Claywell.

32:204 7 October. Peter Dent (g, PG)
exhibited:
- bond of Mary Cooke administratrix of
  Ambrose Cooke. Sureties: James Lee
  (p), John Candler (p). Date: 24
  August 1748.
- bond of Richard Rolings
  administrator of Joseph Tereney.
  Surety: Joseph Turner (p). Date: 21
  September 1748.
- inventory of William Davis.
- inventory of Peter Brightwell.
- inventory of John Lewis.
- inventory of James Downing.
- inventory of James Magruder, Jr.

Court Session: 1748

13 October. John Thompson (g, CE)
exhibited:
- will of John Kankey. Also, bond of
  Anne Kankey administratrix.
  Sureties: John Hyland, William
  Bristow. Date: 13 May 1748.
- will of John Cox. Also, bond of
  William Cox administrator.
  Sureties: David Ricketts, Joseph
  Penington. Date: 1 August 1748.
- will of Nathan Phillips. Also, bond
  of James Boulding & Johannes Arrants
  administrators. Sureties: Michael
  Lum, Thomas Price. Date: 10 June
  1748.
- will of Hugh Terry. Also, bond of
  William Terry, Ruth Terry, & Sarah
  Terry administrators. Date: 1
  August 1748.
- will of King Robearts. Also, bond
  of Samuel Griffin administrator.
  Sureties: John Smith, Benjamin
  Starrat. Date: 5 August 1748.
- will of Christian Peters. Also,
  bond of Unite Peters administratrix.
  Sureties: Edward Means, Tobias Burk.
  Date: 9 August 1748.
- will of Joshua Meakins. Also, bond
  of Benjamin Pearce administrator.
  Sureties: John Money, John
  Penington, Jr. Date: 6 September
  1748.
- bond of Rachel Ewing & William Ewing
  administrators of Nathaniel Ewing.
  Sureties: Joshua Ewing, James
  Breading. Date: 27 September 1748.
- bond of Catherine Ball
  administratrix of Thomas Ball.
  Sureties: Mary Campbell, Alexander
  Scott. Date: 19 September 1748.
- bond of Hukill Guilder administrator
  of Samuel Seal. Sureties: John
  Jones, John Brookes. Date: 19 July
  1748.
- bond of John James administrator of
  Sarah James. Sureties: John Cooker,
  William Abbott. Date: 15 August
  1748.
- bond of Thomas Kenedy administrator
  of George Knox. Sureties: John
  Smith, James Stinson. Date: 26
  August 1748.

Court Session: 1748

- bond of Margaret Smith administratrix of Richard Smith. Sureties: Thomas Severson, Bartlet Smith. Date: 16 August 1748.
- inventory of John Husband.
- inventory of Jonathon Hynds.
- inventory & additional inventory of Charles Heath.
- inventory of John Young.
- inventory of Alphonso Cosden.
- inventory of Richard Dobson.
- inventory of William Carr.
- inventory of Harmana Vanbebber.
- inventory of James Armstrong.
- inventory of William Chambers.
- accounts of John Cooper administrator of Mark Don.

32:205

18 October. Exhibited from QA:
- accounts of John Hall & William Hall executors of Lawrence Hall.

Exhibited from CH:
- will of Robert Hanson.

19 October. Exhibited from CH:
- inventory of John Courts.

Gabriel Parker (g, CV) exhibited:
- will of William Cox, Sr.
- bond of Anna Young administratrix of John Young. Sureties: James Bowen, Ellis Slater. Date: 20 September 1748.
- bond of Sutton Isaack administrator of Mary Scott. Sureties: James Heighe, Ellis Slater. Date: 15 OCtober 1748.
- additional inventory of William Dawkins, Jr.
- inventory of John Wilkinson.
- inventory of Francis Hutchins.
- accounts of Mary Card administratrix of Abraham Card.
- accounts of Dorcas Dawkins executrix of William Dawkins, Jr.

Thomas Aisquith (g, SM) exhibited:
- will of Edward Aloysius Doyne.
- will of Henry Price.
- additional inventory of John Heard.
- inventory & LoD of Thomas Payn.

Page 164

- inventory & LoD of Ignatius Knott.
- inventory & LoD of Francis Hayden.
- inventory & LoD of Henry Bacon.
- inventory & LoD of John Knott.
- inventory & LoD of John Medley.
- inventory & LoD of Basil Cooper.
- accounts of James Heard executor of John Heard.
- accounts of Joseph Hopewell administrator of Thomas Francis Hopewell.
- accounts of John Horn administrator of John Horn.
- accounts of Prissilla Chesher administratrix of John Chesher.

32:206 Walter Hanson (g, CH) exhibited:
- will of John Philbert.
- will of John Barker, constituting Eleanor Barker & William Barker executors. Said executors were granted administration. Sureties: William Dent, Bayne Smallwood. Date: 15 July 1748.
- will of Samuel Adams.
- will of Henrietta Wharton.
- bond of James Hamilton administrator of John Frazier. Sureties: Bennet Coombs, Bartholomew Coombs. Date: 16 September 1748.
- inventory of Daniel Baden.
- inventory of John Barker.

Exhibited from QA:
- additional inventory of Richard Mason. Also, accounts of James Lane & his wife Rebecca widow & administratrix.

Exhibited from BA:
- accounts of Ann Acton executrix of Richard Acton.

Nehemiah King (g, SO) exhibited:
- bond of William Shores administrator of John Shores. Sureties: John Shores, Henry Newman. Also, renunciation of John Shores, Henry Spear, & Henry Dorman, recommending William Shores. Date: 15 October 1748. Witnesses: R. King, Jr., Nehemiah King.

Court Session: 1748

- inventory of William Weatherly.
- inventory of Peter Mills.
- accounts of Abraham Heath administrator of Mary Wilson.
- accounts of Rachell Roach administratrix of Charles Roach.

20 October. William Young (g, BA) exhibited:
- will of Robert West, Sr.
- will of Francis Jewkes, constituting James Walter (AA) executor. Said executor was granted administration. Sureties: James Perkins, Abraham Eaglestone. Date: 7 October 1748.
- will of Thomas Renshaw, constituting Jane Renshaw executrix. Said executrix was granted administration. Sureties: Robert Clark, James Ball. Date: 15 October 1748.
- bond of Edward Martin administrator of German Williams. Surety: Stephen Onion. Date: 15 October 7148.

32:207 21 October. Exhibited from QA:
- accounts of Henry Williams executor of Matthew Williams.
- accounts of Samuel Osborne administrator of William Osborne

Exhibited from FR:
- bond of John Darnall as Deputy Commissary (FR). Sureties: Osborn Sprigg, Esq. (PG), Stephen Bordley (g, AA). Date: 10 September 1748.

22 October. Exhibited from TA:
- additional inventory of John Powell. Also, accounts of Daniel Dickenson executor.
- additional inventory of Susannah Powell. Also, accounts of Daniel Dickinson administrator.

Exhibited from QA:
- additional inventory & LoD of John Hawkins. Also, accounts of Deborah Hawkins executrix.

24 October. Appointment of Mr. Henry Hooper as Deputy Commissary (DO).

25 October. Peter Dent (g, PG)
exhibited:
- bond of Robert Debutts administrator of Isaac Bloomfield. Sureties: James Smith (g), Thomas Baker (g). Date: 3 October 1748.
- bond of George Matthews executor of Isaac Wells. Sureties: Henry Ballinger, Daniel Matthews. Date: 11 June 1747.
- bond of Thomas Hodgkin administrator of William Cocks. Surety: Ignatius Digges (g). Date: 4 October 1748.
- bond of Blanford Beavin administrator dbn of Henry Beavin. Sureties: William Bright (g), William Miles (g). Date: 19 October 1748.
- inventory of Rev. Joseph Jenings.
- accounts of Mary Downes administratrix of Henry Downes.

Mr. Peter Dent (PG) to examine accounts of:
- Mary Barker executrix of Samuel Barker (PG).
- Jane Pelley executrix of James Pelley (PG).
- Elisabeth Massey administratrix of Henry Massey (PG). Additional accounts.

Mr. Nehemiah King (SO) to examine accounts of:
- Outerbridge Horsey acting executor of Nathaniel Horsey (SO).

32:208 27 October. Mr. Henry Hooper, Jr. (DO) to examine additional accounts of:
- Elinor Eccleston executrix of Thomas Eccleston (DO).

Exhibited from BA:
- inventory of John Cockey, Jr.

29 October. Rebecca Clawle widow of Gilbert Clawle (AA) & Cean Clawle daughter & only child of said dec'd vs. Benjamin Clawle (p, AA). Sheriff (AA) to summon defendant to render answer to libel. Said Rebecca is guardian to said Cean.

Court Session: 1748

30 October. William Wilmer who married only child of John Blackiston (KE) vs. John Garrett & his wife Sarah administratrix of said dec'd. Sheriff (KE) to summon defendant to render additional inventory.

4 November. John Tucker & his wife Elisabeth one of children of Daniel Laughland (CV) vs. Comfort Laughland (AA) widow & administratrix of said dec'd. Sheriff (AA) to summon defendant to show cause why she does not pay plaintiff her portion of her father's estate, & her portion of estate of Richard Laughland (another one of children, died under age).

James Calder (g, KE) exhibited:
- will of Charlton Waltham.
- will of Richard Gwinap, constituting Lewis Williams (chyrurgeon) executor. Said executor was granted administration. Sureties: Daniel Bryan (merchant), James Tibbit (p). Date: 4 July 1748.
- will of Charles Smith, constituting Joseph Smith executor. Said executor was granted administration. Sureties: John Smith (p), George Smith (p), Thomas Smith (p). Date: 1 September 1748.
- will of William Harris, constituting Ariana Margaritta Harris executrix. Said executrix was granted administration. Sureties: Daniel Cheston (merchant), Joseph Nicholson (merchant). Date: 2 September 1748.
- will of David Pirkins, constituting Rebecca Pirkins & David Pirkins executors. Said executors were granted administration. Sureties: Thomas Wilkins (p), John Burgin (p). Date: 8 October 1748.
- **32:209** bond of John Batterskill administrator of Amos Atkinson. Sureties: Charles Smith (p), William Hall (p). Date: 31 May 1748.
- bond of James Henly administrator of Christopher Henly. Sureties: Isaac Milton (p), Henry Hosier (p). Date: 4 June 1748.

- bond of Jane Bowers administratrix of William Bowers. Sureties: Benjamin Ricaud (p), Edward Canady (p). Date: 4 June 1748.
- bond of Risetta Hall administratrix of Cuthbert Hall. Sureties: Peter Cole (p), Matthew Smith (p). Date: 10 June 1748.
- bond of Elisabeth Hull administratrix of Ferdinando Hull. Sureties: Richard Wilson (p), John Burgin (p). Date: 20 June 1748.
- bond of Samuel Wallis administrator of Elisabeth Tenant. Sureties: John Wallis, John Hurt. Date: 8 July 1748.
- bond of John Wallace administrator of Samuel Gooding. Sureties: William Murray (chyrurgeon), George Copper, Jr. (p). Date: 9 July 1748.
- bond of Martha Hurt administratrix of Morgan Hurt. Sureties: John Williamson (g), John Waltham (g). Date: 23 July 1748.
- bond of John Brown administrator of Mary Younger. Sureties: John Brooks (p), Edmund Linch (p). Date: 7 August 1748.
- bond of James Sutton administrator of Alexander Sutton. Sureties: Daniel Smith (p, QA), Benjamin Smith (p, QA). Date: 2 August 1748.
- bond of Anne Coley administratrix of Nathaniel Coley. Sureties: Samuel Tibbet (p), Thomas Urick (p). Date: 16 August 1748.
- bond of Hannah Cunningham administratrix of Daniel Cunningham. Sureties: John Falconar (p), Joseph Ricketts (p). Date: 17 August 1748.
- bond of Elinor Walker administratrix of William Walker. Sureties: Lewis Williams (chyrurgeon), John James (p). Date: 14 September 1748.
- bond of Susannah Smith & Solomon Smith administrators of John Worley Smith. Sureties: Thomas Massy (p), John Whealy (p). Date: 8 October 1748.
- inventory of Thomas Farmer.
- additional inventory of James Coarse.

- inventory of John James.
- additional inventory & LoD of Robert Dunn.
- inventory of Elisabeth Thorp.
- inventory of Elisabeth Tennant.
- inventory & LoD of William Bowers.
- inventory of Amos Atkinson.
- inventory of Richard Tibbet.
- inventory of Richard Gwinap.
- inventory of Cuthbert Hall.
- additional inventory of John Wallis.
- inventory of Hannah Hosier.
- additional inventory & LoD of James Greenwood.
- inventory & LoD of Nathaniel Cooley.
- inventory of Morgan Hurt.

32:210 Mr. Henry Hooper, Jr. (DO) to examine additional accounts of:
- William Edmondson & Elisabeth Edmondson executors of William Edmondson (DO).

7 November. William Rogers (g, AA) exhibited:
- will of Thomas Lloyd. Also, bond of James Dick surviving executor. Sureties: William Roberts (merchant), Stephen West, Jr. (merchant). Date: 11 October 1748.
- will of William Ashley, constituting John Ashley executor. Said executor was granted administration. Sureties: John Williams (lawyer), William Hammond (p). Date: 21 October 1748.
- will of Thomas Tucker, constituting Thomas Tucker executor. Said executor was granted administration. Sureties: Sele Tucker (p), Richard Beard (p). Date: 29 October 1748.
- bond of Joseph Peirpoint acting executor of Charles Peirpoint. Sureties: Francis Peirpoint (p), Henry Peirpoint (p). Date: 10 October 1748.
- bond of Margaret Mattox administratrix of Edward Mattox. Sureties: Thomas Johnson (p), James Sargent (p). Date: 30 August 1748.
- bond of Ann Trott administratrix of James Trott. Sureties: John Trott

Court Session: 1748

(p), Anthony Guishard (p). Date: 27
October 1748.
* additional inventory of Gassaway
  Watkins.
* inventory of Henry Budd.
* widow's election of Rachel Phelps on
  estate of William Phelps. Date: 24
  September 1748.

Court Session: 8 November 1748

32:211 Docket:
* Patrick Grey (BA) vs. Patrick Doran
  (AA) administrator of John Handling
  (AA). Sheriff (AA) to render
  attachment to defendant to render
  accounts. Accounts exhibited.
  Discontinued.
* E.D. for John Tootell & his wife
  Rosannah (DO) vs. S.B. for Thomas
  Woolford & John Woolford executors
  of Roger Woolford. Libel, answer by
  Thomas Woolford.
* Executors of Samuel Young (CV) vs.
  Richard Young (AA) surviving
  executor of Col. Samuel Young (AA).
  Sheriff (AA) to render attachment to
  defendant to render final accounts.
  Said Richard is dead. Abated.
* Daniel Dulany, Jr. Esq. for William
  Grantham & his wife Sarah (DO) vs.
  S.B. for William Kennerly only
  surviving executor of Joshua
  Kennerly. Libel, answer, general
  replication.
* S.B. for John Hammond Dorsey & his
  wife Frances (BA) vs. D.D., Jr. for
  Walter Tolley executor of James
  Tolley. Libel, answer

32:212 * Nicholas Clouds administrator of
  Sarah Price (QA) vs. Benjamin Kirby
  (QA). Sheriff (QA) to show cause
  why he does not deliver to plaintiff
  effects of dec'd.
* Rev. Mr. John Urquhart creditor to
  estate of John Graves (SM) vs.
  George Graves (SM). Sheriff (SM) to
  summon defendant to show cause why
  he conceals estate of dec'd.
* Rev. Mr. John Urquhart creditor to
  estate of John Graves (SM) vs.
  Margaret Graves (SM) administratrix

of said dec'd. Sheriff (SM) to
summon defendant to render final
accounts.

- E.D. for William Ryan & his wife Ann
  (PG) vs. Thomas Dorset executor of
  John Bowen.
- W.C. for John Medley & his wife
  Frances (SM) vs. John Smith
  administrator of Richard Smith.
  Libel.
- William Wilmer who married only
  child of Ebenezar Blackiston (KE)
  vs. John Garrett & his wife Sarah
  administratrix of said dec'd.
  Sheriff (KE) to summon defendant to
  render additional inventory.
  Defendant exhibited petition to pass
  accounts. Struck off.
- D.D., Jr. for Rebecca Clawle (AA)
  vs. Benjamin Clawle. Libel.
  Mentions: William Thorton (sheriff,
  AA).

32:213
- John Tucker & his wife Elisabeth one
  of children of Daniel Laughland (CV)
  vs. Comfort Laughland (AA) widow &
  administratrix of said dec'd.
  Sheriff (AA) to summon defendant to
  show cause why she does not pay
  plaintiff her portion of her
  father's estate, & her portion of
  estate of Richard Laughland (another
  one of children, died under age).
  Mentions: William Thornton (sheriff,
  AA).

Court Session: 1748

9 November. William Tilghman (g, QA)
exhibited:
- will of Richard Glandon. Also,
  widow's election.
- will of Sarah Chapman.
- will of Henry Neale.
- bond of Thomas Circum administrator
  of Thomas Jackson. Sureties: John
  Gilbert (p), John Sallaway (p).
  Date: 8 September 1748.
- bond of John Sallaway administrator
  of Daniel Chapman. Sureties:
  William Elbert (p), Thomas Circum
  (p). Date: 15 September 1748.
- bond of Catharine Chaires & Sarah

Chaires acting executrices of Thomas
Chaires. Sureties: Edward Browne
(p), James Chaires (p). Date: 22
September 1748.

- bond of Mary Ward executrix of
  Littleton Ward. Sureties: Phelemon
  Banam (p, TA), William Banam (p,
  TA), Quilton Banam (p, TA). Date:
  29 September 1748.
- bond of Sarah Starkey administratrix
  of William Starkey. Sureties: Isaac
  Boon (p), Nathan Harrington (p).
  Date: 27 October 1748.
- additional inventory & LoD of Robert
  Jones.
- inventory of Benjamin Chaires
- inventory & LoD of Robert Jarman.
- additional inventory of John Nevil.
- inventory of Isaac Hollingsworth.
- 2nd additional inventory of Richard
  Jones.
- inventory of Richard Leech.
- inventory & LoD of John Irons.

Exhibited from PG:
- inventory & LoD of George Kersner.

11 November. Mr. Walter Hanson (CH) to
examine additional accounts of:
- Mary Willson executrix of Alexander
  Willson (CH).
- Jane Mankin administratrix of Tubman
  Mankin (CH).
- Elisabeth Douglass administratrix of
  Benjamin Douglass (CH).

32:214 16 November. Mr. Gabriel Parker (CV)
to examine accounts of:
- Robert Greeves & his wife Elisabeth
  administratrix of Barrington Pardo
  (CV).
- Ann Day administratrix of Robert Day
  (CV).
- James Morsell & his wife Elisabeth
  administratrix of John Gough (CV).
  Additional accounts.

18 November. Thomas Bullen (g, TA)
exhibited:
- bond of Thomas McLaughlin
  administrator of John Davis.
  Sureties: Thomas Ray (p), Philemon

Horney (p). Date: 14 October 1748.
- inventory & LoD of John Lowe.
- inventory & LoD of Edward Elliott.
- inventory of Matthew Hardakin.
- inventory of William Vickars.

Mr. Thomas Bullen (TA) to examine accounts of:
- Thomas Powell & his wife Mary executrix & Richard Dudley executor of Sa. Dudley (TA).
- Tamson Eubanks executrix of Richard Eubanks (TA).
- James Robass & his wife Elisabeth acting executrix of Varty Sweat (TA).

Gabriel Parker (g, CV) exhibited:
- will of Richard Hellen, Jr., constituting Elisabeth Hellen executrix. Said executrix was granted administration. Sureties: John Hellen, John Greeves, Jr. Date: 22 October 1748.
- will of John Washington. Also, bond of James Heighe administrator. Sureties: Richard Johns, William Lyle. Date: 24 October 1748.
- will of Elisabeth Bowen. Also, bond of John Robinson, Jr. administrator. Sureties: William Lyles, Robert Lyles. Date: 14 November 1748.
- will of John Whinfield. Also, bond of John Robinson, Jr. administrator. Sureties: William Lyles, Robert Lyles. Date: 14 November 1748.
- inventory of Everard Taylor.
- inventory of Jane Pattison.
- accounts of Thomas Gray administrator of Jasper Floyd.
- accounts of Susannah Blake executrix of Richard Blake.
- accounts of Margaret Perrie administratrix of Samuel Perrie (CH).

21 November. Mr. William Tilghman (QA) to examine accounts of:
- Lemon Swift & his wife Frances administratrix of Fairclough Wright (QA).
- Rebecca Williams administratrix of

John White (QA).
- James Massey, Sr. & John Hadley, Sr. executors of John Gibb (QA).

32:215 22 November. Mr. John Thompson (CE) to examine accounts of:
- Mary Ward, Peregrine Ward, & Henry Ward executors of Col. John Ward (CE).

23 November. William Young (g, BA) exhibited:
- will of John Coan, Sr.
- bond of Edward Martin administrator of Edward Abbyss. Surety: Stephen Onion. Date: 28 October 1748.
- bond of Thomas Sligh administrator of Thomas Daviss. Sureties: Thomas Sheredine, John Metcalf. Date: 4 November 1748.
- bond of William Bennett administrator of Thomas Shaw. Surety: John Serjant. Date: 22 October 1748.
- bond of Dorcas Thomas executrix of Joseph Thomas. Sureties: Christopher Sutton, Adam Hendrickson. Date: 25 October 1748.
- inventory of William Denton.
- inventory of Mathew Beck.
- inventory of Mary Ingram.
- inventory of Solomon Stansbury.
- inventory of William Wood.

26 November. Mr. James Calder (KE) to examine accounts of:
- Jacob Glenn acting executor of Jacob Glenn (KE).
- Rosetta Hall (late Rosetta Holman) acting executrix of Edward Holman (KE).
- Samuel Wallis administrator of Elisabeth Tenant (KE).
- James Corse executor of James Corse (KE).
- Elisabeth Wallace administratrix of John Wallace (KE).
- James Course & Ebenezar Perkins executors of Francis Barney (KE).

Mr. William Young (BA) to examine accounts of:

- William Denton & John Denton executors of William Denton (BA).
- Henry Waters & his wife Ann administratrix of Mathew Beck (BA).
- Laurence Clark & his wife Jane executrix of Isaac Butterworth (BA).
- Charles Ridgely administrator of John Higgins (BA).
- Ann Wood administratrix of William Wood (BA).
- Susannah Butler executrix of Henry Butler (BA). 2nd additional accounts.

Mr. William Tilghman (QA) to examine accounts of:
- James Gould & his wife Mirimi administratrix of Edward Brown (QA).
- Penelope Jarman executrix of William Jarman (QA).
- Mary Ann Jarman executrix of Robert Jarman (QA).

Mr. Thomas Bullen (TA) to examine accounts of:
- William Herrington & his wife Rachel administratrix of Thomas Thompson (TA).

32:216　28 November. Mr. John Thompson (CE) to examine accounts of:
- George Nock & his wife Mary administratrix of Robert Story (CE).
- Catharine Wooliston administratrix of Richard Wooliston, Sr. (CE).
- William Bailey administrator of William Bailey (CE).
- Nicholas Hyland administrator of William Beeke (CE).
- Charles Bullard & his wife Mary administratrix of John Belarmine (CE).
- John Foster surviving executor of William Foster (CE). Additional accounts.
- Teresa Alman & Dr. Hugh Matthews administrators of Joseph Alman (CE). Additional accounts.

Mr. Nehemiah King (SO) to examine accounts of:
- Mary Cox executrix of William Cox

(SO).
- Mary White & Thomas White executors of Francis White (SO).
- Samuel Phebus executor of George Phebus (SO).

29 November. Peregrine Brown executor of Rachel Paca executrix of Aquila Paca (BA) vs. John Paca, Jr. (BA). R. Boyce (sheriff, BA) to summon defendant to show cause why he refused to sign inventory of said dec'd, as one of next of kin. Said John signed the inventory. Struck off.

30 November. Exhibited from CE:
- inventory of Rev. John Bradford, in QA & in CE. Also, accounts of Elisabeth Bradford (QA) administratrix.
- additional inventory of William Smith. Also, additional accounts of William Currier & his wife Rachel administratrix.

Exhibited from AA:
- accounts of Mary Henderson executrix of Thomas Henderson.

1 December. William Rogers (g, AA) exhibited:
- will of Edward Parrish. Also, bond of Thomas Norris acting executor. Sureties: Samuel Galloway (g, AA), Thomas Williamson (innholder, AA). Date: 1 December 1748. Also, renunciation of Rachel Parish (widow),

32:217   recommending Mr. Thomas Norris. Date: 19 November 1745. Witnesses: Ber. Hewit, Elisabeth Knight.

2 December. Peter Dent (g, PG) exhibited:
- will of Robert Wheeler. Also, bond of Grace Wheeler acting executrix. Sureties: Rignall Odall (g), James Ellitt (g). Date: 23 October 1748. Also, renunciation of Robert Wheeler (son). Date: 23 November 1748.
- will of Thomas Mullikin, constituting Elisabeth Mullikin

executrix. Said executrix was granted administration. Sureties: John Bowie (g), William Mullikin (g). Date: 23 November 1748.

- bond of Thomas Chittam administrator of Josiah Chittam. Surety: Thomas Owen (g). Date: 23 November 1748.
- bond of Van Swearingen administrator of Edward Dawson. Sureties: John Jones (g), Peter Rench (g). Date: 26 November 1748.
- inventory & LoD of John Pyburn.
- inventory of Basil Cramphin.
- accounts of Jayne Pelley executrix of James Pelley.

3 December. Exhibited from AA:
- bond of Elisabeth Pearce administratrix of Daniel Pearce. Sureties: John Jacob (p), Joseph Bazill (joyner). Date 3 December 1748.

6 December. Exhibited from PG:
- accounts of Richard Talbott & his wife Martha widow & administratrix of Charles Burgess, Jr.

7 December. Mr. Peter Dent (PG) to examine accounts of:
- Col. Thomas Lee surviving executor of Philip Lee, Esq. (PG).

32:218 Mr. James Calder (KE) to examine accounts of:
- Henry Hosier executor of Hannah Hosier (KE).

Benton Harris (g, WO) exhibited:
- will of David Hazard, constituting William Hazard & John Hazard executors. Said executors were granted administration. Sureties: Joshua Morss, William Dirickson. Date: 4 November 1748.
- inventory of John Massey.
- inventory of James Oneal.

8 December. Mr. Benton Harris (WO) to examine accounts of:
- Rous Fassitt executor of William Fassitt (WO).

Court Session: 1748

Exhibited from TA:
- 4th additional accounts of David Hall & his wife Sarah administratrix of John Guy Williams.

9 December. Exhibited from TA:
- accounts of David Hall & his wife Sarah executrix of Thomas Clark.

10 December. William Young (g, BA) exhibited:
- will of John Bowen.
- will of James Carroll Croxall. Also, bond of Richard Croxall acting executor. Surety: Charles Croxall. Date: 29 November 1748. Also, renunciation of Charles Croxall (brother), recommending his brother Richard Croxall.
- bond of Edward Carvin executor of John Carvin. Sureties: John Pribble, James Pritchard. Date: 3 November 1748.
- bond of Thomas Sligh administrator of William Jones. Surety: Samuel Harryman. Date: 30 November 1748.
- inventory & LoD of Maj. Aquila Paca.
- inventory of John Jones.

32:219 12 December. William Tilghman (g, QA) exhibited:
- will of Bridget Primrose. Also, bond of David Neal acting executor. Sureties: James Ponder (p), William Ponder (p). Date: 3 November 1748.
- will of Richard Ponder.
- will of John Sayer Blake.
- bond of Elisabeth Daley administratrix of William Daley. Sureties: John Deford (p), Edward Young (p). Date: 10 November 1748.
- bond of Mary Harper administratrix of Thomas Harper. Sureties: Jacob Alquier (p), Stephen Weeks (p). Date: 22 November 1748.
- bond of Ann Glandon executrix of Richard Glandon. Sureties: Matthew Dockery (p), William Durding (p). Date: 29 November 1748.
- bond of Ann Young administratrix of John Young. Sureties: Thomas Lee

(p), Solomon Scott (p). Date: 23 November 1748.
- bond of Susannah Jumpe administratrix of John Jones. Sureties: Thomas Jumpe (p), Vaughan Jumpe (p). Date: 22 November 1748.
- additional inventory & LoD of John Gibbs.
- inventory of Thomas Fisher.
- inventory of Patrick Lindsey.
- inventory of Thomas Jackson.
- additional inventory of Thomas Keld.
- inventory & LoD of Caleb Esgate.
- inventory of John Browne.
- inventory of Daniel Chapman.
- accounts of Charles Birmington executor of John Birmington.
- accounts of Solomon Glanding & his wife Mary administratrix of John Silvester.

Exhibited from BA:
- accounts of Peregrine Brown executor of Rachel Paca executrix of Aquila Paca.

13 December. Mr. William Young (BA) to examine accounts of:
- Samuel Jones administrator of John Jones (BA).

Ennalls Hooper (late Deputy Commissary, DO), by Henry Hooper, Jr. (g, DO), exhibited:
- will of Thomas Lewis.
- will of Roger Wright, constituting Elisabeth Wright executrix. Said executrix was granted administration. Sureties: William Newton (p), Daniel Pain (p). Date: 28 September 1748.
- bond of Thomas Ennalls administrator of John Deflin. Surety: Moses Pool. Date 18 October 1748.
- bond of Ann Edmondson administratrix of James Edmondson. Sureties: John Stevens, Thomas McKeel. Date: 8 May 1748.

32:220
- inventory of John Lewis.
- inventory & LoD of Peter Taylor.
- inventory of John Soward.
- inventory of Esther Edmondson.

- inventory & LoD of Thomas Cannon.
- inventory of John Dawhely.
- additional inventory of Lewis Griffith.
- accounts of Frances Brannock administratrix of John Brannock.
- accounts of Philemon Lecompte administrator of John Ogden.

Exhibited from AA:
- bond of John Stinchcomb administrator of Charles Stinchcomb. Sureties: Lewis Stinchcomb, John Gray, Jr. (son of John Gray, Sr.). Date: 13 December 1748.

John West & his wife Elisabeth vs. Joseph Lane (AA) acting executor of Samuel Maccubbin (BA). Sheriff (AA) to summon defendant to render answer to libel.

14 December. Gabriel Parker (g, CV) exhibited:
- will of Walter Smith. Also, widow's election.

Exhibited from QA:
- accounts of Jonathan Evans surviving executor of John Evans.

Matthew Howard who married Catharine one of daughters of Catharine Howard (AA) vs. John Howard (son of Benjamin, BA) administrator of said dec'd. Sheriff (AA) to summon defendant to render inventory.

15 December. Joseph Griffith who married Ann daughter of Thomas Smith (DO) vs. William Smith (DO) & John Stevens Smith (DO) executors of said dec'd. Sheriff (DO) to summon defendants to render additional inventory.

Henry Hooper, Jr. (g, DO) exhibited:
- will of Flower Fisher, constituting William Fisher executor. Said executor was granted administration. Sureties: Thomas Fisher (p), John Cook (p). Date: 21 November 1748.

- bond of Roger Hodson administrator
of Joseph Piper. Sureties: Thomas
Hicks (g), John Hicks (g). Date: 24
November 1748.
- inventory & LoD of Godfry Meddice.
- inventory of John Miller.

32:221
- accounts of Rachel Draper
administratrix of William Draper.
- accounts of John Pattison
administrator of James Pattison.
- accounts of Rosannah Lewis
administratrix of John Lewis.

Mr. Peter Dent (PG) to examine accounts
of:
- Lucy Hatton executrix of Joseph
Hatton (PG).

Catharine Jenings vs. Robert Debutts
(FR) administrator of Rev. Joseph
Jenings (PG, now FR). Sheriff (FR) to
summon defendant to render accounts.

21 December. William Rogers (g, AA)
exhibited:
- will of Benjamin Allen, constituting
Mary Allen executrix. Also, widow's
election. Said executrix was
granted administration. Sureties:
Philip Allingham (mariner, CV),
William Tillard (p, AA). Date: 21
December 1748.

Exhibited from AA:
- bond of Elisabeth Carpenter
administratrix of John Carpenter.
Sureties: Charles Carroll (surgeon,
Annapolis, AA), John Gassaway (g,
Annapolis, AA). Date: 21 December
1748.

22 December. Nehemiah King (SO)
exhibited:
- will of John Read, Sr., constituting
Obadiah Read executor. Also,
widow's election. Said executor was
granted administration. Sureties:
Thomas Humphris, William More, Jr.
Date: 26 November 1748.
- will of Edward Corley. Also, bond
of Anne Corley administratrix.
Sureties: Daniel Cordary, Evans

Collier. Date: 26 November 1748.
- will of Edward Willin, constituting
John Willin (DO) executor. Said
executor was granted administration.
Sureties: John Fowler, Stephen
Winright. Date: 6 December 1748.
- will of George Givan.
- will of John Read, Jr., Also,
widow's election. Also, bond of
Martha Read administratrix.
Sureties: Benjamin Venables, William
Givan. Date: 29 November 1748.
- nuncupative will of Robert Givan.
Also, bond of Jean Givan
administratrix. Sureties: Day
Givan, Levin Farrington. Date: 29
November 1748.
- bond of Mary Ackworth administratrix
of Henry Ackworth. Sureties: Day
Givan, Levin Farrington. Date: 9
December 1748.

32:222
- bond of William Givan administrator
of George Givan. Sureties: Benjamin
Venables, Day Givan. Also,
renunciation of John Givan
(brother), recommending his brother
William Givan. Date: 29 November
1748. Witnesses: Robert Twilley,
Day Givan.
- inventory of Simon Burn.
- inventory & LoD of Nathaniel Horsey.
Also, accounts of Outerbridge Horsey
acting executor.

24 December. Exhibited from KE:
- LoD on estate of Richard Walters.
Also, accounts of Daniel Cheston
administrator.

Exhibited from SO:
- accounts of Randol Reavill & William
Reavill executors of Charles
Reavill.

E.D. for Rachel Richardson (AA) vs.
Thomas Richardson surviving executor of
Richard Richardson. Attachment issued
to defendant, against a decree in July
1747 Court.

31 December. Peter Dent (g, PG)
exhibited:

Court Session: 1748

- additional accounts of Elisabeth Massey administratrix of Henry Massey.

5 January. William Young (g, BA) exhibited:
- will of Elisabeth Cloyd.
- bond of Elisabeth Odell administratrix of William Odell. Sureties: Edward Ousler, John Hurd. Date: 24 December 1748.

Court Session: 10 January 1748

32:223 Docket:
- Edward Dorsey, Esq. procurator for John Tootle & his wife Rosannah (DO) vs. Thomas Woolford & John Woolford executors of Roger Woolford. Libel, answer by Thomas Woolford.
- D.D., Jr. for William Grantham & his wife Sarah (DO) vs. William Kennerly only surviving executor of Joshua Kennerly. Libel, answer, general replication.
- S.B. & Edward Dorsey, Esq. for John Hammond Dorsey & his wife Frances (BA) vs. D.D., Jr. for Walter Tolley executor of James Tolley. Libel, answer, replication. Sheriff (BA) to summon to testify for plaintiff: Stephen Onion, Capt. Tobias Stansbury, Thomas Sligh.
- Rev. Mr. John Urquhart creditor to estate of John Graves (SM) vs. George Graves (SM). Sheriff (SM) to summon defendant to show cause why he conceals estate of dec'd.
- Rev. Mr. John Urquhart creditor to estate of John Graves (SM) vs. Margaret Graves administratrix of said dec'd. Sheriff (SM) to summon defendant to render final accounts.

32:224
- W.C. for John Medley & his wife Frances (SM) vs. John Smith administrator of Richard Smith. Libel.
- E.D. for William Ryan & his wife Ann & Kessiah Baven (PG) vs. Thomas Dorset executor of John Baven. Libel.
- D.D., Jr. for Rebecca Clawle, etc.

Court Session: 10 January 1748

(AA) vs. Stephen Bordley, Esq. for Benjamin Clawle. Libel. John Gassaway (sheriff, AA) to summon defendant.

- John Tucker & his wife Elisabeth one of children of Daniel Laughland (CV) vs. Comfort Laughland (AA) administratrix of said dec'd. Sheriff (AA) to summon defendant to show cause why she does not pay plaintiff her portion of her father's estate & her portion of estate of Richard (dec'd) another one of the children.
- D.D., Jr. for John West & his wife Elisabeth (AA) vs. Joseph Lane acting executor of Samuel Maccubbin. Libel. John Gassaway (sheriff, AA) to summon defendant.
- Matthew Howard who married Catherine one of daughters of Catharine Howard (AA, dec'd) vs. John Howard (son of Benjamin, AA) administrator of said dec'd. John Gassaway (sheriff, AA) to summon defendant to render inventory.

32:225 • Joseph Griffith who married Ann one of the daughters of Thomas Smith (DO, dec'd) vs. William Smith (DO) & John Stevens Smith (DO) executors of said dec'd. Sheriff (DO) to summon defendants to render additional inventory.

- Catharine Jenings vs. Richard Debutts (FR) administrator of Rev. Joseph Jenings (PG, now FR). Sheriff (FR) to summon defendant to render accounts.
- E.D. for Rachel Richardson (AA) vs. Thomas Richardson surviving executor of Richard Richardson. John Gassaway to render attachment to defendant, on a decree.

Court Session: 1748

17 January. Exhibited from FR:
- bond of Zachariah Magruder & Josiah Magruder administrators of Samuel Magruder. Sureties: Samuel Beall, Jr. (p), Nathaniel Beall, Jr. (p). Date: 17 January 1748.

Court Session: 1748

William Young (g, BA) exhibited:

- will of William Hughes, constituting Hannah Hughs executrix. Said executrix was granted administration. Sureties: Robert North, Greenberry Dorsey. Date: 3 January 1748.
- will of Thomas Ford, Sr., constituting Thomas Ford executor. Said executor was granted administration. Sureties: Charles Robinson, D. Buckler Partridge. Date: 4 January 1748.
- bond of Ann Yates administratrix of William Yates. Sureties: Daniel Dawney, John York. Date 6 January 1748.

32:226

- bond of Isaac Risteau administrator of Samuel Orman. Date: 28 December 1748. [Note: no sureties.]
- bond of Thomas Shey administrator of Henry Oneal. Surety: John Heaven. Date: 11 January 1748.
- inventory of Joshua Alender.

William Wallace (FR) & James Wallace (FR) to appraise estate of Samuel Magruder (FR).

28 January. Walter Hanson (g, CH) exhibited:

- will of James Cole, constituting William Love executor. Said executor was granted administration. Sureties: Samuel Turner (p), William McPherson (p). Date: 11 November 1748.
- will of James Kenam.
- will of George Elgin.
- will of John Ashfeald.
- bond of Edward Milstead & Anne Gow executors of James Gow. Sureties: Augustine Ward (p), Dennis Dowen (p). Date: 3 November 1748.
- bond of Peter Harot administrator of Samuel Purnell. Sureties: James Mankin (p), John Brooks (p). Date: 14 December 1748.
- bond of William Southerland administrator of David Southerland. Sureties: John Cunninghame, David Stone. Date: 12 November 1748.

Court Session: 1748

- bond of Charity Adams executrix of Samuel Adams. Sureties: Charles Courts, Francis Adams. Date: 29 October 1748.
- bond of Thomas Sanders administrator of Virlinda Sanders. Sureties: Henry Barnes, Jr., Edward Sanders. Date: 12 December 1748.
- inventory of Henry Ridge.
- inventory of Edward Kellet.
- inventory of John Frazier.
- accounts of Mary Willson executrix of Alexander Willson.
- accounts of Elisabeth Douglass administratrix of Benjamin Douglass.
- accounts of Jane Mankin administratrix of Tubman Mankin.

3 February. Thomas Cockey one of sureties on estate of John Cockey (BA) vs. William Cockey (BA) & Joshua Owings (BA) executors of said dec'd. Sheriff (BA) to summon defendants to render a complete inventory.

32:227 4 February. William Young (g, BA) exhibited:
- will of Elisabeth Mathews.
- will of Sarah Knight.
- will of William Maccomas.
- will of Roger Donohue, constituting Samuel Gilbert executor. Said executor was granted administration. Sureties: Robert Bryarly, Andrew Thompson. Date: 31 January 1748.
- bond of David McCullock administrator of Uriah Bond (blacksmith). Sureties: William Dallam (g), Talbot Risteau (g). Date: 31 January 1748.
- inventory & LoD of Leonard Wheeler.

10 February. Exhibited from AA:
- accounts of Thomas Reynolds administrator of John Alston.

Gabriel Parker (g, CV) exhibited:
- will of Richard Smith, constituting Althea Smith executrix. Said executrix was granted administration. Sureties: John Smith, Hutcheson Parker, Young

Page 187

Parran. Date: 19 December 1748.

- will of Walter Smith, Jr.
- will of Benjamin Hance, Jr., constituting Joseph Hance & Benjamin Johns executors. Said executors were granted administration. Sureties: Benjamin Hance, William Harris. Date: 10 December 1748.
- will of John Gardner, constituting William Gardner executor. Said executor was granted administration. Sureties: James Kershaw, Richard Everitt. Date: 17 December 1748.
- will of Mary Dare.
- will of Richard Johns.
- will of William Blackburn. Also, bond of William Blackburn acting executor. Sureties: Edward Blackburn, Gideon Turner. Also, renunciation of Edward Blackburn (son). Date: 26 January 1748. Witness: J. Broome.
- will of Daniel Rawlings, constituting Margaret Rawlings & Nancey Rawlings executrices. Said executrices were granted administration. Sureties: John Gray, Joseph Kent. Date: 4 February 1748.
- will of Francis Hollonshead.
- bond of Althea Smith administratrix of Walter Smith (St. Leonard's). Sureties: John Smith, Young Parran, John Broome. Date: 19 December 1748.

32:228
- bond of William Allnutt & Thomas Morgan administrators of William Coster. Sureties: Benjamin Johns, James Heighe. Date: 13 December 1748.
- bond of George Wade administrator of John Wade. Sureties: John Winman, George Wade, Jr. Date: 6 December 1748.
- bond of James Dodson administrator of John Dodson. Sureties: John Winnell, John Howell. Date: 2 December 1748.
- bond of George Johnson administrator of James Casteel. Sureties: Robert Lyles, Benjamin Griffith. Date: 8 December 1748.

- bond of John Brome administrator of John Brome. Sureties: John Smith, James Duke, Jr. Date: 19 January 1748.
- inventory of William Everrist.
- inventory of John Wade.
- inventory of John Young.
- inventory of Mary Scott.
- inventory of Elisabeth Bowen.
- inventory of John Whinfield.
- additional accounts of James Morsell & his wife Elisabeth administratrix of John Gough.

11 February. Mr. William Young (BA) to examine accounts of:
- Mary Allender acting executrix of Joshua Allender (BA).
- Cordelia Holland executrix of Francis Holland (BA).
- Thomas Wheeler executor & William Clemons & his wife Ann executrix of Leonard Wheeler (BA).
- William Denton & John Denton executors of William Denton (BA).
- Lawrence Clark & his wife Jane executrix of Isaac Butterworth (BA).
- Charles Ridgely administrator of John Huggins (BA).
- Ann Wood administratrix of William Wood (BA).
- Susannah Butler administratrix of Henry Butler (BA).
- Cordelia Holland administratrix dbn of Susannah Holland (BA).

13 February. Exhibited from AA:
- accounts & additional accounts of Benjamin Yealhall executor of Gilbert Yealhall.

14 February. Benton Harris (g, WO) exhibited:
- will of James Bratten.
- will of William Bratten, constituting William Bratton executor. Said executor was granted administration. Sureties: Patrick Glasgow, Daniel Wells. Date: 27 January 1748.
- nuncupative will of Adam Bell. Also, bond of Mary Ann Bell

Page 189

administratrix. Sureties: Patrick
Glasgow, George Johnson. Date: 10
December 1748.
* bond of Thomas Midgley administrator
of Ursla Greer. Sureties: Robert
Richardson, Bartholomew Bainum.

32:229 Also, renunciation of Bartholomew
Bainum, Robart Richardson, & William
Smith, recommending Thomas Midgley.
Date: 31 January 1748.

16 February. Mr. Nehemiah King (SO) to
examine accounts of:
* Sarah Holbrook & Thomas Holbrook
administrators of Thomas Holbrook
(SO).

Exhibited from BA:
* LoD on estate of John Cockey, Jr.

Mr. Benton Harris (WO) to examine
accounts of:
* Daniel Cox & his wife Rebecca
administratrix of Thomas Perkins
(WO).
* Mary Martin executrix of James
Martin (WO).

20 February. Exhibited from PG:
* additional accounts of William
Cumming (Annapolis, AA)
administrator of Capt. Joseph
Shakespear.

Exhibited from BA:
* additional inventory of John Cockey,
Jr. Also, accounts of William
Cockey administrator.

22 February. Exhibited from AA:
* will of Rev. Mr. John Lang.

24 February. William Bennett (BA)
administrator of William Shaw (BA) vs.
William Shaw (BA). Sheriff (BA) &
sheriff (AA) to summon defendant to show
cause why he refuses to deliver chattel
of dec'd in his possession.

27 February. Thomas Bullen (g, TA)
exhibited:
* will of John Cuckoe. Also, widow's

election.
- will of John Bartlet.
- will of Mary Davis. Also, renunciation of 1 executor. Also, bond of Perry Benson acting executor. Sureties: Thomas Bruff (g), Richard Bruff (g). Date: 16 December 1748.

32:230
- will of William Sharp (surgeon), constituting Ann Sharp & Peter Sharp executors. Also, widow's election. Said executors were granted administration. Sureties: William Martin (g), Thomas Martin, Jr. (g), William Dickinson (g). Date: 24 December 1748.
- will of John Hoult.
- will of Rev. Henry Nicols.
- bond of Margaret Slater administratrix of James Slater. Sureties: Tristram Thomas (g), Samuel Abbott (miller). Date: 14 November 1748.
- bond of Mary Harwood administratrix of John Harwood. Sureties: Samuel Cockayne (p), Thomas Perkins (p). Date: 9 December 1748.
- bond of John Robinson administrator of William Sinkler. Sureties: John Wilson (p), John Spencer (p). Date: 16 December 1748.
- bond of Dianah Wafford administratrix of William Wafford. Sureties: James Barnwell (p), James Barnwell, Jr. (p). Date: 27 January 1748.
- additional inventory of Thomas Thompson.
- inventory of Isaac Rew.
- inventory of Samuel Sharp.
- inventory of John Angley.
- accounts of William Harrington & his wife Rachel widow & administratrix of Thomas Thompson.

Nehemiah King (g, SO) exhibited:
- will of George Dashiell. Also, bond of Clement Dashiell & Louther Dashiell administrators. Sureties: Benjamin Cottman, Isaac Dashiell. Date: 14 February 1748.
- will of Roger Kellett.

- will of Rev. James Robertson.
  Also, bond of Mary Robertson
  administratrix. Sureties: Thomas
  Williams, Thomas Denwood. Date: 2
  January 1748.
- will of Lewis Beard, constituting
  Rachel Beard executrix. Said
  executrix was granted
  administration. Sureties: Elihu
  Mezick, Joseph Hurst. Date: 1
  January 1748.
- will of John Gray, constituting Jean
  Gray & James Gray executors. Said
  executors were granted
  administration. Sureties: William
  Walton, John Anderson. Date: 26
  January 1748.
- will of William Richardson. Also,
  bond of Benjamin Richardson
  administrator. Sureties: Isaac
  Sirman, Wilson Ryder. Date: 28
  January 1748.
- will of Ann Gilliss.
- will of Thomas Goslee, constituting
  Graves Boardman executor. Said
  executor was granted administration.
  Sureties: Daniel Dulany, Joseph
  Venables. Date: 13 February 1748.
- will of Joseph Cottman.

32:231
- bond of George Gale administrator of
  Matthias Gale. Sureties: David
  Wilson, John Elzey, Sr. Date: 31
  January 1748. Also, renunciation of
  Margaret Gale (widow), recommending
  her brother George Gale. Date: 30
  January 1748.
- bond of Judeth Larramur
  administratrix of Thomas Larramur.
  Sureties: Archibald Ritchie, James
  Larramur. Date: 31 January 1748.
- bond of Randol Phethian
  administrator of Thomas Phethian.
  Sureties: Thomas Banister, Thomas
  Mitchell. Date: 3 February 1748.
- bond of Daniel Henderson
  administrator of Robert Henderson.
  Sureties: George Collier, Archibald
  Ritchie. Date: 31 January 1748.
- bond of Day Scott administrator of
  Thomas Farrill. Sureties: John
  White (merchant), William Smith.
  Date: 14 February 1748.

- inventory of John Read, Jr.
- accounts of Mary Cox executrix of William Cox.
- accounts of Mary White & Thomas White executors of Francis White.
- accounts of Samuel Phebus executor of George Phebus.
- accounts of Isaac Surman administrator of William Surman.

Exhibited from AA:
- inventory of John Galloway.

28 February. Exhibited from AA:
- additional accounts of Mary Elliott administratrix of Matthew Elliott.

Exhibited from QA:
- accounts of Jane McClean administratrix of Daniel McClean.

Mr. James Calder (KE) to examine accounts of:
- James Ohagan & his wife Mary administratrix of Bryan Powell (KE).

1 March. Exhibited from SO:
- bond of George Gale surviving executor of Levin Gale. Sureties: Henry Waggaman (g), Thomas Gillis (g). Date: 28 February 1748.

32:232 Exhibited from BA:
- bond of Charles Carroll (surgeon, Annapolis, AA) administrator of Henry Wise. Surety: Charles Carroll, Jr. (g, Annapolis, AA). Date: 1 March 1748.

2 March. Mr. Thomas Bullen (TA) to examine accounts of:
- Sarah Robins administratrix of Standly Robins (TA).
- Ann Sharp executrix of Samuel Sharp (TA).
- Rebeckah Bounton executrix of Thomas Bounton (TA).
- Rachel Mackey executrix of William Mackey (TA).

3 March. Joshua Yates (AA) & John Gardiner (AA) to appraise estate of

Court Session: 1748

Capt. John Cockey (BA) in AA.

<u>4 March</u>. William Young (g, BA)
exhibited:
- will of Thomas Harris.
- will of Isaac Jackson.
- will of John Willmott.
- bond of William Bond administrator
  of John Beaven. Sureties: Henry
  James, Nathan Nichols. Date: 14
  February 1748.
- bond of Lyde Goodwin administrator
  of William Tiffin. Sureties:
  William Hammond (g), Brian Philpot,
  Jr. (g). Date: 13 February 1748.
- inventory of Frances Holland.
- inventory of Edward Abbyss.
- inventory of German Williams.
- inventory of Rachel Paca.
- accounts of Samuel Jones
  administrator of John Jones.
- accounts of Cordelia Holland
  executrix of Francis Holland.
- accounts of Cordelia Holland
  administratrix dbn of Susannah
  Holland.

<u>8 March</u>. Mr. James Calder (KE) to
examine accounts of:
- Isabell Denning administratrix of
  George Denning (KE).

Henry Hooper, Jr. (g, DO) exhibited:
- bond of Robert Wimseet administrator
  of John Marsh. Sureties: John
  Nicolls, Jr. (p), John Deane (p).
  Date: 21 January 1748.
- bond of Elisabeth Cremeen
  administratrix of John Cremeen.
  Sureties: George Andrew (p), John
  Cremeen (p). Date: 22 February
  1748.
- bond of Sarah Nevett administratrix
  of Thomas Nevett. Sureties: William
  Goldsborough (g), John Henry (g),
  Henry Hooper (g). Date: 24 February
  1748.
- bond of Elisabeth Macknatt
  administratrix of William Macknatt.
  Sureties: William Adams, William
  Kemmey. Date: 24 January 1748.
- bond of Thomas Nevett administrator

32:233

Page 194

of William Galloway. Surety: John
Woolford (g). Date: 26 December
1748.

9 March. William Young (g, BA)
exhibited:
* bond of Hannah Maccomas & Daniel
  Maccomas executors of William
  Maccomas. Sureties: Thomas Tredway,
  William Amos, Jr. Date: 27 February
  1748.

Mr. William Young (BA) to examine
accounts of:
* Peregrine Browne executor of Rachel
  Paca (BA).
* Peregrine Browne executor of Rachel
  Paca executrix of Aquila Paca (BA).
  Additional accounts.

10 March. Mr. Henry Hooper, Jr. (DO)
to examine accounts of:
* Edward Trippe executor of Edward
  Russum (DO).
* Sarah Philips administratrix of
  Thomas Philips (DO).
* Anne Andrew administratrix of
  Richard Andrew (DO).
* Martha Wright executrix of Edward
  Wright (DO).
* Mary Perry administratrix of Richard
  Perry (DO).
* Mary Rotten administratrix of Henry
  Rotten (DO).
* Anne Billings executrix of James
  Billings (DO).
* Catharine Dehorty & George Dehorty
  executors of John Dehorty (DO).
* Rev. Thomas Airey administrator of
  John Pitt (DO). Additional
  accounts.
* Joannah Alcock administratrix of
  Burtonwood Alcock (DO). Additional
  accounts.
* Ann Billings executrix of James
  Billings executor of Charles Rider
  executor of John Rider (DO).
  Additional accounts.

11 March. William Tilghman (g, QA)
exhibited:
* nuncupative will of John Cage,

constituting John Alley executor.
Said executor was granted
administration. Sureties: John
Davis, Jr. (p), Christopher Cross
Ruth (p). Date: 19 January 1748.

- will of William Eagle.
- will of Francis Rochester,
constituting Francis Rochester &
Henry Rochester executors. Said
executors were granted
administration. Sureties: Daniel
Smith (p), Benjamin Roberts (p),
John Spry (p), James Massey, Jr.
(p). Date: 2 February 1748.

32:234
- will of John Kininmont, constituting
Ambrose Kininmont (p, QA) & John
Kininmont (p, TA) executors. Said
executors were granted
administration. Sureties: John Cole
(p, QA), Henry Jones (p, QA). Date:
14 February 1748.
- bond of Mary Nelson administratrix
of Thomas Nelson. Sureties:
Nathaniel Wright (p), John Cheshire
(p). Date: 22 December 1748.
- bond of George Webb executor of
Timothy Webb. Sureties: William
Baley (p), James Wilkinson (p).
Date: 6 January 1748.
- bond of William Hopper administrator
of John Read, during minority of
Charles Read (son of John). Surety:
John Tillotson (g). Date: 23
January 1748.
- bond of Thomas Hadley administrator
of Joseph Tryal. Sureties:
Nathaniel Read, Jr. (p), Edward
Hadley (p), William Carman (p).
Date: 31 January 1748.
- bond of Benjamin Roberts
administrator of Robert Crump.
Surety: Francis Rochester (p).
Date: 2 February 1748.
- bond of Daniel Jurrel (KE)
administrator of Cornelius Redle.
Sureties: Matthew Dockery, Ernault
Hawkins. Also, renunciation of Jane
Redle (widow). Date: 20 December
1748. Witness: Matthew Dockery.
- inventory of Nathaniel Clough.
- inventory of William Starkey.
- inventory of Margaret Berry.

Court Session: 1748

- inventory of John Walker.
- inventory of James Cohee.
- inventory of Thomas Chaires.
- inventory of Jeremiah Praut.
- accounts of James Massey, Sr. & John Hadley, Sr. executors of John Gibb.
- accounts of Penelope Jarman executrix of William Jarman.
- renunciation of Joshua Cook (son of James Cook) on his father's estate. Date: 19 January 1748. Witness: Richard Tilghman.

13 March. John Cawood (CH) vs. Stephen Cawood (CH), Thomas Cawood (CH), & William Cawood (CH). Sheriff (CH) to summon defendants to show cause why administration on estate of Mary Cawood (CH) should not be granted to plaintiff.

Court Session: 14 March 1748

32:235 Docket:
- E.D. for John Tootell & his wife Rosannah (DO) vs. S.B. for Thomas Woolford & John Woolford executors of Roger Woolford. Libel, answer by Thomas Woolford, general replication.
- D.D., Jr. for William Grantham & his wife Sarah (DO) vs. S.B. for William Kennerly surviving executor of Joshua Kennerly. Libel, answer, general replication.
- S.B. & E.D. for John Hammond Dorsey & his wife Frances (BA) vs. D.D., Jr. for Walter Tolley executor of James Tolley. Libel, answer, general replication. Sheriff (BA) to summon to testify for plaintiff: Stephen Onion, Capt. Tobias Stansbury, Thomas Sligh.
- Rev. Mr. John Urquhart creditor to estate of John Graves (SM) vs. George Graves (SM). Robert Chesley (sheriff, SM) to summon defendant to show cause why he conceals estate of dec'd.
  - Said George Graves deposed. Dismissed.
- Rev. Mr. John Urquhart creditor to estate of John Graves (SM) vs.

Margaret Graves (SM) administratrix of said dec'd. Robert Chesley (sheriff, SM) to summon defendant to render final accounts. Continuance granted.

32:236 • E.D. for William Ryan & his wife Ann & Kessiah Bowen (PG) vs. Thomas Dorset executor of John Bowen. Libel.

• W.C. for John Medley & his wife Frances vs. John Smith administrator of Richard Smith. Libel. Richard Chesley to summon defendant to render answer.

• D.D., Jr. for Rebecca Clawle (AA) vs. S.B. for Benjamin Clawle. Libel, answer.

• John Tucker & his wife Elisabeth one of children of Daniel Laughland (CV, dec'd) vs. Comfort Laughland (AA) widow & administratrix of said dec'd. John Gassaway (sheriff, AA) to summon defendant to show cause why she doesn't pay plaintiff her portion of her father's estate, & her portion of estate of Richard (one of children who died under age). NEI.

• Daniel Dulany, Jr. Esq. for John West & his wife Elisabeth (AA) vs. Joseph Lane acting executor of Samuel Maccubbin. Libel.

• Matthew Howard who married Catharine one of daughters of Catharine Howard (AA, dec'd) vs. John Howard (son of Benjamin, AA) administrator of said dec'd. Sheriff (AA) to summon defendant to render inventory. Inventory exhibited. Discontinued.

• Joseph Griffith who married Ann daughter of Thomas Smith (DO, dec'd) vs. William Smith (DO) & John Stevens Smith (DO) executors of said dec'd. Sheriff (DO) to summon defendant to render additional inventory.

32:237 • Catharine Jennings vs. Robert Debutts (FR) administrator of Joseph Jennings (PG, now FR). Sheriff (FR) to summon defendant to render accounts.

• Thomas Cockey one of sureties on

estate of John Cockey (BA) vs.
William Cockey (BA) & Joshua Owings
(BA) executors of said dec'd. Ro.
Boyce (sheriff, BA) to summon
defendants to render a complete
inventory.

- William Bennett (BA) administrator
of Thomas Shaw vs. William Shaw
(BA). John Gassaway (sheriff, AA)
to summon defendant to show cause
why he refuses to deliver to
plaintiff certain chattel.
  - Said William Shaw deposed.
Discontinued.

- John Cawood (CH) vs. Stephen Cawood
(CH), Thomas Cawood (CH), & William
Cawood (CH). Samuel Hanson
(sheriff, CH) to summon defendants
to show cause why administration on
estate of Mary Cawood (CH) should
not be granted to plaintiff. LoA
granted to plaintiff. Discontinued.

Court Session: 1748

32:238 14 March. Thomas Aisquith (g, SM)
exhibited:
- bond of Samuel Eskridge (BA)
administrator of Joshua Dixon.
Sureties: Stephen Chelton, Thomas
Palmer Waughop. Date: 4 October
1748.
- bond of Jonathan Seal administrator
of John George Baptis Johnson.
Sureties: John Raley, Jr., Cuthbert
Abell. Date: 19 December 1748.
- inventory & LoD of William Mekin.
- inventory & LoD of Clare Shirbine.
- inventory of Ezebell Greentree.
- accounts of George Hayden
administrator of Peter Johnson.

15 March. Exhibited from PG:
- accounts of Joseph Waters (AA)
executor of Elisabeth Waters.

16 March. Exhibited from AA:
- inventory of Benjamin Allien.

20 March. Mr. William Tilghman (QA) to
examine additional accounts of:
- Deborah Hawkins executrix of John

Court Session: 1748

Hawkins (QA).

22 March. Mr. Benton Harris (WO) to
examine accounts of:
• John Hudson & his wife Elisabeth
  administratrix of James Stephen
  Bredell (WO).

Gabriel Parker (g, CV) exhibited:
• will of Sarah Burke. Also, bond of
  Littleton Waters acting executor.
  Sureties: Nehemiah Birckhead, Samuel
  Birckhead. Also, renunciation of
  Neh. Birckhead, recommending
  Littleton Waters. Date: 16 March
  1748/9.
• bond of Margaret Johns executrix of
  Richard Johns. Sureties: Benjamin
  Johns, James Heighe. Date: 17 March
  1748.
• bond of Sarah Smith executrix of
  Walter Smith, Jr. Sureties: Richard
  Harrison, Benjamin Harrison. Date:
  2 February 1748/9.
• inventory of John Dotson.
• inventory of James Shanks.
• inventory of Richard Hellen, Jr.
• inventory of John Washinton.

24 March. Mr. Thomas Bullen (TA) to
examine accounts of:
• Mesheck Botfield & his wife Sarah
  executrix of Richard Greason (TA).

Mr. Thomas Aisquith (SM) to examine
accounts of:
• Astin Sanford administrator dbn of
  Stephen Mackey (SM).

Court Session: 1749

32:239 25 March. Thomas Bullen (g, TA)
exhibited:
• bond of Rebeckah Taylor & John
  Walker executors of Issabell Taylor.
  Sureties: Jonathan Taylor (p),
  Robert Greenwood (p). Date: 7 March
  1748.
• inventory & LoD of Lambert Clayland.
• inventory of John Sedar.
• inventory of William Williams.

Page 200

Court Session: 1749

27 March. Exhibited from BA:
- bond of Godfrey Walters (AA) administrator of Henry Walters. Surety: Charles Carroll (phisician, Annapolis, AA). Date: 27 March 1749. Appraisers (BA): George Presbury, Nathan Richardson. Appraisers (AA): Joseph Foreman, Jacob Allwell.

28 March. William Young (g, BA) exhibited:
- will of John Harryman, constituting John Harryman & Charles Harryman executors. Said executors were granted administration. Sureties: Walter Dallas, Valentine Carback. Date: 8 March 1748.
- will of Hannah Hendon.
- will of Sarah Robertson.
- will of John Serjant, constituting John Yoston Gerswick executor. Said executor was granted administration. Sureties: Samuel Sollers, Samuel Bowen. Date: 7 March 1748.
- will of Thomas Spicer.
- bond of Mary Jackson executrix of Isaac Jackson. Sureties: James Maxwell, William Hill. Date: 10 March 1748.
- bond of Jacob Giles administrator of Henry Rhodes. Surety: Amos Garrett. Date: 3 March 1748/9.
- bond of Thomas Sligh administrator of John Boswith. Surety: Staly Dunham. Date: 9 March 1748.
- bond of William Shaw executor of John Shaw. Sureties: Aquila Gorswick, John Bays. Date: 9 March 1748.
- bond of John Paca administrator of John Nowall. Surety: William Dallam. Date: 27 February 1748.
- bond of Walter Dallas administrator of Charles Crooke. Sureties: John Harryman, Charles Harryman. Date: 8 March 1748.
- inventory of Dr. Robert Holliday.
- inventory of Samuel Orman.

32:240 Exhibited from PG:
- bond of Elisabeth Roberts

administratrix of Reubin Roberts. Sureties: William Reynolds (hatter, Annapolis), Simon Duff (house carpenter, Annapolis). Date: 28 March 1749.

Exhibited from QA:
- additional accounts of Edward Browne & his wife Rachel executrix of John Griffith.

Exhibited from KE:
- additional accounts of Hanse Hanson & his wife Margaret executrix of Glanville Rolph.
- accounts of Hanse Hanson & his wife Margaret administratrix of William Sheild.

29 March. Exhibited from QA:
- accounts of Hannah Burroughs & Thomas Burroughs executors of William Burroughs.

1 April. Peter Dent (g, PG) exhibited:
- will of Ninian Mariarte. Also, bond of Osborn Sprigg administrator. Sureties: Col. Edward Sprigg (g), Thomas Owen (g). Date: 3 February 1748.
- will of Joseph Newton.
- bond of Thomas Tucker administrator of Thomas Tucker. Sureties: Samuel Wright (p), John Welch (p). Date: 3 March 1748/9.
- bond of John Welch administrator of Joseph Lovejoy. Sureties: Samuel Wright (p), John Tucker (p). Date: 3 March 1748/9.
- bond of Henry Brookes administrator of Sollomey Large. Sureties: John Orme (minister), Dr. John Sprigg. Date: 9 February 1748.
- inventory of Henry Beavin.
- additional inventory of Philip Lee, Esq. in PG & in DO.
- accounts of Mary Barker executrix of Samuel Barker.
- accounts of Thomas Lee surviving executor of Philip Lee, Esq.
- accounts of Lucy Hatton executrix of Joseph Hatton.

4 April. Mr. Peter Dent (PG) to
underline examine accounts of:
- Lucy Hatton executrix of Joseph
  Hatton (PG).

Mr. Thomas Aisquith (SM) to examine
accounts of:
- James Pike & his wife Ann executrix
  of Henry Bacon (SM).

Mr. William Tilghman (QA) to examine
accounts of:
- Tabitha Nevitt administratrix of
  William Nevitt (QA).
- James Gould & his wife Mirime
  administratrix of Edward Browne
  (QA).

32:241 Mr. Benton Harris (WO) to examine
accounts of:
- John Dolby executor of Peter Dolby
  (WO).
- William Hazard & John Hazard
  executors of David Hazard (WO).
- Rachel Oneal administratrix of James
  Oneal (WO).

6 April. Sheriff (AA) to summon Philip
Hammond, Esq. (AA) administrator of
James Williams (AA) to render inventory.

10 April. Walter Hanson (g, CH)
exhibited:
- will of John Shaw, constituting
  Elisabeth Shaw executrix. Said
  executrix was granted
  administration. Sureties: Philip
  Jenkins (p), John Jenkins (p).
  Date: 8 March 1748.
- will of Joseph Green, constituting
  Jane Green executrix. Said
  executrix was granted
  administration. Sureties: Thomas
  Jameson, William McPherson, Jr.
  Date: 7 February 1748.
- will of Luke Adams.
- will of Thomas Matthews,
  constituting Mary Matthews &
  Maximilian Matthews executors. Said
  executors were granted
  administration. Sureties: Thomas
  Stone (g), Gerrard Fowke (g). Date:

9 March 1748.
- bond of Posthuma Groves administratrix of John Groves. Sureties: Edward Ford (p), Edward Smoot (p). Date: 21 March 1748.
- bond of Elisabeth Elgin acting executrix of George Elgin. Sureties: Francis Demington, Benjamin Maddox, John Elgin. Date: 24 January 1748.
- inventory of George Lewis.
- inventory of James Gow.
- inventory of Cornelius Standford.
- inventory of James Cole.
- inventory of David Southerland.
- inventory of Virlinda Sanders.
- inventory of Samuel Purnell.
- accounts of Margaret Ridge administratrix of Henry Ridge.
- accounts of Matthew Breeding executor of Stephen Mankin.

11 April. Mr. William Tilghman (QA) to examine accounts of:
- Nathan Wright executor of Robert Norrest Wright (QA).

12 April. William Young (g, BA) exhibited:
- will of Peter Bond.
- will of Christopher Duke, constituting Christopher Duke executor. Said executor was granted administration. Sureties: John Long, Isaac Raven. Date: 25 March 1749.
- will of Samuel Fortt, constituting Susannah Fortt executrix. Said executrix was granted administration. Sureties: Luke Trotten, Thomas Norris. Date: 4 April 1749.

32:242
- will of Mary Marshall, constituting John Hall (Swan Town) executor. Said executor was granted administration. Sureties: Col. John Hall, Susannah Smith. Date: 8 April 1749.
- will of William Waller, constituting Elisabeth Waller executrix. Said executrix was granted administration. Sureties: John

Steavin, Richard Wilmot. Date: 16
March 1748.

- bond of Susanna Smith administratrix
  of Winstone Smith. Sureties:
  Richard Dallam, John Hall (Swan
  Town). Date: 8 April 1749.
- bond of John Paca, Jr. administrator
  of Charles Baily. Surety: John Hall
  (Swan Town). Date: 16 March 1748.
- bond of Jacob Starkey administrator
  of Robert Kibble. Surety: Jonathan
  Starkey. Date: 29 March 1749.
- bond of Henry Garland administrator
  of William Garland. Sureties:
  Benjamin Hanson, George
  Hollandsworth. Date: 16 March 1748.
- bond of Samuel Smith administrator
  of Joseph Smith. Sureties: William
  Dallam, George Presbury. Date: 18
  March 1748.
- inventory of John Coulston.
- inventory of Sarah Ruff.
- inventory of Francis Jewkes.
- additional inventory of William
  Wood.
- accounts of Laurence Clark & his
  wife Jane executrix of Isaac
  Butterworth.
- accounts of Mary Allender acting
  executrix of Joshua Allender.
- accounts of Ann Wood administratrix
  of William Wood.

Mr. William Young (BA) to examine
accounts of:
- John Bull acting executor of Sarah
  Ruff (BA).
- Thomas Presbury executor of James
  Presbury (BA).

Mr. John Thompson (CE) to examine
accounts of:
- George Rock & his wife Mary
  administratrix of Robert Story (CE).

Exhibited from AA:
- inventory of William Phelps.

32:243 13 April. Exhibited from TA:
- accounts of Philemon Hambleton
  executor & Fiddeman Rolle & his wife
  Lydia executrix of John Sherwood.

Court Session: 1749

18 April. Tobias Hall administrator of
James Ashley (AA) vs. Ann Ashley
(widow, AA). Sheriff (AA) to summon
defendant to show cause why she conceals
estate of dec'd.

28 March. MM Thomas Harwood & Philip
Pindle to appraise estate of Reubin
Roberts (PG).

26 April. Mr. Peter Dent (PG) to
examine accounts of:
• Anne Brightwell executrix of Peter
  Brightwell (PG).

28 April. Thomas Bullen (g, TA)
exhibited:
• will of Samuel Bounton, constituting
  Mary Bounton executrix. Also,
  widow's election. Said executrix
  was granted administration.
  Sureties: William Burgess (p),
  Lambert Kirby (p). Date: 24 March
  1748.
• will of Hugh Lynch. Also, widow's
  election. Also, bond of Rebeckah
  Lynch administratrix. Sureties:
  Thomas Stevens (p), John Lee (p).
  Date: 8 April 1749.
• bond of Pooley Jones administrator
  of Vincent Jones, during minority of
  Sarah Jones. Sureties: Edward
  Knott, John Ploughman. Date: 15
  April 1749.
• bond of Thomas Powell administrator
  dbn of Samuel Dudley. Sureties:
  Daniel Powell, Abner Parratt.
  Sureties: Date: 24 March 1748.
• additional inventory of William
  Parratt.
• additional inventory of Thomas
  Bounton.
• accounts of Richard Marshall & his
  wife Sarah administratrix of Denton
  Carroll.
• accounts of Thomas Baynard acting
  executor of Richard Hall.
• accounts of Peter Comerford
  administrator dbn of William
  Parratt.

Mr. Thomas Bullen (TA) to examine accounts of:
- Thomas Powell administrator dbn of Samuel Dudley (TA).
- David Hall & his wife Sarah executrix of Thomas Clark (TA). Additional accounts.

32:244 11 May. Peter Dent (g, PG) exhibited:
- will of Edm. Hanbury. Also, renunciation of executor.
- bond of Anne Newton executrix of Joseph Newton. Sureties: Thomas Hillery (g), Ninian Magruder, Sr. (g). Date: 30 March 1749.
- bond of Mary Lisby administratrix of Aaron Lisby. Sureties: Samuel Brashair (p), John Prather, Jr. (p). Date: 29 March 1749.
- inventory of Richard Condon.
- additional accounts of Patrick Redding & his wife Sarah executrix of John Maudesly.
- accounts of Cathrine Condon administratrix of Richard Condon.

5 May. Exhibited from BA:
- will of Robert North, constituting Alexander Lawson (g) executor. Said executor was granted administration. Sureties: James Wardrop (merchant, PG), George Maxwell (merchant, CH). Date: 1749.

10 May. William Tilghman (g, QA) exhibited:
- will of Richard Scrivener, constituting Margaret Scrivener & Joseph Scrivener executors. Also, widow's election. Said executors were granted administration. Sureties: John Lloyd (p), William Coventon (p). Date: 16 March 1748.
- will of Sarah Roe.
- will of Edward Roe, constituting John Roe & Samuel Roe executors. Said executors were granted administration. Sureties: James Knotts (p), Benjamin Thomas (p). Date: 9 March 1748.
- will of John Collins, Sr.
- will of Henry Cielly.

- will of John Webb, constituting William Webb executor. Said executor was granted administration. Sureties: Jonathon Nicols, Hawkins Downes. Date: 19 April 1749.
- bond of Elisabeth Monsieur administratrix of William Monsieur. Surety: Thomas Roe (p). Date: 30 March 1749.
- bond of Sarah Countess administratrix of William Countess. Sureties: Jeremiah Jadin (p), Emanuel Swift (p). Date: 29 March 1749.
- bond of Rebecca Chaires administratrix of Joseph Chaires. Sureties: Matthew Dockery (p), George Smith (p). Date: 27 April 1749.
- bond of Philemon Bannan administrator of Littleton Ward, during minority of Rachel Ward. Sureties: William Bannan (TA), Quilton Bannan (TA). Date: 20 April 1749.
- bond of Sarah Newton administratrix of William Newton. Sureties: Thomas Ringgold (p), William Elliott, Jr. (p). Date: 9 March 1748.

32:245
- bond of Thomas Wilkinson administrator of Christopher Wilkinson, during minority of Richard Wilkinson. Surety: Nathan Wright, Jr. (g). Date: 9 March 1748.
- bond of John Sertain executor of John Collins, Sr. Sureties: Nathan Wright, Jr. (p), John Atkinson (p). Date: 12 March 1748.
- inventory & LoD of Cornelius Comegys.
- additional inventory of Arthur Emory.
- inventory & LoD of John Jones.
- additional inventory & LoD of Robert Norrest Wright.
- inventory & LoD of Timothy Web.
- inventory & LoD of William Daley.
- inventory of John Reed.
- inventory of John Cage.
- inventory of Thomas Beton.
- inventory of Joseph Tryal.

- accounts of Lemon Swift & his wife Frances administratrix of Fairclough Wright.

11 May. Mr. Nehemiah King (SO) to examine accounts of:
- Solomon Long administrator of Wonney McClemmy (SO).

12 May. Nehemiah King (g, SO) exhibited:
- will of Joseph Bounds. Also, bond of Hezekiah Read administrator. Sureties: John Hufington, Jr., Joshua Jackson. Date: 22 March 1748.
- will of Thomas Covington. Also, bond of Abraham Covington (DO) administrator. Sureties: William Jones, Daniel Jones. Date: 17 March 1748.
- will of Benjamin Cottman. Also, bond of William Cottman administrator. Sureties: William Robison, Joseph Reed. Date: 10 March 1748.
- will of John Hardy, constituting Joseph Callaway executor. Said executor was granted administration. Sureties: John Langford, John Callaway. Date: 13 March 1748.
- will of Thomas Covington (Stepney Parish), constituting Mary Covington & John Covington executors. Said executors were granted administration. Sureties: John Shockley, Allan Gray. Date: 20 March 1748.
- will of George Olliver.
- will of James Nicholson.
- will of Robert Hardy, constituting Sarah Hardy executrix. Also, widow's election. Said executrix was granted administration. Sureties: John Goslee, Jacob Cordary. Date: 22 March 1748.
- will of John Hoffington, constituting John Hoffington executor. Said executor was granted administration. Sureties: Michael Disharoon, Hezekiah Read. Date: 22 March 1748.

- will of William Brady. Also, bond of Mary Brady administratrix. Sureties: Thomas Byrd, Purnell Johnson. Date: 23 March 1748.
- will of William Bozman. Also, widow's election. Also, bond of Sarah Bozman acting executrix. Sureties: Booz Wallston, William Roach. Date: 8 April 1749.
- will of Daniel Uniack Dulany, constituting David Polk executor. Said executor was granted administration. Sureties: William Davis (WO), Joseph Allen (WO). Date: 5 April 1749.

32:246
- will of John Turpin, constituting Whittey Turpin executor. Said executor was granted administration. Sureties: John Waters, Sr., Marcy Fountain. Date: 22 April 1749.
- will of Solomon Coulbourn. Also, widow's election. Also, bond of Isaac Coulbourn acting executor. Sureties: John Waters, Sr., Patrick Mackenny. Also, renunciation of Rachell Colbourn (widow), recommending her son Isaac Colbourn. Date: 1 May 1749.
- bond of Susanna Nicholson administratrix of James Nicholson, Sr. Sureties: John Hufington, Hezekiah Read. Date: 22 March 1748.
- bond of Sarah Browne administratrix of Thomas Browne. Sureties: Thomas Dasheill, Thomas Denwood. Date: 24 March 1748.
- bond of Susanna Boardman administratrix of Graves Boardman. Sureties: Willson Ryder, William More, Jr. Date: 29 April 1749.
- bond of John Bell administrator of Christopher Husbands. Sureties: Alexander Maddux, John Shore, Jr. Also, renunciation of Elisabeth Husbands (widow), recommending John Bell. Date: 27 March 1749.
- bond of Thomas Marshall (Northamton Co. VA) administrator of Elisabeth Dashiell. Sureties: William Allen (WO), John Waters (SO). Date: 24 March 1748.
- bond of Zekell Jones administrator

of Thomas Collins. Sureties: John Langford, Jr., Isaac Jones. Date: 20 March 1748.

- bond of Outerbridge Horsey administrator of Robert Bell. Sureties: Samson Wheatley, John Waters. Date: 24 March 1748.
- bond of Eunice Kellett executrix of Roger Kellett. Sureties: John Handy, Thomas Moore. Date: 14 March 1748.
- inventory of John Read, Sr.
- inventory of Edward Corby.
- inventory of Edward Willin.
- inventory of William Richardson.
- inventory of Robert Givan.
- inventory of Henry Ackworth.
- inventory of Lewis Beard.
- inventory of Thomas Larremore.
- inventory of Robert Henderson.
- inventory of Robert Hardy.
- inventory of Wonney McClemmy.
- inventory of Thomas Phithian.
- inventory & LoD of Abraham Covington.
- accounts of Sarah Holbrook & Thomas Holbrook administrators of Thomas Holbrook.

32:247 Thomas Aisquith (g, SM) exhibited:
- will of Henry Greenfield. Also, bond of Thomas Greenfield administrator. Sureties: William Cartwright, Mev. Lock. Date: 7 March 1748/9.
- will of John Hayes.
- will of William Harrison, constituting William Jones & Peter Mugg executors. Said executors were granted administration. Sureties: Charles Smith, Peter Smith. Date: 14 March 1748/9.
- will of Solomon Jones, constituting Cathrine Jones executrix. Also, widow's election. Said executrix was granted administration. Sureties: Denniss Burne, James Burne. Date: 24 April 1749.
- will of Justinian Jordan, constituting Mary Jordan executrix. Also, widow's election. Said executrix was granted

administration. Sureties: Justinian
Jordan, John Llewellin. Date: 3 May
1749.
- bond of Gilbert Ireland
administrator of Hugh Hambleton.
Sureties: John Llewellin, Enoch
Fenwick. Date: 7 March 1748/9.
- bond of Ann Lucus administratrix of
William Lucus. Sureties: William
Lucus, Charles Lucus. Date: 7 March
1748/9.
- bond of Richard Forrest
administrator dbn of Patrick
Forrest. Sureties: William Hebb,
Jr., Matthew Hebb. Date: 27 March
1748/9.
- bond of James Bissco executor of
Sarah Mackey. Sureties: Charles
King, Hugh Hopewell, Jr. Date: 11
April 1749.
- inventory & LoD of John Greaves.
- inventory & LoD of John Tippitt.
- accounts of Elisabeth Blackman
administratrix of Thomas Blackman.
- accounts of Elisabeth Payn executrix
of Thomas Payn.
- accounts of William Joseph & his
wife Elisabeth executrix of Charles
Ganyott.
- accounts of Ann Norriss
administratrix of John Norriss.

Court Session: 9 May 1749

32:248 Docket:
- E.D. for John Tootle & his wife
Rosanna (DO) vs. S.B. for Thomas
Woolford & John Woolford executors
of Roger Woolford. Libel, answer by
Thomas Woolford, general
replication.
- D.D., Jr. for William Grantham & his
wife Sarah (DO) vs. S.B. for
William Kennerly only surviving
executor of Joshua Kennerly. Libel,
answer, general replication.
- S.B. & E.D. for John Hammond Dorsey
& his wife Frances (BA) vs. D.D.,
Jr. for Walter Tolley executor of
James Tolley. Libel, answer,
general replication. Summons to
testify for plaintiff to: Stephen

Court Session: 9 May 1749

Onions, Capt. Tobias Stansbury, Thomas Sligh.

- W.C. for John Medley & his wife Frances (SM) vs. John Smith administrator of Richard Smith. Libel.
- E.D. for William Ryann & his wife Ann & Keziah Bowen (PG) vs. Thomas Dorset executor of John Bowen. Libel.
- D.D., Jr. for Rebecca Clawle, etc. (AA) vs. S.B. for Benjamin Clawle. Libel, answer.
- John Tucker & his wife Elisabeth one of children of Daniel Laughland (CV, dec'd) vs. Comfort Lawland (AA) widow & administratrix of said dec'd. John Gassaway (sheriff, AA) to summon defendant to show cause why she doesn't pay plaintiff her portion of her father's estate, & her portion of estate of Richard (one of children who died under age).
- D.D., Jr. for John West & his wife Elisabeth (AA) vs. Joseph Lane acting executor of Samuel Maccubbin. Libel. John Gassaway (sheriff, AA) to render attachment to defendant.
- 32:249 • Joseph Griffith who married Ann daughter of Thomas Smith (DO, dec'd) vs. William Smith (DO) & John Stevens Smith (DO) executors of said dec'd. Sheriff (DO) to summon defendants to render additional inventory. Additional inventory exhibited. Discontinued.
- Catharine Jennings vs. Robert Debutts (FR) administrator of Rev. Joseph Jennings (PG, now FR). Sheriff (FR) to summon defendant to render accounts.
- Thomas Cockey one of sureties on estate of John Cockey (BA) vs. William Cockey (BA) & Joshua Owings (BA) executors of said dec'd. Sheriff (BA) to summon defendants to render complete inventory. Inventory exhibited. Discontinued.
- John Gassaway (sheriff, AA) to summon Philip Hammond, Esq. (AA) administrator of James Williams (AA)

Court Session: 9 May 1749

to render inventory.
- Tobias Hall administrator of James Ashley (AA) vs. Ann Ashley (widow). John Gassaway (sheriff, AA) to summon defendant to show cause why she conceals estate of dec'd.

Court Session: 1749

13 May. Warrant issued for new appraisers on estate of Constant Pettys.

James Mills administrator of Constant Pettys (AA) vs. Thomas Johnson (AA) & George Bare (AA). Sheriff (AA) to summon defendants to show cause why they conceal estate of dec'd.

15 May. Henry Counsill one of sureties on estate of Trustram Thomas (QA) vs. Jane Thomas (QA) & Benjamin Thomas (QA) executors of said dec'd. Sheriff (QA) to summon defendants to render accounts.

32:250 13 May. Exhibited:
- inventory of Constant Pettey (AA). Administrator: William Mills. It is not received because it was not signed by either creditors or relations.

16 May. Henry Hooper, Jr. (g, DO) exhibited:
- will of Thomas Eccleston.
- will of Dorothy Miller, constituting John Mace executor. Said executor was granted administration. Sureties: Patrick Reed (p), William Tregoe (p). Date: 15 March 1748.
- will of William Standford, constituting Elisabeth Standford executrix. Said executrix was granted administration. Sureties: Thomas Staplefort for William Standford (p), Joseph Wallace (p). Date: 10 April 1749.
- will of David Melvill, Jr., constituting Sarah Melvill executrix. Said executrix was granted administration. Sureties: John Rix (p), John Harper (p). Date: 15 April 1749.

Page 214

Court Session: 1749

- will of Henry Wheeler, constituting Mary Wheeler executrix. Said executrix was granted administration. Sureties: Obadiah Dawson (p), John Wheeler (p). Date: 28 April 1749.
- will of William Broadaway, constituting James Broadaway executor. Said executor was granted administration. Sureties: John Oldfield (p), William Oldfield (p). Date: 2 May 1749.
- will of Jonathan Williams, constituting Hannah Williams executrix. Said executrix was granted administration. Sureties: Daniel Kelley (p), John Linch (p). Date: 11 May 1749.
- bond of Bethewly Ross administratrix of Thomas Ross. Sureties: John Vickars (p), William Jones (p). Date: 15 March 1748.
- bond of Mary Williams administratrix of Isaac Williams. Sureties: John Smith (p), Thomas Hinds (p). Date: 1 May 1749.
- bond of Mary Langfitt administratrix of Jervice Langfitt. Sureties: William Smith (g), John Hicks (g). Date: 12 May 1749.
- bond of Sarah Nevett administratrix of Amos Bunt. Sureties: John Henry (g), Joseph Cox Gray (g). Date: 11 April 1749.
- bond of John Wheeler administrator of Thomas Stinson. Sureties: Solomon Wheeler, Obadiah Dawson. Date: 28 April 1749.
- bond of Sarah Charles administratrix of Isaac Charles. Sureties: John Brown (p), Jacob Charles (p). Date: 20 March 1748.
- bond of Elisabeth Foster administratrix of Nathaniel Foster. Sureties: Joseph Records (p), Daniel Jones (p). Date: 14 April 1749.
- bond of John Caile administrator of Edward Grant. Sureties: Thomas Stuart (g), William Gray (g). Date: 9 May 1749.
- bond of John Eccleston & William Bestpitch administrator of William

Page 215

West. Sureties: Moses Lecompte (g), Edward Pritchard, Jr. (g). Date: 10 April 1749.

- bond of Mary Creek administratrix of John Creek. Sureties: Thomas Thompson (p), William Addams (p). Date: 13 May 1748.
- bond of Thomas Wall administrator of William Wall. Sureties: Thomas Willson (p), Henry Wall (p). Date: 14 April 1749.

32:251

- bond of Rebecca Noble administratrix of Francis Noble. Sureties: Daniel Jones (p), Benjamin Records (p). Date: 14 April 1749.
- bond of Thomas Loockerman administrator of Peter Lecompte. Sureties: Thomas MacKeel (g), Peter Cooke (g). Date: 8 May 1749.
- bond of Ennalls Hooper administrator of John Dunbar. Sureties: John Hicks (g), Francis Hayward, Jr. (g). Date: 1 March 1748.
- bond of Rosannah Tootell administratrix of John Tootell. Sureties: Richard Tootell (g, AA), Thomas Stewart (g, DO). Date: 28 March 1749.
- bond of Patrick Reed administrator of Thomas Howarth. Sureties: Charles Beckwith (p), Patrick Stark (p). Date: 17 March 1748.
- bond of Alice Rawley administratrix of James Rawley. Sureties: William Rawley (p), Daniel Willcox (p). Date: 5 April 1749.
- bond of Mary Langfitt administratrix of Abraham Oneal. Sureties: William Smith (g), John Hicks (g). Date: 12 May 1749.
- bond of Sarah Snelson administratrix of John Snelson. Sureties: Patrick Reed (p), Patrick McCallister (p). Date: 10 April 1749.
- bond of Anne Bond administratrix of Joseph Bond. Sureties: Obediah Dawson (p), John Wheeler (p). Date: 28 April 1749.
- bond of William Cartwright administrator of William Kelley. Sureties: Thomas Hutchings (p), John Cremeen (p). Date: 10 March 1748.

Court Session: 1749

- bond of Rachel Tregoe administratrix of Philip Tregoe. Sureties: George North (p), Thomas North (p). Date: 11 April 1749.
- inventory of Richard Francis.
- additional inventory of Peter Taylor.
- inventory of Roger Wright.
- inventory & LoD of George Staplefort.
- inventory of George Grayham.
- inventory of Richard Harrington.
- inventory & LoD of Cornelius Riley.
- additional inventory of Edward Russum.
- inventory & LoD of James Edmondson.
- additional accounts of Eleanor Eccleston acting executrix of Thomas Eccleston.
- accounts of Mary Perry administratrix of Richard Perry.
- accounts of Daniel Sulivane administrator of Peter Taylor.
- accounts of Edward Trippe executor of Edward Russum.
- accounts of Martha Wright executrix of Edward Wright.
- accounts of John Oldfeild executor of Cornelius Ryley.
- additional accounts of Joannah Alcock administratrix of Burtenwood Alcock.

Benton Harris (g, WO) exhibited:
- will of Ursla Greer. Also, bond of Tabitha Greer administratrix of John Greer executor. Sureties: Daniel Steel, Samuel Williams. Date: 14 March 1748.
- will of John Christopher. Also, widow's election.
- will of William Hayman.
- will of Dormon Donohoe, constituting Cornelius Dickeson executor. Said executor was granted administration. Sureties: William Wharton, Moses Mills. Date: 3 April 1749.
- will of Monseur Cart.
- will of Robert Melvin.
- bond of Nathan Brittingham administrator of Joseph Brittingham. Sureties: Isaac Covington, Obed

32:252

Page 217

Gault. Date: 14 March 1748.
- inventory & LoD of David Hazard.
- inventory of Adam Bell.
- inventory of Col. James Martin.
- accounts of Mary Smith administratrix of William Taylor.
- accounts of Daniel Cox & his wife Rebeckah administratrix of Thomas Purkins.

Gabriel Parker (g, CV) exhibited:
- will of Thomas Breckenden.
- will of John Peters, constituting Fanne Peters executrix. Said executrix was granted administration. Sureties: Richard Chew, Thomas Reynolds. Date: 2 May 1749.
- bond of Benjamin Hungerford administrator of Mathew Howard. Sureties: Richard Day, William Blackburn. Date: 21 March 1748.
- bond of James Williamson administrator of John Booker. Surety: Thomas Ireland, Jr. Date: 24 March 1748.
- bond of Ann Driver administratrix of Martin Driver. Sureties: John Bond, John Gray. Date: 8 April 1749.
- bond of Thomas Reynolds administrator of Daniel Pront. Surety: Thomas Gray. Date: 3 April 1749.
- bond of Sarah Walston administratrix of Henry Walston. Surety: Philip Dowell. Date: 14 April 1749.
- bond of Thomas Reynolds administrator of Mary Cobreth. Surety: William Lyle. Date: 2 May 1749.
- bond of Walter Hellen administrator of John Hellen. Sureties: Samuel Parran, John Dorrumple. Date: 6 May 1749.
- bond of Issabella Hollingshead executrix of Francis Hollingshead. Sureties: Job Hunt, Jacob Deall. Date: 2 May 1749.
- inventory of James Casteel.
- additional inventory of Robert Day.
- additional accounts of Cesar Jones acting executor of Peter Poore.

- accounts of Robert Greeves & his wife Elisabeth administratrix of Barrington Pardo.
- accounts of Ann Day administratrix of Robert Day.
- accounts of Elisabeth Hunt executrix of Thomas Hunt.
- additional accounts of Isaack Monett & his wife Elisabeth administratrix of John Williams.

32:253 Exhibited from BA:
- inventory in BA & in AA of Henry Walters.

17 April. John Darnall (g, FR) exhibited:
- will of William Norris, constituting Elisabeth Norris executrix. Said executrix was granted administration. Sureties: Stephen Hampton, Abraham Neighbours. Date: 13 March 1748.
- will of John Peter Hofman, constituting Apolonia Hofman executrix. Said executrix was granted administration. Sureties: James Storm, Christian Thomas. Date: 11 March 1748.
- will of Charles Scraggs, constituting Elisabeth Scraggs executrix. Said executrix was granted administration. Sureties: Joseph Beall, Stephen Hampton. Date: 18 April 1749.
- will of Thomas Ball.
- will of John Jones, constituting Elisabeth Jones executrix. Said executrix was granted administration. Sureties: John Cramptin, Cleburn Simms. Date: 29 April 1749.
- bond of Mary Tannehill administratrix of William Tannehill. Sureties: James Perry, Ninian Tannehill. Date: 10 May 1749.
- bond of Mary Stoner administratrix of Jacob Stoner. Sureties: John Brawner, Casper Miers. Date 17 January 1748.
- bond of Ann Wickham administratrix of Robert Wickham. Sureties:

Nathaniel Wickham, Jr., Kennedy
Farrell, Capt. Robert Debutts.
Date: 17 January 1748.

- bond of Mary Sparks administratrix
  of Joseph Sparks. Sureties: James
  MacDaniel, William Kerley. Date: 23
  March 1748/9.
- bond of John Lindsey (Frederick Co.
  VA) administrator of John Grist.
  Sureties: Van Swearingen, Joseph
  Chaplin. Date: 22 March 1748.
- bond of Abraham Miller administrator
  of John Hussey. Sureties: Francess
  Wise, Stephen Julien. Date: 11
  March 1748.
- bond of Charles Hedges administrator
  of Catharine Bloomfield. Sureties:
  Joseph Wood, Joseph Hedges. Date:
  10 May 1749.
- bond of William Bowel administrator
  of John Roberts. Surety: Van
  Swearingen. Date: 23 March 1748.
- bond of John Lindsey (Frederick Co.
  VA) administrator of Thomas Alben.
  Sureties: Van Swearingen, Joseph
  Chaplin. Date: 22 March 1748.
- bond of Elisabeth Harden
  administratrix of John Harden.
  Sureties: Velando Griffith, William
  Davis. Date: 7 April 1749.
- accounts of Margaret James executrix
  of John James.

32:254 Exhibited from KE:
- 2nd additional accounts of Philip
  Kennard & William Ringgold executors
  of Sarah Kennard surviving executrix
  of Philip Kennard.

18 May. Exhibited from FR:
- bond of Ann Richardson
  administratrix of William
  Richardson. Sureties: Richard
  Richardson (p, FR), Joseph
  Richardson (p, AA). Date: 18 May
  1749.

Exhibited from BA:
- will of Christopher Grindell.

Thomas Bullen (g, TA) exhibited:
- will of David Kirby, constituting

Elisabeth Kirby & John Kirby
executors. Also, widow's election.
Said executors were granted
administration. Sureties: Michael
Kirby, Richard Kirby. Date: 5 May
1749.

- bond of Deborah Dudley
administratrix of Richard Dudley.
Sureties: Thomas Dudley (p), Thomas
Powell (p). Date 5 May 1749.
- bond of Sarah Perkins administratrix
of Thomas Perkins. Sureties: Samuel
Cockayne (g), Nathaniel Conner (g).
Date: 12 May 1749.
- additional inventory of William
Mackey.
- accounts of Thomas Coben acting
executor of James Coben.
- accounts of Rebeckah Bounton
executrix of Thomas Bounton.
- accounts of Rachel Mackey executrix
of William Mackey.

19 May. Exhibited from DO:
- accounts of William Smith acting
executor of Thomas Smith. Also,
additional inventory.

Exhibited from BA:
- inventory of Thomas Ford.

Exhibited from FR:
- inventory of Samuel Magruder.

Exhibited from AA:
- inventory of John Burle.

20 May. Exhibited from PG:
- will of John Welsh.

22 May. Exhibited from AA:
- LoD on estate of Dr. Samuel
Stringer. Also, accounts of Lydia
Stringer executrix.

32:255   23 May. Exhibited from CH:
- accounts of Jane Parnham & Francis
Parnham administrators of John
Parnham.

24 May. John Thompson (g, CE)
exhibited:

- will of William Manson.
- will of Furgus Smith.
- will of Susannah Ward.
- will of Joshua George.
- will of Robert Money.
- will of Francis Elliot.
- will of James Murreen.
- will of Thomas Polten.
- will of Henry Penington, Sr.
- will of Ann Williams.
- will of Arthur Ellis.
- will of William Ellis.
- will of Hugh Hall.
- will of Jane Phillips.
- bond of James Macky & George Lawson administrators of William Manson. Sureties: Samuel Hill, William Young. Date: 23 August 1748.
- bond of Elenor Dagnal administratrix of John Dagnal. Sureties: William Pearce, James OHagan. Date: 24 March 1748/9.
- bond of Temperance Calk & John Calk administrators of Isaac Calk. Sureties: Oliver Calk, Thomas Baird. Date: 30 January 1748/9.
- bond of Benjamin Chew administrator of Stephen Hollaway. Sureties: John Stump, Benjamin Starrat. Date: 21 November 1748.
- bond of James Redus administrator of Jonathan Leedam. Sureties: Bartholomew Hukill, Richard Hukill, Jr. Date: 20 October 1748.
- bond of John Ricketts administrator of John Harbert. Sureties: Archbald Armstrong, William Wallace. Date: 24 October 1748.
- bond of William Cheek administrator of Henry McDonnaugh. Sureties: John Cheek, Jr., Cornelius Woolliston. Date: 16 February 1748.
- bond of Peter Bayard administrator of Philip Debarres. Sureties: Alexander Lunan, Cornelius Brady. Date: 25 February 1748/9.
- bond of Alexander Lunan & John Beatty administrators of Peter Watts. Sureties: William Farrell, Patrick Keran. Date: 25 February 1748/9.
- bond of Sarah Penington

administratrix of Joseph Penington.
Sureties: Benjamin Benson, James
Copin. Date: 3 March 1748/9.

- bond of Jethro Browne administrator
of Thomas Miller. Sureties: James
Grady, John Jones. Date: 16 March
1748/9.
- bond of Aaron Latham administrator
of Aaron Latham, Jr. Sureties: John
Latham, Jacob Hamm. Date: 28
February 1748/9.
- bond of John Ricketts administrator
of David Leach. Sureties: Thomas
Ricketts, Andrew Barnett. Date: 19
February 1748.
- bond of William Bristow
administrator of Benjamin Tayler.
Sureties: Henry Baker, Peter Boyer.
Date: 4 May 1749.

32:256
- bond of Benjamin Ridge, James Ridge,
& Elisabeth Ridge administrators of
William Ridge. Sureties: John
Ryland, William Jones. Date: 22
January 1748.
- bond of Samuel Gilpin administrator
of Thomas Booth. Sureties: Zebulon
Hollingsworth, John Bing. Date: 23
January 1748.
- bond of George Hardman administrator
of Robert Poage. Sureties: Jacob
Hamm, Ephraim Thompson. Date: 3
April 1749.
- bond of Richard Steadman (Notingham,
Chester Co.) administrator of John
Kempson. Sureties: Thomas
Underhill, Richard Norton, Jr.
Date: 1 May 1749.
- bond of Margaret Brumfield
administratrix of Francis Brumfield.
Sureties: Daniel Brumfield, Edward
Brumfield. Date: 1 May 1749.
- bond of James Smith administrator of
Andrew Ellis. Surety: Martin
Alexander. Date: 1 May 1749.
- bond of James Elliott administrator
of John Brown. Sureties: Andrew
Elliott, William Elliott. Date: 20
April 1749.
- bond of Rebecca Alexander
administratrix of Jacob Alexander.
Sureties: Thomas Beatle, Edward
Armstrong. Date: 20 March 1748/9.

- inventory of Nathan Phillips.
- inventory of Richard Smith.
- inventory of Richard Rutter.
- inventory of Sarah James.
- inventory of Christopher Elsbury.
- inventory & LoD of John Kankey.
- inventory of Joshua Meakins.
- inventory of Archibald Douglas.
- inventory of Mary Douglas.
- inventory of John Melvin.
- inventory of Christian Peters.
- additional inventory of John Ward.
- inventory of Bartholomew Johnson.
- inventory of William Richardson.
- inventory of John Ryland.
- inventory of James Hill.
- inventory of Susanna Ward.
- inventory of John Cox.
- inventory of Brison Blackburn.
- inventory of John Brown.
- inventory of Samuel Archibald.
- inventory of Steven Alloway.
- inventory of William Manson.
- inventory of John Gray.
- inventory & LoD of James Forster.
- inventory & LoD of Forgus Smith.
- LoD on estate of William Beck.
- accounts of Thomas Elliot administrator of Thomas Jordan.
- accounts of Nicholas Hyland executor of William Beck.
- William Baily administrator of William Baily.
- accounts of Mary Ward, Peregrine Ward, & Henry Ward executors of Col. John Ward.
- accounts of Elisabeth McKnitt executrix of John McKnitt
- accounts of Peter Bayard administrator of James Hill.

GENERAL INDEX

Allien
    Benjamin 199
Allinder
    Joseph 140
    Joshua 140
    Mary 140
Allingham
    Philip 182
Allistree
    William 126
Allman
    Abraham 24
    Abram 24
    Joseph 23, 58
    Margaret 24
    Terresa 23
Allnutt
    William 188
Alloway
    Steven 224
Allwell
    Jacob 201
Alman
    Joseph 98, 129, 176
    Teresa 98, 176
    Terressa 129
Alquier
    Jacob 179
Alston
    John 187
Alstone
    Thomas 9, 10
Alvey
    Joseph 126
    Margaret 126
    Margret 9
Amos
    James 112
    William 34, 195
Anderson
    John 192
Anderton
    John 153
Andrew
    Anne 84, 195
    Elisabeth 143
    George 14, 84, 194
    James 144
    Jemima 144
    Richard 84, 195
    William 113, 143
Andrews
    Alice 46, 49, 54
    James 157

William 157
Angley
    John 114, 191
Aprice
    Edward 107
Arbuckel
    William 51
Arbuckle
    William 51
Archer
    Thomas 143
Archibald
    Samuel 142, 224
Ardery
    William 2
Armstrong
    Archbald 222
    Archibald 142
    Edward 58, 223
    Francis 7, 161
    Henry 115
    James 142, 164
    John 24
    Martha 142
    Russell 124
Arnatt
    Andrew 85
    Margaret 85
    William 85
Arnett
    Andrew 37
    Margaret 37
    William 37
Arnold
    David 94
Arono
    James 129
Arrants
    Johannes 163
Ashcraft
    Daniel 76
Ashfeald
    John 186
Ashley
    Ann 206, 214
    James 206, 214
    John 170
    William 170
Ashman
    Elias 99
    George 106
Askin
    Vincent 1, 20, 63,
        90, 117

Besom
    Margaret 46
    Nicholas 46
Bessicks
    Absolem 3
Bestpitch
    William 215
Beton
    Elisabeth 156
    Thomas 156, 208
Bettesworth
    John 48
Bettice
    Robert 44
Bevans
    Anne 90
    Charles 90
Bevine
    Blanford 92
Bickerton
    Joseph 17, 66
Biggs
    John 68, 70
Billings
    Ann 153, 195
    Anne 195
    James 153, 154, 195
Billingsley
    William 107
    William Sumner 107
Billingsly
    Bowles 9
    Rachel 9
    William 74
    William Sumner 74
Bing
    John 223
Binks
    John 91, 116, 118,
        147
Birckhead
    John 91
    Matthew 91
    Neh. 200
    Nehemiah 91, 200
    Samuel 91, 200
    Solomon 134, 145
Bird
    John 43
Birkhead
    John 126
Birmingham
    Charles 62, 156
    John 62, 80, 81

Birmington
    Charles 180
    John 180
Bissco
    James 212
    Thomas 125
Black
    Alex. 48
Blackbourn
    Briceson 142
    Robert 142
Blackburn
    Brison 224
    Edward 188
    William 188, 218
Blackiston
    Ebenezar 130, 172
    John 168
Blackman
    Elisabeth 106, 212
    Thomas 106, 116,
        212
Blackstone
    Richard 116, 122,
        130, 133
    Thomas 116, 122,
        130, 133
Blackwood
    John 25
Bladen
    Thomas 49
Blake
    John Sayer 179
    Richard 63, 86,
        133, 174
    Susannah 63, 133,
        174
Blakiston
    Ebenezar 32, 109
    Sarah 32, 109
Blakistone
    Ebenezar 60
Blewer
    James 47, 118, 151
    John 33
    Margaret 47, 118,
        151
Blewett
    John 38, 135
Blewitt
    John 162
Bloomfield
    Catharine 220
    Isaac 167

Page 230

Blunt
  Samuel 7
Boardman
  Graves 192, 210
  Susanna 210
Bodien
  Henry 11, 102
Body
  Stephen 53, 67, 77
Bond
  Anne 216
  George 134
  John 34, 116, 218
  Joseph 216
  Peter 204
  Thomas 34, 75, 112
  Uriah 187
  William 194
Bonner
  Matthew 142
Booker
  John 218
Boon
  Abraham 156
  Benjamin 113, 156
  Esther 156
  Isaac 173
  Jacob 144
  John 9
  Margaret 81
Boone
  Benjamin 113
  Thomas 83, 94, 105
Booth
  Thomas 128, 223
Bordley
  Stephen 6, 28, 30,
    48, 55, 66, 104,
    139, 140, 166,
    185
  Thomas 136
Bostock
  Thomas 22
Boswell
  Benjamin 19, 29
Boswith
  John 201
Botfield
  Mesheck 200
  Sarah 200
Boulding
  James 127, 142, 163
  Richard 127
Boulen

  Edman 146
Boult
  Ann 27
  Kenelm 27
  Thomas 27
Bounds
  Joseph 209
Bounton
  Mary 206
  Rebeckah 114, 193,
    221
  Samuel 206
  Thomas 114, 124,
    193, 206, 221
Bourne
  Jesse 10, 51, 124,
    149
Boushel
  Peter 142
Bowdle
  Loftus 1
Bowel
  William 220
Bowen
  Benjamin 160
  Charles 142
  Edward 160
  Elisabeth 174, 189
  James 164
  John 152, 159, 172,
    179, 198, 213
  Jonas 34
  Kesiah 159
  Kessiah 152, 198
  Keziah 213
  Martha 34, 70
  Samuel 34, 70, 201
Bower
  William 102
Bowers
  Jane 169
  William 169, 170
Bowie
  Allen 61
  James 150
  John 178
  Thomas 150
Bowly
  Daniel 80
  Elisabeth 80
Bowyer
  Robert 65, 110
Boyce
  Daniel 139

R. 177
Ro. 199
Roger 105, 111, 140
Boyd
    Archibald 59
    George 10
Boyer
    Elisabeth 59
    James 59, 60
    Margaret 59
    Peter 223
    William 59, 103
Bozman
    Risdon 22, 50
    Sarah 210
    Thomas 8, 23, 26,
        50
    William 210
Bradburne
    William 36, 68
Bradford
    Elisabeth 177
    George 112
    John 80, 177
    William 55
Brady
    Cornelius 128, 222
    Mary 210
    William 210
Bramble
    Jacob 14
    Thomas 84
Branan
    John 39
Brannock
    Frances 40, 181
    John 40, 84, 181
Branthwaite
    Joseph 143
Brashair
    Samuel 207
Bratten
    Hugh 31
    James 189
    William 189
Bratton
    William 189
Brawner
    Henry 119, 132
    John 219
Breading
    James 163
Breckenden
    Thomas 218

Bredell
    Elisabeth 119
    James Stephen 119,
        139, 200
Breeding
    Matthew 116, 204
Brent
    Jane 25, 69
    William 25, 69
Brereton
    Henry 99
    Richard 137
Brerewood
    Thomas 34
Bright
    James 40
    William 167
Brightwell
    Anne 123, 206
    Peter 121, 123,
        162, 206
Brisco
    Alexander 11
Briscoe
    John 104
Bristow
    George 86, 128
    William 57, 163,
        223
Brittingham
    Joseph 217
    Nathan 217
Broadaway
    James 215
    Samuel 161
    Sarah 115
    William 215
Brome
    John 35, 189
Bromwell
    Jacob 131
Brook
    John 64
    Martha 64
Brooke
    Isaac 69
    John 10, 149
    Martha 149
    Thomas 131
Brookes
    Henry 202
    James 143
    John 163
Brooks

Bunt
    Amos 215
Burch
    John 104
    Rachael 4
    William 4
Burdus
    Richard 111, 121,
        135, 138, 139
Burgess
    Charles 178
    Martha 178
    Richard 157
    Samuel 1, 63, 90
    William 206
Burgin
    John 168, 169
Burk
    John 61
    Tobias 163
Burke
    Sarah 200
Burle
    John 73, 221
Burley
    Mary 137
Burn
    Michall 10
    Pricilla 10
    Simon 150, 183
    William 153
Burne
    Denniss 211
    James 67, 211
    Michael 39
    Pricilla 39
Burney
    Thomas 55, 108
Burross
    Pricilla 13
    Prissilla 65
    Warren 13, 65
Burroughs
    Hannah 123, 202
    Thomas 123, 202
    William 113, 123,
        156, 202
Burrus
    Presilla 80
    Warren 80
Burt
    Henry 155
Burton
    Frances 31

John 3, 31, 33, 57
Joshua 31
William 31
Busey
    John 69, 132, 149
    Sarah 132, 149
Bussey
    Charles 13
    Hezekiah 11, 70
    Rachel 10, 70
Butler
    Elisabeth 16, 20
    Henry 12, 55, 79,
        176, 189
    Peter 16, 20
    Susanna 12, 55, 79
    Susannah 176, 189
Butt
    John 106
Butterworth
    Isaac 34, 112, 176,
        189, 205
    Jane 34
Buttler
    Chrispin 60
    Crispin 32
Byrd
    Thomas 210

Cadle
    Ann 41, 55
    Benjamin 41, 55
Cage
    John 195, 208
Cahell
    John 4
Cail
    John 39
Caile
    John 215
Caill
    John 153
Calder
    James 109, 120,
        129, 130, 136,
        152, 168, 175,
        178, 193, 194
Caldwell
    James 73
    John 4, 82, 83, 94,
        105, 117
    Joshua 83, 94, 105
    Mary 4, 82, 83, 94,

105
Rachel 73
Rachell 110
Samuel 83, 94, 105
William 33
Calk
Ann 136, 162
Isaac 222
John 222
Oliver 222
Peter 72, 136, 162
Temperance 222
Callahan
James 91
Callaway
John 209
Joseph 74, 209
Camden
Hary 46
Campbel
Mary 30
Campbell
John 30, 120, 135,
139, 162
Mary 163
Canady
Edward 169
Mary 127
Candler
John 162
Cannon
Catherine 152
Hugh 14
Thomas 152, 181
Carback
Philip 141
Valentine 201
Card
Abraham 35, 63,
148, 164
Mary 35, 148, 164
Carey
Dennis 40, 84
Esther 40
Carlise
John 78
Carlisle
John 141
Carman
John 44, 156
William 196
Carmichall
William 43
Carpenter

Elisabeth 182
John 182
Carr
Jane 142
Thomas 55
William 142, 164
Carradine
Thomas 41
Carroll
Charles 32, 138,
182, 193, 201
Denton 117, 145,
206
Dom. 87
Dominick 26, 95
Sarah 117
Carrow
Henry 61
Carruthers
Ann 63, 87, 95
Francis 63, 87, 95
Cart
Monseur 217
Carter
Jacob 81
John 61, 108
Robert 55
Sarah 61
Valentine 61
Cartman
Caleb 143
Cartwright
William 211, 216
Carvin
Edward 179
John 179
Carwarden
Edward 11, 32
Casey
James 88
Casson
Henry 61
John 61
Casteel
James 188, 218
Catteratt
Thomas 99
Caulk
Isaac 32
Jacob 32, 58
Cawood
John 197, 199
Mary 197, 199
Stephen 197, 199

Andrew 1, 20, 25
John 20
Richard 1, 25
Cielly
 Henry 207
Circum
 Thomas 172
Cissell
 Luke 126
 Matthew 146
Civil
 Thomas 46, 81
Clagett
 Charles 97
 John 8
 Sabrit 8
Clarak
 Thomas 145
Clarey
 Benjamin 26
Clark
 Abraham 6, 18, 28,
  44, 47
 Elisabeth 44
 George 59
 Jane 176, 189, 205
 Laurence 176, 205
 Lawrence 189
 Leonard 104
 Margaret 6, 18, 28,
  47
 Mary 59
 Robert 166
 Sarah 22
 Susanna 18, 28, 47
 Susannah 6
 Thomas 6, 18, 22,
  28, 47, 124,
  134, 179, 207
 William 23
Clarke
 Mary 29
 Peter 29
Clarkson
 Phillis 37, 85
 Robert 37, 85
 William 152
Clary
 Benjamin 30
Clawle
 Benjamin 167, 172,
  185, 198, 213
 Cean 167
 Gilbert 167

Rebecca 167, 172,
 184, 198, 213
Clayland
 Elisabeth 161
 James 50, 119, 145
 Jannet 88
 John 155
 Lambert 161, 200
 Thomas 13
Claypoole
 James 32
Clayton
 George 59
 John 58, 59
 Solomon 156
 William 22
Claywell
 Lucretia 3, 38,
  135, 162
 Peter 3, 30, 38,
  57, 135, 162
 Selby 3
Clement
 William 160
Clemons
 Ann 189
 William 189
Clifton
 George 133
 John 40, 133
 Michael 133
 Rachel 133
 Sarah 40, 133
 William 40, 84
Clocker
 Daniel 68
Clouds
 Elisabeth 4, 17, 91
 Nicholas 17, 130,
  140, 144, 158,
  171
Clough
 Nathaniel 144, 196
 Susanna 144
Cloyd
 Elisabeth 184
Clubb
 John 1
 Matthew 1
Coale
 William 155
Coan
 John 175
Coarse

James 169
Coastin
  Roase 151
Coben
  <torn> 124
  James 124, 161, 221
  Thomas 221
Cobreth
  Mary 218
Coburn
  Anne 37, 85
  Samuel 85
  Stephen 37
Cockayne
  Samuel 191, 221
Cockey
  Elisabeth 33
  John 4, 33, 70, 71,
    83, 89, 94, 97,
    98, 105, 106,
    131, 167, 187,
    190, 194, 199,
    213
  Thomas 33, 71, 83,
    89, 94, 105,
    187, 198, 213
  William 33, 71, 74,
    83, 89, 94, 97,
    105, 106, 131,
    187, 190, 199,
    213
Cockran
  John 58
Cocks
  William 167
Cockson
  John 24
Coe
  Daniel 56
Coffen
  Thomas 80
Coffin
  John 56
  Mary 119, 120
  Thomas 56, 119,
    120, 139
Coghill
  Smallwood 149
Cohee
  James 156, 197
  Martha 156
Colbourn
  Isaac 210
  Rachell 210

Cole
  Jacob 131
  James 186, 204
  John 12, 97, 107,
    196
  Peter 169
  Samuel 85
Coleman
  Frances 34
  John 50
  Josiah 50
  Margaret 50
  Mordecai 96
  Nicholas 34, 112
  Thomas 1
Coley
  Anne 169
  Nathaniel 169
Collier
  Evans 183
  George 192
Collins
  John 114, 207, 208
  Samuel 33, 51
  Thomas 211
  William 33
Colson
  Henry 22
Colston
  Henry 118
Colvill
  Thomas 98, 148
Combest
  Jacob 34
  John 34
Comegys
  C. 155
  Cornelius 155, 208
  E. 155
  Mary 155
Comerford
  Peter 206
Commerford
  Peter 96, 115
Compton
  Matthew 89
Condon
  Cathrine 149, 207
  Richard 149, 207
Connant
  Charles 96
  Dorcas 64
  Robert 64
Conner

John 66
Nathaniel 115, 221
Connerly
  Martha 15
  Owen 15
Connor
  Bridget 161
  Charles 17, 71, 81
  John 161
  Mary 71
Cooch
  Thomas 127
Cook
  Hercules 10
  James 44, 123, 197
  John 99, 181
  Joshua 197
  Thomas 154
Cooke
  Ambrose 162
  Hercules 44
  John 98, 121
  Mary 162
  Peter 216
  Richard 125
Cooker
  John 128, 163
Cooksey
  William 148
Cooley
  Nathaniel 170
Coombs
  Bartholomew 165
  Bennet 165
Coop
  Richard 160
Cooper
  Amelia 9
  Basil 165
  Bassil 125
  Benjamin 2
  John 24, 127, 130,
    164
  Lydia 19
  Samuel 19, 55
  Thomas 9
Copin
  James 223
Copper
  George 169
Copsey
  Roger 72
  William 4
Copson

John 148
Corby
  Edward 211
Cordary
  Daniel 182
  Jacob 209
Corke
  Mary 8, 19
  Peter 8, 19
Corley
  Anne 182
  Edward 182
Cornish
  Samuel 15
Corse
  James 102, 175
  John 102
Cosden
  Alphonso 127, 164
Coster
  William 188
Costin
  Henry 5, 17, 22
  Isaac 118, 151
  Rebecca 5, 22
  Richard 113
  Rose 118
Cotman
  Joseph 110
Cotter
  William 89
Cottman
  Benjamin 191, 209
  Joseph 192
  William 209
Couch
  Joseph 41
Coulbourn
  Isaac 210
  Solomon 210
  William 150
Coulston
  John 160, 205
Counsill
  Henry 214
Countess
  Sarah 208
  William 208
Countiss
  Peter 3, 82, 101,
    108
Course
  James 175
Coursey

William 41, 113
Court
    Joseph 58
Courts
    Charles 187
    John 117, 164
    William 117
Covel
    Mary 52
Covell
    Jeremiah 64
    Mary 64
Coventon
    William 207
Covill
    Mary 8
Covington
    Abraham 150, 209, 211
    Henry 91, 114
    Isaac 217
    Isbel 150
    John 91, 114, 156, 209
    Mary 209
    Thomas 209
Covinton
    Jeremiah 59
Cowman
    Joseph 98, 137
Cox
    Daniel 190, 218
    James 20
    John 163, 224
    Mary 117, 176, 193
    Rebecca 190
    Rebeckah 218
    William 117, 151, 163, 164, 176, 193
Cramphin
    Basil 149, 178
    Henry 16, 109, 132, 149
    Mary 16, 109, 132, 149
Crampkin
    John 99
Cramptin
    John 219
Crandall
    Francis 64
Cranford
    Elisabeth 51

James 51, 75
Thomas 35, 149
Craxon
    John 63, 90
Creagh
    Patrick 5
Creek
    John 15, 216
    Mary 216
Cremeen
    Elisabeth 194
    John 194, 216
Crocker
    Robert 1, 87
Crockett
    John 100, 102
    Mary 102
Croker
    Robert 63
Cromwell
    Joseph 75
Crook
    Anne 76, 88
    John 76, 88
Crooke
    Charles 201
Crouch
    James 56
Crow
    Isaac 21, 60
    James 54
    John 54
    William 12, 21, 31, 60
Croxall
    Charles 179
    James Carroll 179
    Richard 179
Crump
    Robert 196
Cuckoe
    John 161, 190
Cullen
    James 14, 37, 86
    William 14, 37, 41, 86
Cullinbur
    Thomas 10
Cumming
    William 6, 28, 29, 91, 94, 104, 146, 190
Cunningham
    Daniel 62, 169

Hannah 62, 169
Cunninghame
  John 131, 186
Curlett
  John 107
Currier
  Rachel 144, 159,
    177
  William 144, 159,
    177
Curtis
  Rebecca 64, 82
  Thomas 44, 64, 82
Cutler
  Ann 42, 72
  William 42, 72

Dagnal
  Elenor 222
  John 222
Dailey
  John 5
Daintry
  Richard 125, 146
Daley
  Elisabeth 179
  James 5, 64
  John 64
  William 179, 208
Dallam
  Richard 3, 12, 34,
    79, 205
  William 34, 48,
    145, 187, 201,
    205
Dallas
  Robert 32
  Walter 201
Daly
  Hugh 16
Dames
  William 7
Dare
  Mary 188
Darnall
  John 157, 166, 219
Dash
  Rebecca 46
  Richard 46
Dasheill
  Thomas 210
Dashiel
  George 151

Matthias 82
William 82
Dashiell
  Clement 191
  Elisabeth 210
  George 46, 110, 191
  Isaac 191
  Isabella 74
  Louther 191
  Mathias 65
  William 65, 74
Dashiells
  Isabella 46
  William 46
Dashiels
  George 118
Davidge
  Hudson 12
Davies
  Allen 20
  James 45, 116
  Jonathan 20
Davis
  Anne 149
  Benjamin 2
  Charles 38
  Daniel 56, 89
  Edward 59, 103
  Elisabeth 56
  John 7, 17, 56,
    136, 144, 162,
    173, 196
  Jonathan 53
  Joseph 38
  Marg. 116
  Margaret 100
  Mary 7, 191
  Phillip 32
  Robert 137
  Tabitha 121
  Thomas 24, 121,
    127, 147
  Walter 149
  William 82, 89,
    149, 162, 210,
    220
Davison
  Elisabeth 150
  John 150
Daviss
  Thomas 175
Dawhely
  John 181
Dawkins

Ann 74, 86
Dorcas 124, 164
Dorcus 35
William 35, 63,
124, 164
Dawney
Daniel 186
Dawson
Edward 178
George 100
John 99
Obadiah 215
Obediah 216
Day
Ann 126, 173, 219
Edward 34, 55, 135
Francis 8, 127,
135, 157
John 34, 135
Richard 218
Robert 126, 149,
173, 218, 219
Samuell 93
Deadman
Mathew 32, 59
Deal
James 46
Deale
Hanah 150
Deall
Jacob 218
Dean
Henry 40, 84
John 40
Deane
John 194
Deaver
Richard 27, 147
Thomas 79
Deavor
Daniel 78, 141
Mary 54
Richard 54
Thomas 56
Deavour
Assilla 27
Sarah 116
William 116
Debarres
Philip 222
Debutts
Richard 185
Robert 53, 56, 167,
182, 198, 213,

220
Deflin
John 180
Deford
Jacob 35
John 179
Dehorty
Catharine 195
Catherine 152
George 152, 195
John 152, 195
Demington
Francis 204
Demmitt
Sophia 141
Thomas 141
Dempster
John 43
Dening
John 59
Denning
George 102, 103,
194
Isabell 194
Issabell 102
Dent
Hanah 61
Peter 13, 16, 17,
20, 36, 42, 46,
60, 69, 76, 83,
87, 92, 97, 99,
109, 121, 123,
132, 149, 162,
167, 177, 178,
182, 183, 202,
203, 206, 207
William 165
Denton
John 141, 160, 176,
189
William 112, 141,
175, 176, 189
Denwood
Thomas 192, 210
Dern
William 70
Deven
Walter 23
Devenish
Ishmael 101
Dever
Richard 68
Deverson
Humphry 20

Dew
    Robert 32, 62
Dick
    James 137, 170
Dickenson
    Daniel 166
    Hannah 101
Dickeson
    Abraham 133
    Charles 117
    Cornelius 217
    Edward 133
Dickinson
    Charles 131
    Daniel 166
    William 124, 191
Dickson
    James 10
Digges
    Ignatius 167
Dirickson
    William 178
Disharoon
    Levin 13
    Michael 209
Dixon
    Isaac 110
    Joshua 199
    Sarah 110
    Thomas 110, 151
Dobbins
    Robert 112
    William 112
Dobson
    Adam 128
    Hannah 96
    Henry 86
    Isaac 96, 131, 161
    James 35
    Jonathan 44
    Richard 128, 164
Dockery
    Matthew 113, 122,
       179, 196, 208
    Thomas 113
Dodd
    Sarah 6, 18, 28, 47
Dodson
    James 188
    John 188
Dolby
    John 139, 203
    Peter 139, 162, 203
Don

    Mark 164
Donahue
    Roger 160
Donaldson
    Elisabeth 104, 125
    John 104, 125
    Parson 104
    Susanna 104
Donohoe
    Dormon 217
Donohue
    Roger 187
Doran
    Patrick 22, 29, 49,
      66, 77, 93, 105,
      111, 121, 139,
      157, 171
Dorman
    Henry 165
    Samuel 117
Dorrell
    Nicholas 24
Dorrumple
    John 218
Dorset
    Thomas 159, 172,
      184, 198, 213
Dorsett
    Thomas 152
Dorsey
    Anne 137
    Basil 56
    Caleb 56, 138
    Comfort 112, 160
    Edward 6, 28, 47,
      48, 66, 75, 122,
      158, 184
    Ely 75, 138
    Frances 110, 111,
      122, 140, 158,
      171, 184, 197,
      212
    Greenberry 186
    Henry 137
    John 75, 138
    John Hammond 110,
      111, 112, 122,
      140, 158, 171,
      184, 197, 212
    Joshua 137
    Nicholas 137
    Philemon 137
    Sarah 53
Dossey

John 91, 92, 118, 147
   Mary 92, 116
Dotson
   James 51
   John 200
Dougal
   James 89
Douglas
   Archibald 224
   Mary 224
   William 127
Douglass
   Archibald 128, 129
   Benjamin 89, 117, 173, 187
   Elisabeth 89, 173, 187
   George 59, 129
   John 62
   Joseph 129
   Mary 128
   Susannah 129
Doull
   James 16, 33
Dove
   Rachel 2
   Richard 2
Dowell
   John 52, 95
   Peter 12, 34, 140
   Philip 66, 218
   Susanna 52, 95
Dowen
   Dennis 186
Downes
   Hawkins 208
   Henry 88, 144, 167
   John 43, 155
   Mary 167
   Nathaniel 122, 156
Downing
   Anne 149
   James 149, 162
Downs
   Charles 113
   Henry 60
   John 81, 123
   Mary 60
   Nathaniel 43
   William 29, 60
Doxkey
   Agnes 10
   William 10

Doyne
   Edward Aloysius 164
Drake
   Francis 10, 35, 64, 126
Drane
   Elisabeth 5
   James 5
Draper
   Alce 118
   Alice 151
   Rachel 41, 182
   William 41, 84, 118, 151, 182
Drayden 10
Dreadman
   Mathew 32
Drewry
   George 40
Driver
   Ann 218
   Martin 100, 218
   Mathew 152
Drury
   Charles 51, 111, 147
Dudley
   Deborah 221
   Richard 96, 119, 174, 221
   Sa. 174
   Samuel 50, 96, 119, 206, 207
   Thomas 8, 50, 221
Dudly
   Thomas 23
Due
   Robert 12, 103
Duff
   Simon 5, 202
Dugliss
   Mary 115
   Thomas 115
Duke
   Christopher 204
   James 189
Dulany
   Daniel 94, 111, 122, 140, 158, 171, 192, 198
   Daniel Uniack 210
   Dennis 53
   Michael 43
   Sarah 67, 77, 102

Page 245

Ellis
Andrew 223
Arthur 128, 222
Philip 6, 19, 28,
48, 66, 77, 93
William 128, 222
Ellitt
James 177
Ellot
Thomas 128
Elsbury
Christopher 224
Elsey
John 33
Elzey
John 192
Emory
Arthur 101, 113,
123, 208
James 113, 123
John 43, 113
Sarah 123
Thomas 41, 113
William 123, 156
Ennalls
Ann 39
Henry 39, 84
Joseph 39, 71, 153
Thomas 39, 85, 180
Ennas
Rebeckah 3
Ennis
Rebecka 139
Rebeckah 108
William 3, 13, 108,
139
Ennolls
Joseph 74
Ensor
John 112
Erwin
Joseph 116
Robert 116
William 116
Esgate
Caleb 80, 156, 180
Esgatte
Dorthy 156
Eskridge
Samuel 199
Eubanks
Richard 8, 101,
119, 174
Tamson 8, 119, 174

Evans
James 63, 87, 153
John 109, 181
Jonathan 31, 109,
181
Mary 144
Richard 57, 143
Rowland 7
Stephen 53
Evens
Ebenezar 162
Everitt
John 59
Richard 188
Everrest
William 126
Everrist
William 189
Evitts
John 75, 157
Ewart
James 13
Ewing
Alexander 129
Joshua 163
Nathaniel 129, 163
Rachel 163
William 163

Falconar
John 169
Fanning
John 36, 68
Fardrey
Nicholas 92
Farguson
Colin 103
Collin 62
Elen 32
Farlow
Thomas 79
Farmer
Peter 3, 12
Thomas 130, 169
Farrell
Edmond 17
John 17
Kennedy 220
Mary 17
William 17, 44, 222
Farrill
Thomas 192
Farrington

James 142
John 176
Nathaniel 215
William 176
Fottrell
Edward 107
Fountain
Marcy 4, 210
Mary 4
Nicholas 4
Samuel 41
Fouracres
John 22
Fowke
Gerrard 1, 25, 69,
203
Sarah 1, 25, 69
Fowler
John 183
Patrick 123
Thomas 106
Foxson
Ann 14
James 14, 84
Fraizer
Alexander 91
Daniel 10
James 10
Francis
Burton 101
Richard 217
Franklin
Isabel 98
Jacob 46
John 46, 98
Richard 98, 155
Thomas 34
William 119
Frazier
John 79, 165, 187
Frederick
John 12, 147
Freeman
Ann 23, 24, 58
Isaac 60
James 51, 52, 90,
132, 148
Jane 90, 131
Janet 52
John 116
William 23, 24, 58
French
Otho 92
Frisby

Mary 55, 108, 141,
160
Peregrine 55, 161
Fryer
Elisabeth 35
John 35
Richard 35
Furgoe
Alexander 39
Mazotin 39
Furnis
James 151
Furroner
Edward 57

Gale
George 192, 193
John 151
Levin 126, 193
Margaret 192
Matthias 126, 192
Gallion
Samuel 99
Galloway
Jane 136
John 48, 89, 98,
137, 193
Samuel 98, 155, 177
William 195
Ganyott
Charles 98, 212
Gardiner
Clement 9, 118, 147
Elenor 147
Elinor 118
John 68, 193
Gardner
Ignatius 1, 20, 63,
90, 117
John 188
William 188
Garey
Jane 50
William 50
Garland
Henry 205
William 205
Garnet
Joseph 32
Garnett
Joseph 130
Garrett
Amos 79, 201

103, 111, 121

Goodin
  Benjamin 140
Gooding
  Samuel 169
Goodrick
  Edward 25, 53
  Francis 25, 53
  Mary 25, 53
Goodson
  William 11
Goodwin
  Ceasar 88
  Lyde 98, 194
  Marmaduke 80
Gordon
  George 138
  Robert 158
Gorsuch
  Charles 68, 160
  John 68
  Sarah 68
  William 68
Gorswick
  Aquila 201
Goslee
  James 4
  John 209
  Mary 4
  Thomas 192
Gossey
  James 142
  John 142
Gough
  John 173, 189
Gould
  James 176, 203
  Mirime 203
  Mirimi 176
  Richard 61, 113
Gover
  Ephraim 46, 56
  Philip 56
  Samuel 56
Gow
  Anne 186
  James 131, 186, 204
Grady
  James 223
Graham
  John 59
Grainger
  Edward 154
  John 7

William 154
Granger
  Ann 90
  Christopher 90, 91
  Edward 152
  Martha 62
  Thomas 62, 108
  William 102, 152
Granohan
  Mary 59
  Thomas 59
Grant
  Edward 215
Grantham
  Sarah 103, 106,
    111, 122, 140,
    158, 171, 184,
    197, 212
  William 83, 103,
    106, 111, 122,
    140, 158, 171,
    184, 197, 212
Graves
  Ann 146
  Elenor 146
  George 146, 147,
    159, 171, 184,
    197
  John 36, 68, 146,
    147, 159, 171,
    184, 197
  Margaret 36, 147,
    159, 171, 184,
    198
  Margret 68
  William 160
Gravs
  Sarah 160
Gray
  Allan 209
  Andrew 88, 120
  Bridget 155
  Bridgett 52
  Elisabeth 31
  Jacob 88, 120
  James 31, 60, 117,
    192
  Jane 124
  Jean 192
  John 52, 75, 116,
    128, 155, 181,
    188, 192, 218,
    224
  Joseph 119

Guilder
    Hukill 163
Guishard
    Anthony 171
Gully
    Rachel 96
    Thomas 96
Gunby
    James 4
    John 4
Guy Williams
    John 134, 145, 161,
        179
Guy
    Sarah 15
    William 15
Guyther
    Owen 91
Gwinap
    Richard 168, 170
Gwinn
    Joseph 117

Hack
    Spencer 51
    Tunstall 51
Hackett
    Michael 103
Haddaway
    William Webb 2, 131
Hadder
    Anthony 101
    Mary 101
Hadley
    Edward 196
    John 88, 175, 197
    Thomas 196
Hagar
    Jonathan 124
Hager
    Robert 91, 92, 115,
        125
Haislip
    Robert 19, 29
Hall
    Avarilla 55
    Cuthbert 169, 170
    Daniel 59
    David 134, 161,
        179, 207
    Edward 9
    George 42, 103
    Hugh 222

John 9, 48, 49, 55,
    101, 122, 144,
    160, 161, 164,
    204, 205
Joseph 86
Lawrence 101, 114,
    164
Parker 12, 34, 54,
    55
Richard 114, 145,
    206
Risetta 169
Robert 50
Rosetta 175
Sarah 134, 161,
    179, 207
Tobias 206, 214
William 101, 164,
    168
Hambleton
    Hugh 212
    Mary 68
    Philemon 76, 205
    William 68
Hamell
    John 67
Hamersley
    Francis 11, 25
    Mary 11, 25
Hamersly
    Francis 119
    Mary 119
Hamill
    John 19, 29, 132,
        145, 159
Hamilton
    James 70, 99, 126,
        165
    John 32
    Mary Ann 70, 99
Hamm
    Jacob 223
Hammond
    John 17
    Mary 6, 19, 29
    Mordecai 27, 45,
        138
    Nicholas 6, 19, 29
    Philip 17, 203, 213
    William 106, 170,
        194
Hamond
    Phil. 48
Hampton

Harrison
  Benjamin 200
  James 99
  John 45, 73
  Joseph Hanson 53
  Richard 200
  Samuel 97
  Thomas 55
  William 27, 92, 211
Harrout
  Peter 148
Harryman
  Charles 201
  John 201
  Samuel 179
Hart
  John 108
Harvey
  James 62
  John 3, 65, 80,
    135, 162
  Martha 3, 65, 135,
    162
  Mary 80
  Richard 86
  William 86
Harwood
  John 191
  Mary 191
  Robert 58, 115
  Solomon 96
  Thomas 71, 206
Hatfield
  John 152
Hattan
  John 12
Hatton
  Bartholomew 25
  Joseph 97, 121,
    182, 202, 203
  Lucy 97, 182, 202,
    203
Hawkins
  Deborah 166, 199
  Ernault 196
  Hanah 109
  Hannah 136, 143
  John 75, 97, 166,
    200
  Robert 109, 136,
    143
  Sarah 21, 41, 119,
    148
  Thomas 21, 41, 119,

                   148
Hayden
  Clement 38
  Elisabeth 125
  Francis 125, 165
  George 38, 199
  Richard 39
Hayes
  John 211
Hayman
  Isaac 51
  James 51
  William 217
Hays
  Charles 13, 69
  John 35, 62
  Nathaniel 69
  Sarah 35, 62
  William 64
Hayward
  Francis 216
  John 40
  Thomas 74
Hazard
  David 178, 203, 218
  John 178, 203
  William 178, 203
Heard
  James 27, 127, 165
  John 27, 68, 127,
    164, 165
  Luke 125
  Matthew 27
Heath
  Abraham 51, 166
  Charles 164
  James Paul 56
Heaven
  John 186
Hebb
  Edward Hilard 68
  Edward Hillard 107
  Edward Hilliard 27
  Matthew 212
  Thomas 108
  William 108, 212
Hedges
  Andrew 124, 134
  Charles 220
  Joseph 134, 220
  William 70, 97
Heighe
  James 63, 164, 174,
    188, 200

Hellen
    Elisabeth 174
    John 174, 218
    Penelope 74, 86
    Peter 51, 74, 86,
      100
    Richard 174, 200
    Susannah 51, 100
    Walter 218
Helsby
    Thomas 114
Henderson
    Daniel 192
    Jacob 19
    Mary 160, 177
    Robert 192, 211
    Thomas 177
Hendon
    Hannah 201
Hendrakesen
    Sarah 59
Hendrickson
    Adam 175
Henly
    Christopher 168
    James 168
    Joseph 79
Henn
    <torn>iel 124
    John 124, 154
Henratee
    Patrick 60
Henry
    John 131, 153, 194,
      215
    Robert Jenckins 151
    Robert Jenkins 51,
      131
Hepburn
    John 78, 121
Herbert
    Mathew 68
Hern
    (N) 38, 49, 66, 77,
      93
    Debborah 118
    Deborah 73, 151
    Edward 38, 49, 66,
      73, 77, 93, 110,
      118, 151
Hernly
    Darby 141
Herrington
    David 22, 156

    Rachel 96, 176
    William 96, 176
Hewit
    Ber. 177
Hickman
    Elisabeth 12
    John 12
    William 116
Hicks
    Ann 17
    Anne 5
    Charles 87, 101
    Giles 5, 17, 115
    James 4, 17
    John 5, 153, 182,
      215, 216
    Joseph 87, 145
    Mary 115
    Thomas 182
Higgens
    Mary 127
    Stephen 127
Higgins
    John 176
    Stephen 135, 157
Higgs
    Aaron 72
    Agnes 72
Hill
    Anne 37
    Daniel 37
    Elisabeth 97, 120
    Hutten 31, 97, 120
    James 128, 224
    Samuel 142, 222
    William 201
Hilleary
    Eleanor 107
    Thomas 16
Hillen
    Elisabeth 141
    Solomon 141
Hillery
    Eleanor 16
    Thomas 16, 207
Hillton
    Francis 125
Hilton
    Andrew 9, 39
    John 9
Hindman
    Jacob 44
Hinds
    Thomas 215

Hines
  Benjamin 35
Hitch
  Elget 151
  Elgett 96, 118, 150
  Elisabeth 118, 151
  Leavin 151
  Solomon 150, 151
Hitchcock
  George 98, 112
Hitchcoke
  Mary 98
Hobbs
  James 113
  John 26, 30
Hodgkin
  Thomas 167
Hodgkins
  Charles 91
  Thomas 9
Hodgson
  Joseph 128, 142
  Solomon 98, 148
Hodson
  John 36, 85
  Roger 182
Hoffington
  John 209
Hofman
  Apolonia 219
  John Peter 219
Hoker
  Hannah 129
  Henry 129
Holbrook
  Sarah 150, 190, 211
  Thomas 150, 151,
    190, 211
Holeadger
  John 32
Holland
  Cordelia 79, 95,
    108, 189, 194
  Frances 194
  Francis 54, 79, 95,
    108, 159, 189,
    194
  Henretter 160
  John 142
  Margaret 96
  Richard 95, 96
  Susanna 79, 95, 99
  Susannah 189, 194
  Thomas 95

William 86
Hollandsworth
  George 205
Hollaway
  Stephen 222
Hollerin
  Erassmus 22
Holliday
  Robert 201
Hollingshead
  Francis 100, 218
  Issabella 218
  Jane 100
Hollingsworth
  Isaac 143, 173
  Rosanna 143
  Zebulon 128, 223
Hollis
  William 55, 79
Hollonshead
  Francis 188
Holly
  John 20
  Thomas 36
Hollyday
  Catharine 35
  Ja. 49
  James 123
  Jonathan 35
  Mary 98
  Robert 98
  William 98
Holman
  Edward 175
  Rosetta 175
Holt
  Arthur 36
Honey
  Sarah 81, 114
  Valentine 81, 114
Hooper
  Enn. 121, 139, 140
  Ennalls 14, 36, 39,
    42, 68, 71, 83,
    130, 148, 152,
    154, 180, 216
  Henry 6, 18, 28,
    47, 166, 167,
    170, 180, 181,
    194, 195, 214
  James 154
  Roger 83
Hopewell
  Hugh 9, 27, 39, 212

John 72
Joseph 9, 72, 125, 133, 165
Thomas Francis 116, 133, 165
Thomas Francis 72
Hopkins
Betty 13
Gerrard 39
Hampton 13, 80
John 40
Joseph 117, 145, 160
Luke 9, 39
Philip 102
Samuel 50
William 161
Hopper
John 92
Mary Ann 113
William 196
Horn
John 9, 72, 107, 133, 165
Horney
Philemon 50, 174
Horsey
John 51
Nathaniel 74, 150, 167, 183
Outerbridge 110, 150, 167, 183, 211
Hosier
Hannah 170, 178
Henry 168, 178
Hoult
John 191
How
Elisabeth 64, 86
Robert 64, 86
Howard
Ambrose 102
Anne 20
Benjamin 138, 181, 185, 198
Catharine 181, 185, 198
Catherine 138, 185
Henry 137
John 18, 89, 138, 181, 185, 198
Mathew 218
Matthew 181, 185,

198
Ruth 75
Samuel 138
Howarth
Thomas 216
Howarton
John 2
Howell
John 188
Howerton
John 35
Hubbert
Daniel 14, 41
Mary 14
Samuel 153
Titus 41
Hudson
Catharine 91
Elisabeth 200
John 200
Mary 13, 38
Richard 13, 38
William 91, 157
Hufington
John 209, 210
Huggins
John 112, 189
Hughes
Thomas 138
William 186
Hughs
Hannah 186
Henry 160
John 15
Hukill
Bartholomew 222
Richard 222
Hull
Elisabeth 169
Ferdinando 169
Humphris
Thomas 182
Humphry
Thomas 59
Hungerford
Benjamin 218
Thomas 117
Hunt
Elisabeth 97, 219
Job 97, 218
John 147
Thomas 97, 116, 219
Hunter
John 46, 49

111, 122, 140,
　158, 171, 184,
　197, 212
William 83, 103,
　106, 111, 122,
　140, 158, 171,
　184, 197, 212
Kennett
　Bridgett 3, 38
　Martin 3, 38
Kent
　Abs. 51, 75
　Absolom 75
　Elisabeth 51, 75
　Joseph 188
Keran
　Patrick 32, 62,
　　103, 222
Kerley
　William 220
Kershaw
　James 188
Kersner
　Anna 124
　George 173
　John George 124
Key
　Mary 122
　Richard 122
Keys
　Richard 144, 157
Kibble
　Robert 205
Killgore
　Thomas 127
King
　Capel 14, 64, 149
　Capell 33
　Charles 212
　John 116, 149
　Nehemiah 1, 4, 33,
　　46, 51, 65, 73,
　　82, 96, 109,
　　117, 118, 135,
　　150, 165, 167,
　　176, 182, 190,
　　191, 209
　R. 165
　Richard 25, 53
　Robert 33
　Sarah 116
　Thomas 88, 157
　Whittington 151
Kininmont

Ambrose 196
John 50, 196
Joseph 72
Samuel 50
Kinnaston
　Edward 48
Kirby
　Benjamin 17, 130,
　　140, 158, 171
　David 220
　Elisabeth 221
　John 221
　Lambert 206
　Michael 221
　Richard 221
Kirkland
　William 157
KirkPatrick
　John 142
Kirkwood
　John 92, 132, 149
Kitely
　William 160
Knight
　Elisabeth 177
　Sarah 187
　William 121
Knock
　Daniell 59
Knott
　Edward 206
　Ignatius 125, 165
　John 146, 165
　William 146
Knotts
　James 207
Knox
　George 163

Lamb
　Francis 11
Lambden
　Thomas 88
Lamphier
　Thomas 131, 148
Lancake
　Francis 162
Lancaster
　Joseph 20
Lane
　James 165
　Joseph 30, 36, 57,
　　136, 140, 147,

158, 181, 185,
198, 213
Rebecca 165
Richard 35, 75
Sarah 75
Timothy 5, 64, 81,
82
Lang
John 190
Langfitt
Jarvis 83
Jervice 215
Mary 215, 216
Langford
John 209, 211
Langril
James 37
Sarah 37
Langston
John 3, 120
Mary 120
Lanham
Edward 123
John 13
Lankford
Benjamin 150
Large
Philip 69, 83, 149
Sollomey 202
Solomey 69
Solomy 149
Larramur
James 192
Judeth 192
Thomas 192
Larremore
Thomas 211
Latham
Aaron 223
John 223
Lathinghouse
Mary 3, 31, 135
William 3, 31, 135
Laughland
Comfort 168, 172,
185, 198
Daniel 168, 172,
185, 198, 213
Richard 168, 172,
185, 198, 213
Lawland
Comfort 213
Lawson
Alex. 48

Alexander 207
David 87, 95
George 142, 222
John 95
Layton
Nicholas 153
Richard 153
William 153
Leach
David 223
Leack
Henry 14
Leak
Henry 14
Lecompt
Mary 37
Moses 37
Nehemiah 40
Lecompte
Anthony 87
John 46, 50, 67, 77
Mary 15, 85
Moses 15, 85, 216
Peter 216
Philemon 181
Samuel 46, 50, 66,
77
Lee
Alexander 80
Ann 54
Anna Maria 99
Arthur 54
Elisabeth 121
Hancock 121
James 162
John 206
Lewis 16
Philip 178, 202
Stephen 39
Thomas 44, 178,
179, 202
Leech
David 128
Rebecca 81
Richard 81, 156,
173
Leedam
Jonathan 222
Legg
John 81
Legross
Elias 48
Lemmon
Neil 112

Letchworth
 Joseph 123
Levin
 Lewis 5
Lewis
 George 204
 Henry 99
 John 16, 123, 154,
   162, 180, 182
 Rosannah 153, 182
 Thomas 180
 William 31, 66
 Winifred 123
Linch
 Alexander 57
 Edmund 169
 John 215
Lindow
 Margaret 1
 Margrett 33
Lindsey
 John 220
 Patrick 155, 180
 Sarah 155
Lingan
 George 75
Linsey
 James 139
 Margrett 139
Linstead
 Hannah 137
 Richard 138, 157
Linton
 John Evans 80
Lisby
 Aaron 207
 Mary 207
Little
 John 17
Littleton
 Mark 153
 William 152, 153
Llewellin
 John 212
Lloyd
 Edward 65
 John 207
 Robert 155
 Thomas 170
Loage
 Manassah 142
Lock
 Mev. 211
 Meverel 79

Meverell 39, 45, 49
Meveril 10, 39
 William 54
Lockwood
 Samuel 137
Logsdon
 John 74, 75, 97
 William 74
Loney
 James 79
Long
 John 34, 42, 204
 Margaret 76, 78, 94
 Sewall 76, 78, 94
 Solomon 151, 209
Longo
 Elisabeth 3
 James 3
Longoe
 James 31
Loockerman
 Dorothy 6, 18, 28,
   48, 66, 77, 93,
   111, 121
 Jacob 161
 Thomas 216
Looker
 William 107, 125
Lookerman
 Dorothy 103
Lord Baltimore
   49 1
Lorton
 John 133
 Susanna 133
Louther
 Elisabeth 45
 Robert 45
Love
 William 186
Loveday
 Grace 45, 73
 Sarah 101
 Thomas 45, 73, 96
Lovejoy
 Joseph 123, 202
Low
 James 112
Lowe
 James 131
 John 131, 174
 Mary 131
 Nicholas 50
Lowes

Henry 118
Loyd
Edward 135
Lucas
James 96, 117
John 9
Lucus
Ann 212
Charles 212
William 212
Ludel
Robert 9
Lum
Michael 163
Lunan
Alexander 222
Lusby
Edward 46
Thomas 138, 157
Lux
Darby 20, 48
Richard 7, 155
Lyle
William 51, 174,
218
Lyles
Robert 174, 188
William 174
Lynch
Anne 11
Edmund 11
Hugh 206
Nicholas 11
Rebeckah 206
Thomas 11
Lyon
Henry 42, 72
William 147

MacClanahan
Nathaniel 136
Maccomas
Alexander 56
Daniel 195
Deborah 56
Hannah 195
William 187, 195
Maccomus
Alexander 79
Deborah 79
Macconikin
John 141
Maccroy

Thomas 55
Maccubbin
Nicholas 45
Samuel 30, 36, 57,
136, 140, 147,
159, 181, 185,
198, 213
Macdanald
James 3
Macdaniel
Daniel 2, 23
Eve 23, 50
James 220
Macdaniell
Daniell 50
Mace
John 214
Macfall
Elisabeth 28
James 28
Macgren
Patrick 24
Mackall
James 35
Mackbee
Jayne 16
Mackclanan
James 96
MacKeel
Thomas 216
Mackenny
Patrick 210
Mackewn
William 24
Mackey
Araminta 106
Hezekiah 118
James 142
Mr. 94
Philip 118
Rachel 114, 193,
221
Robert 118
Sarah 115, 125, 212
Stephen 115, 125,
146, 200
William 114, 118,
128, 193, 221
Mackie
William 95
Macklannen
James 5
Macknatt
Elisabeth 194

William 194
Macky
  Araminta 54
  James 222
  John 54
Macnamara
  Elisabeth 67
  Laurence 67
Macnemara
  Elisabeth 6, 19,
    25, 28, 46, 50,
    145, 159
  Laurence 145, 159
  Lawrence 6, 19, 25,
    28, 46, 50
  Margaret 32
Macotter
  Alexander 101
  Hezekiah 114
Macquain
  Dugal 34
Maddox
  Benjamin 204
  John 11, 146, 148
  Samuel 11
Maddux
  Alexander 210
Maffett
  Agnes 57
  Samuel 57
  William 57
Maffitt
  Samuel 87
Magee
  John 95
Magraw
  Robert 110
Magruder
  Alexander 17, 60
  Cave 87
  Enoch 157
  James 87, 162
  John 18
  Josiah 185
  Nathaniel 18, 35
  Ninian 207
  Robert 39
  Samuel 185, 186,
    221
  Sarah 39
  Susanna 17, 60
  Zachariah 185
Malden
  Sarah 14, 64

Maloney
  James 84
Malony
  John 20
Mankin
  James 136, 148, 186
  Jane 89, 173, 187
  Stephen 116, 132,
    204
  Tubman 89, 90, 173,
    187
Manning
  Cornelius 115
  John 126, 146
  Thomas 14
Mansfield
  Samuel 59
Manson
  William 222, 224
Mapp
  Francis 46, 49, 54,
    137
Marbury
  Luke 97
March
  Geor Henry 55
  George Henry 34
  John 11
Mariarte
  Ninian 202
Marrall
  Luke 92
  Mary 92
Marrott
  John 40
Marsh
  John 194
Marshall
  Isaac 80
  Mary 204
  Richard 206
  Sarah 206
  Thomas 210
  William 99
Martin
  Ann 1
  Edward 166, 175
  James 119, 190, 218
  John 117, 119
  Mary 119, 190
  Samuel 45, 73
  Samuell 73
  Thomas 191
  William 1, 45, 73,

James 142
McFall
    Elisabeth 29
McGrahan
    Patrick 58
McGuire
    Hugh 126
Mchard
    Hugh 59
McHone
    Elisabeth 21, 41
    Robert 21, 41
McKeel
    Thomas 84, 180
McKey
    John 32
McKnitt
    Elisabeth 142, 224
    John 142, 143, 224
McKormack
    Christian 41
Mckorn
    Elisabeth 90
    Robert 90
McLachlan
    James 128
McLaughlin
    Thomas 173
McLoud
    Alexander 20
McNeille
    Neille 43
McPherson
    William 186, 203
Mcquire
    Hugh 97
Meakins
    Elisabeth 127
    Joshua 127, 163,
        224
Means
    Edward 163
Mears
    Adam 15
Meconikin
    John 88
Meconnekin
    John 43
Meddice
    Godfry 182
Meddis
    Godfrey 153
    Sarah 153
Medford

Butman 58, 103
    George 58
    Sarah 58
Medley
    Clement 126, 146
    Frances 154, 159,
        172, 184, 198,
        213
    John 146, 154, 159,
        165, 172, 184,
        198, 213
    Sarah 146
Meeds
    William 123
Meeks
    Benjamin 130
Mekin
    William 199
Meloney
    James 40
    Michael 115
Meloyd
    Thomas 43
Melvill
    David 214
    Sarah 214
Melvin
    John 224
    Robert 217
Meradith
    Thomas 123
Mercer
    Robert 24
Merchant
    James 45, 73
    Mary 45, 73
Meredith
    Rees 48, 49
Metcalf
    John 175
Mezick
    Elihu 192
Mickell
    John 146
    Tersia 146
    William 146
Middagh
    Johannes 124
    John 70, 124
Middlemore
    Josias 49
Middleton
    James 1, 20, 63,
        90, 117

Samuel 71, 117
William 20
Midgley
  Thomas 190
Miers
  Casper 219
Milbourn
  John 117
Miles
  Margaret 9
  William 33, 124,
    167
Miller
  Abraham 220
  Ann 8, 100
  Anne 36, 109, 132,
    149
  Arthur 130
  Dorethy 152
  Dorothy 214
  Elisabeth 12
  John 9, 152, 182
  Martha 21, 60
  Michael 103
  Michaell 58
  Nathaniel 12
  Samuel 21, 58, 60
  Thomas 223
Millis
  John 75
Millit
  William 32
Mills
  James 9, 125, 214
  Moses 217
  Peter 166
  William 40, 214
Milner
  Godfrey 6, 19, 29,
    48, 89
  Isaac 7, 48, 89
Milstead
  Edward 186
Milton
  Isaac 168
Milvill
  John 57
Mirick
  Roger 24
Mitchell
  Collin 131
  Francis 92
  Joshua 57, 139
  Thomas 141, 150,

192
Mockbee
  Jane 33
Mollehone
  John 68
Monett
  Elisabeth 219
  Isaack 219
Money
  Ann 22
  Elisabeth 87
  Hesther 143
  John 163
  Patrick 22
  Robert 87, 222
  Thomas 87
Monro
  Thomas 20
Monsieur
  Elisabeth 208
  William 208
Moody
  James 123, 144
  Mary 123
Moor
  Charles 61
  Josias 15
Moore
  Isaac 152
  James 141
  John 19, 29, 67,
    145, 159
  Josias 37, 85
  Thomas 211
More
  William 182, 210
Morgan
  Edward 79, 128
  Henry 5, 18, 28,
    47, 67, 77, 94
  Samuel 161
  Thomas 35, 188
Morison
  Thomas 48
Morisson
  Thomas 28
Morris
  Daniel 39
  Darby 27
  Robert 22
  Samuel 59
Morrison
  John 99
  Thomas 6, 19, 66,

Nennam
    Joseph 10
    Sarah 10
Nevett
    Sarah 194, 215
    Thomas 40, 153, 194
Nevil
    John 61, 81, 114,
      173
    William 22
Nevill
    William 44, 144,
      157
Nevitt
    Tabitha 113, 203
    William 113, 203
Newbold
    Purnall 52
    Purnell 33
    Thomas 33, 52
Newman
    Boxley 113
    Daniel 113
    Henry 165
    Joseph 108, 113,
      156
    Sarah 156
    William 113
Newnam
    Joseph 43
    Sarah 43, 44
    William 43
Newton
    Anne 207
    Joseph 202, 207
    Sarah 208
    William 180, 208
Nichollson
    Nathan 141
Nichols
    Nathan 194
Nicholson
    James 209, 210
    John 115
    Joseph 7, 168
    Nathan 141
    Susanna 210
    Thomas 123
Nickolls
    Sarah 39, 45, 49
    Thomas 39, 45, 49
Nicolls
    John 154, 194
Nicols

Henry 191
    Jeremiah 8
    Jonathon 208
Night
    John 9
Nilson
    Jared 142
Noble
    Francis 216
    George 115
    Rebecca 216
Nock
    George 176
    Mary 176
Noell
    Septimus 46, 50,
      66, 77
Norfolk
    John 97
Norman
    John 144
    Nicholas 64, 137
    Sarah 62
    Thomas 62, 108, 136
Norris
    Benjamin 13
    Elisabeth 219
    Thomas 177, 204
    William 219
Norriss
    Ann 125, 212
    John 125, 126, 212
    Mark 125
    Thomas 72
North
    George 217
    Robert 106, 186,
      207
    Thomas 217
Norton
    Alexander 20
    Anne 20
    Richard 223
Norwood
    Philip 138
Notingham
    Athanasius 27
    Stephen 27
Nowall
    John 201
Nowland
    Edward 112
Nuttawell
    Richard 15

Nutter
Thomas 152

Odall
Rignall 177
Odell
Elisabeth 184
William 184
Offutt
Mary 157
Nathaniel 157
Ogden
John 181
Mary 91, 94, 106
Nehemiah 106
Ogle
Joseph 90, 132
Ogleby
James 24, 58
John 24, 58
Ohagan
James 193, 222
Mary 193
Oldfeild
John 217
Oldfield
Henry 8
John 152, 215
William 215
Olliver
George 209
Oneal
Abraham 216
Henry 186
James 162, 178, 203
John 162
Peter 91
Rachel 162, 203
Onion
Stephen 166, 175,
184, 197
Onions
Stephen 213
Opey
Linsy 126
Opie
LIndsy 107
Orchard
John 16, 69
Orem
Andrew 114
Orman
Samuel 186, 201

Orme
John 202
Osborn
James 12
John 42
Samuel 81
William 81, 108
Osborne
Samuel 166
William 166
Oshahanus
William 3
Oston
Thomas 76
Otley
James 65, 133
Sarah 65
Ottley
James 110
Sarah 110
Oumphrie
Thomas 59
Ousler
Edward 184
Outten
Abraham 2, 80, 139
Rhoda 80
Owen
Francis 40, 84, 85
Thomas 178, 202
Owens
Joseph 9
Joshua 83
Sarah 44, 123
Owing
Alexander 95
Joshua 94
Nathaniel 95
Owings
John 16
Joshua 33, 71, 89,
97, 105, 106,
131, 187, 199,
213
Samuel 48, 52
Oxenham
Mary 92, 115
William 92, 113,
115

Paca
Aquila 49, 177,
179, 180, 195

Mary 68, 132
Perry 68, 132
St. Leeger 85
St. Leger 15, 38
Pattyson
  Mary 69
  Perry 69
Pavett
  Isaac 39
  Joseph 39
Payn
  Elisabeth 125, 212
  Mathew 80
  Thomas 125, 164,
    212
Pearce
  Beatrice 62
  Benjamin 163
  Daniel 178
  Elisabeth 178
  Gideon 62
  John 126
  Mary 32
  William 128, 222
Pearkins
  Ebenezar 102
Peek
  Peter 27
Peirce
  Richard 63
  William 63
Peirpoint
  Charles 157, 170
  Francis 5, 170
  Henry 170
  Joseph 157, 170
  Sidney 157
Pelley
  Constant 70
  James 69, 100, 167,
    178
  Jane 167
  Jayne 69, 178
Pembrook
  John 10
Penhallow
  Joseph 54
Penington
  Henry 222
  John 87, 163
  Joseph 127, 163,
    223
  Mary 87
  Sarah 222

Pennington
  John 58, 63
  Mary 63
Perce
  Ann 67
  John 67
Perigoe
  Avarilla 70
Perkins
  David 70, 78, 94,
    105, 111, 122,
    140, 158
  Ebenezar 175
  James 166
  Rebecca 70, 78, 94,
    105, 111, 122,
    140, 158
  Rebekah 158
  Sarah 158, 221
  Thomas 190, 191,
    221
  William 48
Perray
  Mary 154
  Ricahrd 154
  Richard 154
  William 15
Perrie
  Hugh 25, 148
  Margaret 148, 174
  Samuel 148, 174
Perrigoe
  Avarilla 34
  Edward 34, 70
Perry
  Hugh 37
  James 219
  Mary 195, 217
  Richard 37, 195,
    217
Persons
  Tabitha 43
  Thomas 22, 43
Peterkin
  David 46, 50, 66,
    77
  James 37, 84
  Mary 37
Peters
  Christian 163, 224
  Fanne 218
  John 218
  Unite 163
Pettey

Constant 214
Pettibone
    Phillip 31
Pettys
    Constant 214
Phebus
    George 110, 177,
        193
    Samuel 177, 193
Phebuss
    George 82
    Samuel 82
Phelp
    William 92
Phelps
    Rachel 157, 171
    Richard 157
    William 157, 171,
        205
Phethian
    Randol 192
    Thomas 192
Philbert
    John 165
Philips
    Sarah 195
    Thomas 195
Phillips
    Catherine 38
    Elinor 15
    James 79
    Jane 222
    John 151
    Nathan 163, 224
    Susanna 151
    Thomas 15, 41, 85
    William 38
Phillups
    Elinor 85
    Sarah 14
    Thomas 14
Philpot
    Brian 194
    Bryan 48
    John 48
Phippard
    Mary 36, 68
    William 36, 68
Phithian
    Thomas 211
Pibon
    John 99
Piburn
    Benjamin 99

Jacob 99
Pickerin
    Francis 161
Pickering
    Francis 115
Pike
    Ann 203
    James 115, 203
Pile
    Joseph 36, 53, 68
Piles
    Francis 69
    Leonard 69
Pindell
    Elisabeth 71
    Philip 71
    Thomas 71
Pindle
    Philip 206
Piner
    Edward 158
Pinkstone
    Peter 124
Piper
    Christopher 46, 73,
        110
    Joseph 182
    Rachell 46, 110
Pirkins
    David 47, 168
    Rebecca 168
    Rebeckah 56
    Thomas 56
Pitt
    John 70, 84, 195
Plant
    James 117
Ploughman
    John 206
Plummer
    James 76
    Jerom 98
    John 101
    Philemon 76
Poage
    Robert 223
Pointer
    Rackleff 139
    Rackliff 120
    Turvil 139
    Turvill 3, 120
Polk
    David 150, 210
Polland

John 208
Joseph 209
Patrick 214, 216
Rosannah 6, 18, 28, 47
Rench
Peter 124, 178
Renshaw
Jane 166
Thomas 166
Ress
William 141
Revell
Charles 33
Randall 33
William 33
Revill
Charles 51
Rew
Isaac 161, 191
Mary 161
Reymer
Ebenezar 94
Sarah 94
Reynell
John 48
Reyner
Ebenezar 47, 70, 78, 105, 111, 122, 140, 158
Sarah 47, 70, 78, 105, 111, 122, 140, 158
Reynolds
John 24
Margaret 24, 26, 98
Richard 24
Robert 4
Thomas 26, 98, 126, 187, 218
William 202
Rhodes
Henry 201
Thomas 51, 100
Ricaud
Benjamin 169
Rice
William 32
Rich
Peter 143, 144, 153
Richard
James 112
Richardson
Ann 66, 81, 220

Anne 129
Anthony 23, 26
Benjamin 192
Joseph 102, 220
Lydia 66
Margaret 43, 81, 114
Mark 66, 98
Mary 66
Nathan 201
Rachel 21, 30, 49, 66, 183, 185
Richard 21, 30, 49, 66, 183, 185, 220
Robart 190
Robert 190
Sam. 49
Thomas 21, 30, 49, 60, 66, 81, 183, 185
William 43, 62, 96, 192, 211, 220, 224
Rickard
Benjamin 130
Rickcords
Ann 73
John 73
Rickets
David 57
John 24, 128
Richard 93
Thomas 24, 128, 142
Ricketts
David 24, 127, 128, 163
John 222, 223
Joseph 169
Thomas 86, 223
Rickford
Thomas 32
Rickords
John 13, 110
Riddle
Cornelius 155
Rider
Charles 195
John 195
Ridge
Benjamin 223
Elisabeth 223
Henry 131, 187, 204
James 223

Willson 210
Wilson 192
Ryland
 John 142, 223, 224
 Rebecca 142
 Thomas 57, 127
Ryley
 Cornelius 217
Ryon
 Ann 152
 Dennis 73
 Elinor 73
 Joseph 69
 William 152

Sadd
 William 13
Safford
 Abram 86
 James 84, 86
Sallaway
 John 156, 172
Salmon
 William 13, 31
Samons
 Ann 150
Sanders
 Edward 187
 Mary 58
 Thomas 58, 60, 187
 Virlinda 187, 204
Sandford
 Charles 136
 Cornelius 148
Sands
 Robert 131
 Thomas 62, 155
Sanford
 Astin 200
Santee
 Nathaniel 7, 92, 119
 Sarah 92
Sargent
 James 170
Sarjant
 John 12
Satterfield
 Joseph 144, 156
 Nathanael 144
 William 144
Satyr
 Henry 98

Saunders
 William 22
Sayers
 James 24, 69
Scandrel
 William 41
Scandrell
 William 41
Scarbrough
 John 13
Scarff
 James 12
 Nicholas 2, 51
 Sarah 2, 51
Scarffe
 James 79
Scholfield
 Benjamin 31
Schoolfield
 Joseph 31
 Sarah 31
Scott
 Alexander 163
 Andrew 36, 82
 Anne 20
 Burridge 1, 15
 Charles 59, 103, 109
 Daniel 48
 Day 110, 192
 James 20
 Mary 36, 82, 164, 189
 Sarah 59, 109
 Solomon 180
 Walter 20
 William 20
Scotten
 Mary 42
 Richard 42, 62
 Thomas 42
Scotton
 John 123
Scraggs
 Charles 219
 Elisabeth 219
Scrivener
 Joseph 207
 Margaret 207
 Richard 207
Scymeter
 Jonathan 114
Sea
 Jemima 117

Robert 117
Seaders
   John 115
Seal
   Jonathan 199
   Samuel 163
Sedar
   John 200
Sedgwick
   Richard 87, 128
Sedwick
   Benjamin 2, 63
   Betty 2, 63
Seele
   Richard 93
Segwick
   Richard 58
Selby
   John 57
   Martha 38, 89, 135,
     162
   Mary 57
   Nathan 51, 111, 147
   Parker 57, 120
   William 38, 89,
     135, 162
Semans
   Solomon 59
Semmes
   Francis 148
   James 19
   Joseph Milburn 19,
     71, 94
   Joseph Milburne 78
   Marmaduke 19
Semms
   Joseph Milburn 78
   Rachell 78
Seney
   Ann 61, 114
   Benjamin 114
   Solomon 61, 114,
     123
Serjant
   John 175, 201
Serjeant
   Michael 62
Sertain
   John 208
Sesson
   William 25
Seth
   John 101
Severson

Thomas 164
Sevil
   Thomas 44
Sewall
   Charles 7
Sexton
   Andrew 85
   Rachel 85
Seymeter
   Jonathan 43, 44
Shakespear
   Joseph 190
Shanks
   James 200
Sharp
   <torn> 124
   Ann 191, 193
   James 113, 116
   Katherine 113
   Peter 191
   Samuel 124, 191,
     193
   William 134, 145,
     191
Sharples
   William 116
Shaw
   Christopher Durbin
     55
   Elisabeth 203
   John 201, 203
   Thomas 175, 199
   William 190, 199,
     201
Sheild
   Solomon 137
   William 202
Sheilds
   Elisabeth 141
   Solomon 141
Sherburn
   Clare 91
   Nicholas 91
Sheredine
   Thomas 12, 48, 49,
     79, 175
Sherwin
   Mary 40
   Robert 40, 84, 154
   Stephen 40
Sherwood
   John 76, 205
   Mary 7
Shey

Lydia 99, 221
Samuel 99, 138, 221
Stuart
  Thomas 215
Studham
  John 7, 45, 76, 87
Stull
  Peter 134
Stump
  John 127, 128, 222
Sturgis
  Joshua 80
Sudler
  Joseph 62, 80, 135
Sulivane
  Daniel 40, 153, 217
Sumner
  William 149
Surman
  Isaac 193
  John 110, 117
  Mary 110
  William 151, 193
Sutton
  Alexander 169
  Ashbury 71
  Benjamin 156
  Christopher 175
  James 169
Swann
  Burch 9
  James 74, 104, 107
  Mary 74, 107
  Robert 88, 138
Swearingen
  Van 178, 220
Sweat
  Varty 174
Sweatman
  Stephen 44
Sweatnam
  Stephen 4
Swift
  Emanuel 156, 208
  Frances 174, 209
  Gideon 113, 156
  John 113
  Lemon 174, 209
  Richard 156
Sworden
  Henry 2, 44
Swormstedt
  Nicholas 97, 100
Sylvester

Benjamin 155
Sympson
  Amos 157
  Thomas 25
  William 24

Ta\<unreadable\>
  Jonathon 93
Talbott
  Daniel 10, 35
  Elisabeth 10
  Joseph 10
  Martha 178
  Richard 10, 178
Taman
  Sarah 12
Tannehill
  Mary 219
  Ninian 219
  William 219
Tanner
  Thomas 62
Tanyhill
  William 56
Tarvin
  Elisabeth 90
  Richard 90
Tayler
  Benjamin 223
Taylor
  Elisabeth 6, 18,
    28, 36, 47, 66,
    77, 84, 86, 93,
    103, 111, 121
  Everard 97, 174
  Henry 156
  Isable 114
  Issabell 200
  James 57
  John 95, 112, 125,
    143, 156
  Jonathan 8, 23, 50,
    107, 200
  Joseph 34, 97, 108
  Mary 143
  Peter 153, 180, 217
  Phillip 130
  Rebeckah 200
  Reuben 4
  Sarah 97
  Thomas 14, 24
  William 12, 218
Tayman

Tibbit
James 168
Tibbitt
James 130
Richard 130
Samuel 130
Tiffin
William 194
Tilden
John 11, 32, 129
Tilghman
Edward 91
James 87
Matthew 87
Richard 197
William 3, 4, 10,
16, 17, 21, 23,
35, 42, 46, 52,
61, 63, 80, 81,
82, 91, 101,
108, 113, 120,
122, 134, 143,
155, 159, 172,
174, 176, 179,
195, 199, 203,
204, 207
Tillard
William 52, 182
Tilley
Rebecca 89, 94, 105
Tillotson
John 196
Tilly
Rebecca 20
Tingle
Daniel 2
Elisabeth 2
Hugh 2
Tippens
Edward 61, 114
Mary 61
Thomas 61
Tippitt
John 212
Tipton
John 52
Toadvine
William 38, 135
Todd
John 138
Lance 48
Lancelott 73
Mary 84
Michael 84, 154

Ruth 138
Todvine
William 162
Tole
John 27, 39
Roger 27
Timothy 92
Tolley
James 110, 111,
122, 140, 158,
171, 184, 197,
212
Walter 110, 111,
122, 140, 141,
158, 171, 184,
197, 212
Tongue
Ann 52
James 52
Thomas 127
Toon
John 146
Tootel
John 111, 122
Rosannah 111, 122
Tootell
John 54, 64, 67,
77, 93, 139,
158, 171, 197,
216
Richard 5, 6, 19,
29, 216
Rosannah 54, 64,
67, 77, 93, 139,
158, 171, 197,
216
Tootle
John 105, 184, 212
Rosanna 212
Rosannah 105, 184
Topham
Christopher 31
Tounsend
James 4
Jane 4
Townsend
Charles 162
James 44
Littleton 3
Train
James 110
Travers
Henry 83
Tredway

Thomas 195
Tregoe
    Anne 37, 85
    James 153
    Philip 217
    Rachel 217
    William 37, 85, 86,
      214
Trew
    William 102, 129
Tribe
    John 131
Trickey
    Mary 22
    Thomas 22, 62
Trippe
    Anne 37
    Edward 37, 83, 195,
      217
    Elisabeth 7
    John 37
    William 7
Troth
    William 124
Trott
    Ann 170
    James 170
    John 170
    Sarah 5
    Thomas 5, 18
Trotten
    Elisabeth 53, 54,
      67, 77
    Luke 53, 54, 67,
      77, 204
Trotter
    Ephraim 37
Truelock
    Henry 12, 130
Truitt
    Elisabeth 2
    George 2, 120
Trussitt
    Rhodam 25
Tryal
    Joseph 196, 208
Tucker
    Elisabeth 168, 172,
      185, 198, 213
    John 168, 172, 185,
      198, 202, 213
    Nathaniel 122, 144
    Sele 170
    Thomas 170, 202

Tull
    Elisabeth 82, 118,
      151
    George 51, 82, 110,
      118, 151
Tully
    Michael 1, 63, 87
    Rachel 1, 63, 87
    Thomas 17
Tunis
    Edward 15
Tunstall
    John 4, 51
Turbutt
    Richard 72
    William 64, 91
Turner
    Elisabeth 37
    Gideon 188
    Henry 15, 37
    Jonathan 11
    Joseph 161, 162
    Samuel 20, 186
Turpin
    John 15, 210
    Whittey 210
Turvill
    John 3
    Margery 3
    William 3, 89
Twilley
    Robert 183
Twyford
    William 15
Ty
    John 99
Tye
    John 98
Tyler
    Robert 16
    William 60
Tyson
    John 39, 45, 49

Underhill
    Thomas 223
Unick
    Thomas 130
Urick
    Thomas 169
Urquhart
    John 146, 147, 159,
      171, 184, 197

Walter
  George 72
  Isaac 72
  James 166
  Thomas 139
Walters
  Godfrey 201
  Henry 201, 219
  Isaac 107
  Richard 183
  Robert 9
Waltham
  Charlton 168
  John 169
Walton
  Martha 31
  William 57, 192
Ward
  Augustina 1
  Augustine 20, 186
  Daniel 73, 92, 115
  Henry 127, 175, 224
  John 1, 34, 127,
    143, 175, 224
  Littleton 155, 173,
    208
  Margaret 87
  Mary 127, 173, 175,
    224
  Peregrine 127, 128,
    175, 224
  Price 152
  Rachel 208
  Susanna 224
  Susannah 222
Warder
  William 29
Wardrop
  James 121, 207
  John 88
Warfield
  Alexander 99
  Richard 99
Waring
  Samuel 16
  Thomas 16
Warren
  Ailce 15
  John 15
Warring
  Samuel 83
Washington
  John 174
Washinton

John 200
Waters
  Ann 176
  Elijah 42, 72
  Elisabeth 39, 69,
    199
  Henry 176
  John 25, 210, 211
  Joseph 39, 199
  Littleton 126, 200
  Samuel 39, 95
  Susanna 119, 148
  Susannah 90
  Thomas 42, 68, 72
  William 90, 119,
    148
Wathen
  Hudson 63, 90
  John 25, 53, 63, 90
Watkins
  Gassaway 5, 171
Watson
  Abraham 58
  Abram 129
  Charles 38
  Elisabeth 129
  John 31, 38, 59,
    120
  Joseph 38
  Lawrence 112
  Robert 31, 38, 80
Watt
  Mary 72
  Thomas 72
Watts
  Jane 10
  John 137, 138
  Peter 222
  William 10
Wattson
  Abraham 23
  Elisabeth 23
  William 23
Waughop
  Thomas Palmer 199
Weatherly
  Eliah 151
  Joseph 151
  Mary 151
  Patience 151
  William 151, 166
Weathers
  John 25, 69, 132
Weaver

Anne 13, 16
Web
   Timothy 208
Webb
   Armerall 11
   Armerell 32
   George 196
   John 11, 12, 32,
     208
   Timothy 155, 196
   William 208
Webster
   Isaac 48
   Samuel 48
Weeks
   John 5, 17
   Matthew 5, 17
   Stephen 5, 17, 179
Weems
   David 54
Welch
   John 202
Wells
   Daniel 2, 3, 189
   Davenport 156
   Humphrey 113
   Humphry 43
   Isaac 56, 110, 150,
     167
   Joseph 56
   Thomas 129
   Zorobabel 156
Welsh
   James 137
   John 221
   Judith 55
   William 52, 55
West
   Benjamin 8, 100
   Elisabeth 181, 185,
     198, 213
   Jane 27
   John 30, 36, 100,
     136, 140, 158,
     181, 185, 198,
     213
   Robert 166
   Stephen 137, 170
   William 27, 95, 216
Westman
   Arthur 52, 90
Wethered
   Richard 107, 130
Wetherell

Francis 12
Whale
   Mary 119
   William 119
Whaley
   John 129
   William 129, 162
Wharton
   Henrietta 165
   Henry 36, 68
   William 123, 217
Whealer
   Charles 85
   Thomas 85
Whealton
   Comfort 154
Whealy
   John 169
Wheatley
   Daniel 21
   John 21, 44
   Samson 211
   Thomas 14
   William 21, 43
Wheatly
   William 113
Wheeler
   Ann 112
   Benjamin 12
   Charles 15, 37
   Grace 177
   Henry 215
   Ignatius 34
   John 215, 216
   Leonard 34, 112,
     187, 189
   Mary 215
   Robert 177
   Solomon 215
   Thomas 12, 37, 40,
     112, 160, 189
   William 52, 155
Wheelton
   Comfort 153
Wherrill
   John 39
Whinfield
   John 174, 189
   Jonah 64
White
   Cassandra 8, 44
   Ebenezar 40
   Francis 109, 110,
     177, 193

John 73, 109, 110,
141, 175, 192
Joseph 157
Mary 109, 177, 193
Thomas 3, 6, 12,
19, 26, 29, 41,
48, 54, 55, 78,
95, 98, 108,
109, 112, 117,
134, 136, 140,
160, 177, 193
William 8, 44, 60
Whiteacre
Joseph 37, 85
Mary 37, 85
Whiteley
Arthur 153
Whitely
Arthur 14
Whittingham
Heber 51, 74, 151
Whittington
Benjamin 61, 114
Elisabeth 61
Joseph 61, 156
Southey 73
Whythill
Elisabeth 1, 63
Robert 1, 63, 119,
146
Wibb
John 32
Wickes
Joseph 120
Samuel 90
Wickham
Ann 219
Nathaniel 90, 220
Robert 219
Wicks
John 62
Joseph 62
Wilcox
Daniel 101
Wildgoose
Thomas 119, 120
Wilkins
Thomas 168
Wilkinson
Christopher 208
James 196
John 10, 164
Richard 208
Thomas 208

William 88
Willcocks
Daniel 123
Willcox
Daniel 216
Willett
Edward 16
William 16
Willey
John 41, 65, 80
Willeys
John 13
Williams
Abraham 4, 43, 81
Ann 222
Benjamin 67
Catherine 36
Cathrine 132, 150
Christopher 43, 62
Daniel 29
Elisabeth 161
George 15, 37, 84,
85
German 166, 194
Hannah 215
Henry 81, 144, 166
Isaac 161, 215
James 203, 213
John 13, 39, 107,
141, 170, 219
John Guy 134, 145,
161, 179
Jonathan 215
Joseph 36, 132, 150
Lewis 32, 168, 169
Margret 141
Mary 215
Matthew 61, 81,
108, 123, 166
Philadelphia 39, 84
Rebecca 4, 109, 174
Samuel 217
Thomas 40, 71, 78,
94, 192
William 2, 35, 116,
161, 200
Williamson
Alexander 91
Alice 115
James 218
John 115, 142, 169
Thomas 17, 97, 138,
177
Willin

Edward 183, 211
John 183
Willitt
Ninian 69
Willmott
John 194
Willobey
John 152
Willson
Alexander 1, 20,
25, 132, 173,
187
John 144
Joseph 76
Joshua 132
Mary 20, 132, 173,
187
Presila 46
Prisila 60
Thomas 46, 60, 216
William 152
Wilmer
Lambert 12
Simon 7
William 32, 168,
172
Wilmot
Richard 205
Wilmott
William 35
Wilson
Ann 4, 155
David 33, 151, 192
Elisabeth 7
George 51
Henry Wright 5, 18,
28, 47, 65, 77
Ishua 117
James 5, 18, 28,
47, 59, 65, 77,
155, 157, 161
John 88, 145, 191
Joseph 5, 18, 28,
47, 65, 77, 78,
93, 103, 106
Lingan 5, 18, 28,
47, 65, 77, 93,
103, 106
Martha 151
Mary 51, 151, 166
Phineas 4
Priscilla 14
Richard 169
Robert 7, 53

Samuel 1, 33, 74,
151
Thomas 14
William 155
Wimseet
Robert 194
Winall
Clarana 2, 10
William 2, 10
Winchester
Jacob 27
Winder
Thomas 118, 151
Windstandley
Thomas 15
Wing
Thomas 74
Wingate
John 83, 154
Rachel 83
Winman
John 188
Winnell
John 188
Winright
Stephen 183
Winston
Rebecca 76, 135
Wise
Christopher 61
Francess 220
Henry 193
John 53, 69, 132
Samuel 13
Withers
Robert 24
Withgot
Henry 153
Wollman
Sarah 7
Wollston
Obid 118
Wolter
Henry 74
Wood
Ann 160, 176, 189,
205
James Greenfield 1
John 26, 63, 75
Joseph 90, 220
Martha 1
William 26, 63,
160, 175, 176,
189, 205

Woodcraft
   William 56, 120
Wooden
   John 108, 109
   Solomon 108, 109
Woodford
   Robert 112, 161
Woodhead
   George 60
Wooding
   John 137
   Solomon 137
Woodward
   Benjamin 40, 152
   John 27
Wooleston
   Catherine 58
Wooley
   Anne 75
   John 74, 97
Woolford
   John 64, 67, 78,
      93, 105, 111,
      122, 139, 158,
      171, 184, 195,
      197, 212
   Robert 161
   Roger 54, 64, 67,
      78, 93, 105,
      111, 122, 139,
      158, 171, 184,
      197, 212
   Thomas 54, 67, 78,
      93, 105, 111,
      122, 139, 158,
      171, 184, 197,
      212
Wooliston
   Catharine 176
   Cornelius 58
   Elenor 58
   Richard 58, 87, 176
Woolliston
   Cornelius 222
Wootters
   John 43
Worrell
   Edward 12, 81, 88
   Mary 81, 88
Wrench
   James 43, 156
   William 81, 123
Wright
   Abraham 141

Ann 7
Benjamin 5
Edward 83, 154,
   195, 217
Elinor 63, 87
Elisabeth 180
Fairclough 174, 209
Henry 21, 31, 47,
   82, 106
James 24, 63, 87
John 14
Joseph 138
Martha 83, 195, 217
Nathan 21, 43, 113,
   204, 208
Nathan Samuel
   Turbutt 113
Nathaniel 196
Peter 7
Robert Norrest 21,
   62, 204, 208
Roger 180, 217
Samuel 202
Thomas 113
Thomas Hynson 101,
   113, 144
William 141, 151
Wye
   Rebecca 98
   William 98
Wyeth
   Ann 131
   Anne 148
Wyle
   William 126

Yates
   Ann 186
   Joshua 193
   Robert 54, 131
   William 36, 68, 186
Yealhall
   Benjamin 189
   Gilbert 189
Yewell
   Mary 115
   Solomon 115
Yoakley
   Marth 78
   Martha 71, 94
Yoe
   Aaron 123
   Jane 80

INDEX OF EQUITY CASES

www.ingramcontent.com/pod-product-compliance
Lightning Source LLC
Chambersburg PA
CBHW060150280326
41932CB00012B/1708